Lecture Notes in Bioinformatics 4230

Edited by S. Istrail, P. Pevzner, and M. Waterman

Editorial Board: A. Apostolico S. Brunak M. Gelfand
T. Lengauer S. Miyano G. Myers M.-F. Sagot D. Sankoff
R. Shamir T. Speed M. Vingron W. Wong

Subseries of Lecture Notes in Computer Science

Corrado Priami   Anna Ingólfsdóttir
Bud Mishra   Hanne Riis Nielson (Eds.)

Transactions on Computational Systems Biology VII

 Springer

Series Editors

Sorin Istrail, Brown University, Providence, RI, USA
Pavel Pevzner, University of California, San Diego, CA, USA
Michael Waterman, University of Southern California, Los Angeles, CA, USA

Editor-in-Chief

Corrado Priami
The Microsoft Research - University of Trento
Centre for Computational and Systems Biology
Piazza Manci, 17, 38050 Povo (TN), Italy
E-mail: priami@dit.unitn.it

Volume Editors

Anna Ingólfsdóttir
Aalborg University
Department of Computer Science
Fr. Bajersvej 7E, Aalborg, Denmark
E-mail: annai@cs.auc.dk

Bud Mishra
Cold Spring Harbor Laboratory
One Bungtown Road
Cold Spring Harbor, NY 11724, USA
E-mail: mishra@nyu.edu

Hanne Riis Nielson
Technical University of Denmark
Informatics and Mathematical Modelling
Richard Petersens Plads, 2800 Lyngby, Denmark
E-mail: riis@imm.dtu.dk

Library of Congress Control Number: 2006935571

CR Subject Classification (1998): J.3, F.1, F.4, I.6

LNCS Sublibrary: SL 8 – Bioinformatics

ISSN   1861-2075
ISBN-10   3-540-48837-5 Springer Berlin Heidelberg New York
ISBN-13   978-3-540-48837-8 Springer Berlin Heidelberg New York

This work is subject to copyright. All rights are reserved, whether the whole or part of the material is concerned, specifically the rights of translation, reprinting, re-use of illustrations, recitation, broadcasting, reproduction on microfilms or in any other way, and storage in data banks. Duplication of this publication or parts thereof is permitted only under the provisions of the German Copyright Law of September 9, 1965, in its current version, and permission for use must always be obtained from Springer. Violations are liable to prosecution under the German Copyright Law.

Springer is a part of Springer Science+Business Media

springer.com

© Springer-Verlag Berlin Heidelberg 2006
Printed in Germany

Typesetting: Camera-ready by author, data conversion by Scientific Publishing Services, Chennai, India
Printed on acid-free paper   SPIN: 11905455   06/3142   5 4 3 2 1 0

Preface

This issue of the journal reports some selected contributions from the workshops *BioConcur 2004* chaired by Anna Ingolfsdottir and Hanne Riis Nielson and *BioConcur 2005* chaired by Bud Mishra and Corrado Priami.

There are three contributions from BioConcur 2004. The first one is by Calder, Gilmore and Hillston on the modelling of signalling pathways using the stochastic process algebra PEPA. The second contribution is by Kuttler and Niehren on gene regulation in π-calculus. The last contribution is by Remy, Ruet, Mendoza, Thieffry and Chsouiya on the relationships between logical regulator graphs and Petri nets.

There are five contributions from BioConcur 2005. The first contribution is by Eccher and Lecca on the automatic translation of SBML models to stochastic π-calculus. The second paper is by Blinov, Yang, Faeder and Hlavacek on the use of graph theory to model biological networks. The third contribution, by Jha and Shyamasundar, introduces biochemical Kripke structures for distributed model checking. The fourth paper is by Phillips, Cardelli and Castagna on a graphical notation for stochastic π-calculus. The last paper is by Remy and Ruet on differentiation and homeostatic behaviour of boolean dynamic systems.

The volume ends with a regular contribution by Margoninsky, Saffrey, Hetherington, Finkelstein and Warner that describes a specification language and a framework for the execution of composite models.

July 2006   Corrado Priami

LNCS Transactions on Computational Systems Biology – Editorial Board

Corrado Priami, Editor-in-chief	University of Trento, Italy
Charles Auffray	Genexpress, CNRS and Pierre & Marie Curie University, France
Matthew Bellgard	Murdoch University, Australia
Soren Brunak	Technical University of Denmark, Denmark
Luca Cardelli	Microsoft Research Cambridge, UK
Zhu Chen	Shanghai Institute of Hematology, China
Vincent Danos	CNRS, University of Paris VII, France
Eytan Domany	Center for Systems Biology, Weizmann Institute, Israel
Walter Fontana	Santa Fe Institute, USA
Takashi Gojobori	National Institute of Genetics, Japan
Martijn A. Huynen	Center for Molecular and Biomolecular Informatics, The Netherlands
Marta Kwiatkowska	University of Birmingham, UK
Doron Lancet	Crown Human Genome Center, Israel
Pedro Mendes	Virginia Bioinformatics Institute, USA
Bud Mishra	Courant Institute and Cold Spring Harbor Lab, USA
Satoru Miayano	University of Tokyo, Japan
Denis Noble	University of Oxford, UK
Yi Pan	Georgia State University, USA
Alberto Policriti	University of Udine, Italy
Magali Roux-Rouquie	CNRS, Pasteur Institute, France
Vincent Schachter	Genoscope, France
Adelinde Uhrmacher	University of Rostock, Germany
Alfonso Valencia	Centro Nacional de Biotecnologa, Spain

Table of Contents

Modelling the Influence of RKIP on the ERK Signalling Pathway Using the Stochastic Process Algebra PEPA

Muffy Calder[1], Stephen Gilmore[2], and Jane Hillston[2]

[1] Department of Computing Science, The University of Glasgow, Glasgow, Scotland
muffy@dcs.gla.ac.uk
[2] Laboratory for Foundations of Computer Science, The University of Edinburgh, Scotland
stg@inf.ed.ac.uk, jeh@inf.ed.ac.uk

Abstract. This paper examines the influence of the Raf Kinase Inhibitor Protein (RKIP) on the Extracellular signal Regulated Kinase (ERK) signalling pathway [5] through modelling in a Markovian process algebra, PEPA [11]. Two models of the system are presented, a reagent-centric view and a pathway-centric view. The models capture functionality at the level of subpathway, rather than at a molecular level. Each model affords a different perspective of the pathway and analysis. We demonstrate the two models to be formally equivalent using the timing-aware bisimulation defined over PEPA models and discuss the biological significance.

1 Introduction

In recent years several authors have investigated the use of Petri nets and process algebras – techniques originating in theoretical computer science – for representing the biochemical pathways within and between cells [15,18,10]. Largely, the previous work has focussed on capturing the appropriate functionality at the molecular level and analysis is through simulation. In this paper we present a preliminary exploration of an alternative approach in which a more abstract approach is taken and the target mathematical representation is a continuous time Markov chain. This involves the analytical application of a process algebra to a biochemical pathway with feedback. Our goal is to develop more than one representation, suitable for different forms of analysis. We prove the two representations to be equivalent (i.e. bisimilar).

The process algebra which we use is Hillston's PEPA [11], a Markovian process algebra which incorporates stochastic durations and probabilistic choices. The system which we consider is the Ras/Raf-1/MEK/ERK signalling pathway, as presented in [5]. We believe that our modelling is novel because we are able to combine performance and different modelling viewpoints. Moreover we demonstrate the feasibility of using process algebra to model signalling pathways in a more abstract style than previously.

C. Priami et al. (Eds.): Trans. on Comput. Syst. Biol. VII, LNBI 4230, pp. 1–23, 2006.
© Springer-Verlag Berlin Heidelberg 2006

We propose that process algebra models are appropriate in this domain for several reasons. First, an algebraic formulation of the model makes clear the interactions between the biochemical entities, or substrates. This is not always apparent in the classical, ordinary differential equation (ODE) models. Second, an algebraic approach permits comparison of high level descriptions. For example, when one is first building up a picture of a pathway from experimental evidence, it may be natural to describe the pathway in a fine-grained, distributed fashion, e.g. each substrate (in this case a protein) is described in terms of its interactions. That is, each (collection of a) protein is a process and all processes run in parallel, synchronising accordingly. But later, we may prefer a higher level view of a pathway which describes how a pathway is composed of (perhaps already well known) sub-pathways. Indeed we may wish to derive the latter from the former, or vice-versa. Third, a stochastic process approach allows reasoning about livelocks, deadlocks, and the performance of the behaviour of the pathway in the long-run.

This paper is an extended version of the earlier paper [2]. As previously, we concentrate primarily on alternative approaches to constructing a representation of a pathway. We show that two contrasting representations can indeed be identified. Moreover they can be formally shown to be equivalent. The novelty of this paper lies in the systematic transformation between the alternative representations which are presented in algorithmic form. The analysis of the model has also been somewhat extended.

In the next section we give a brief overview of cell signalling and the Ras/Raf-1/MEK/ERK pathway. In section 3 we give two different PEPA formulations of the pathway: the first is reagent-based (i.e. distributed) and the second is pathway-based. In section 4 we compare the two models and show them to be bisimilar. Section 5 contains some analysis of the underlying continuous time Markov model. Transformation between the two styles of representation is presented in section 6. There follows a discussion of further analysis, related work and our conclusions.

2   RKIP and the ERK Pathway

The most fundamental cellular processes are controlled by extracellular signalling [7]. This signalling, or communication between cells, is based upon the release of signalling molecules, which migrate to other cells and deliver stimuli to them (e.g. protein phosphorylation). Cell signalling is of special interest to cancer researchers because when cell signalling pathways operate abnormally, cells divide uncontrollably.

The Ras/Raf-1/MEK/ERK pathway (also called Ras/Raf, or ERK pathway) is a ubiquitous pathway that conveys mitogenic and differentiation signals from the cell membrane to the nucleus. Briefly, Ras is activated by an external stimulus, it then binds to and activates Raf-1 (to become Raf-1*, "activated" Raf) which in turn activates MEK and then ERK. This "cascade" of protein interaction controls cell differentiation, the effect being dependent upon the activity of ERK. A current area of experimental scientific investigation is the role the kinase inhibitor protein RKIP plays in the behaviour of this pathway: the hypothesis is that it inhibits activation of Raf and thus can "dampen down" the ERK pathway. Certainly there is much evidence that RKIP inhibits the malignant transformation by Ras and Raf oncogenes in cell cultures and it is reduced in tumours. Thus good models of these pathways are required to understand the role of RKIP and develop new therapies. Moreover, an understanding of the functioning and structure of this pathway may lead to more general results applicable to other pathways.

Here, we consider how RKIP regulates the activity of the Raf-1/MEK/ERK module of the ERK pathway, as presented in [5]. This paper [5] presents a number of mathematical models in the form of nonlinear ODEs and difference equations representing the (enzyme) kinetic reactions, based on a graphical representation given in Figure 1. This figure is taken from [5], with some additions. Specifically, we have added MEK and an associated complex, following discussions with the authors[1].

We take Figure 1 as our starting point, and explain informally, its meaning. Each node is labelled by the protein (or substrate, we use the two interchangeably) it denotes. For example, Raf-1, RKIP and Raf-1*/RKIP are proteins, the last being a complex built up from the first two. It is important to note that Raf-1*/RKIP is simply a *name*, following biochemical convention; the / symbol is not an operator (in this context). A suffix -P or -PP denotes a phosphorylated protein, for example MEK-PP and ERK-PP. Each protein has an associated concentration, denoted by $m1$, $m2$ etc. *Reactions* define how proteins are built up and broken down. We refer to the former as an association, or forward reaction, and the latter as a disassociation, or backward reaction. Associations are typically many to one, and disassociations one to many, relations. In the figure, bi-directional arrows denote both forward and backward reactions; unidirectional arrows denote disassociations. For example, Raf-1* and RKIP react (forwards) to form Raf-1*/RKIP, and Raf-1/RKIP disassociates (a backward reaction) into Raf-1* and RKIP. Reactions do not necessarily come in pairs; for example, Raf-1*/RKIP/ERK-PP disassociates into Raf-1*, ERK and RKIP-P. Each reaction has a rate denoted by the rate constants $k1$, $k2$, etc. These are given in the rectangles, with $kn/kn+1$ denoting that kn is the forward rate and $kn+1$ the backward rate. So for example, Raf-1* and RKIP react (forwards) with rate $k1$, and Raf-1/RKIP disassociates with rate $k2$.

Initially, all concentrations are unobservable, except for m_1, m_2, m_7, m_9, and m_{10} [5].

Figure 1 gives only a static, abstract view of the pathway; the dynamic behaviour is quite complex, particularly because some substrates are involved in more than one reaction. In the next section we develop two process algebraic models which capture that dynamic behaviour.

---

[1] Analysis of our original model(s) indicated a problem with MEK and prompted us to contact an author of [5] who confirmed that there was an omission.

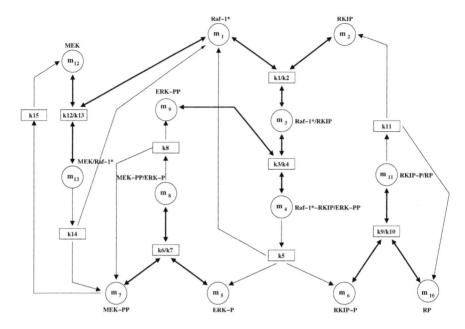

Fig. 1. RKIP inhibited ERK pathway

3   Modelling the ERK Signalling Pathway in PEPA

In this section we present two stochastic process algebra models of the ERK signalling pathway.

The two models presented here encode different views of the underlying biochemistry. The first is a reagent-centric view, focussing on the variations in concentrations of the reagents, fluctuating with phosphorylation and product formation, i.e. with association and disassociation reactions. This model provides a fine-grained, distributed view of the system. The second is a pathway-centric view, tracking the legitimate serialisations of activities. This model provides a coarser grained, more abstract view of the same system.

For some purposes in biological study the former view provides the right conceptual tools and powers the programme of analysis. For other purposes the pathway-centric view brings to the fore the dynamics of greatest interest. A major contribution of this paper is the unification of both views.

We express both models in the PEPA stochastic process algebra [11]. We assume some familiarity with this process algebra; a brief introduction to PEPA is contained in Appendix A. All activities in PEPA are timed. Specifically, their durations are quantified using exponentially-distributed random variables. The PEPA algebra supports multi-way cooperations between components: the result of synchronising on an activity α is thus another α, available for further synchronisation. The multi-way synchronisation of PEPA makes this process algebra ideally suited to this domain.

Each reaction in the pathway is represented by a multi-way synchronisation – on the reagents of the reaction[2]. We refer to reagents as *producers* and *consumers*, depending upon their role within the reaction. Table 1 gives the producers and consumers for reactions in the pathway. The first column names the reaction using the following convention. Reactions which are forward and backward are called *react*, with a prefix which is the associated rate constant. For example, *k1react* is the name of the reaction between Raf-1* and RKIP, to produce Raf-1*/RKIP. Thus *k1react* is a 3-way synchronisation. Reactions which are only disassociations are called *product* (because they produce *products*); again, the prefix denotes the associated rate constant. Table 1 gives only the forward reactions for the reactions which are both forward and backwards; to obtain the associated backward descriptions, replace Producer by Consumer and vice-versa.

Table 1. Reactions in the pathway

Reaction	Producer(s)	Consumer(s)
k1react	{ Raf-1*, RKIP }	{ Raf-1*/RKIP }
k3react	{ ERK-PP, Raf-1*/RKIP }	{ Raf-1*/RKIP/ERK-PP }
k6react	{ MEK-PP, ERK-P }	{ MEK-PP/ERK }
k9react	{ RKIP-P, RP }	{ RKIP-P/RP }
k12react	{ MEK, Raf-1* }	{ MEK/Raf-1* }
k5product	{ Raf-1*/RKIP/ERK-PP }	{ ERK-P, RKIP-P, Raf-1* }
k8product	{ MEK-PP/ERK }	{ MEK-PP, ERK-PP }
k11product	{ RKIP-P/RP }	{ RKIP, RP }
k14product	{ MEK/Raf-1* }	{ Raf-1*, MEK-PP }
k15product	{ MEK-PP }	{ MEK }

3.1 Modelling Centred on Reagents

The reagent-centred model is presented in Figures 2 and 3. In this view, we represent concentrations by a discrete number of abstract values. Here, we consider the coarsest possible discretisation: there are two values representing (continuous) concentrations; we refer to the two values as *high* and *low*. The former implies that a reagent *can* participate (as a producer) in a forward reaction; the latter implies that a reagent *can* participate (as a consumer) in a product, or (as a producer) in a backward reaction. Otherwise, the substrate is inert, with respect to a reaction. We discuss the effect of a finer granularity of abstract concentration on the model in Section 7.

We define the behaviour of each substrate in turn, for each concentration. Thus there are $2n$ equations, where n is the number of proteins. We adopt the naming convention that high concentrations have a H subscript and low concentrations have a L subscript.

Most equations involve a choice between alternative behaviours (notated by $+$). For example, even in one of the simplest cases, RKIP, where there is a simple

---

[2] We agree with the authors of [15] – reactions are fundamentally synchronous.

$$\text{Raf-1}^*_\text{H} \stackrel{def}{=} (k1react, k_1).\text{Raf-1}^*_\text{L} + (k12react, k_{12}).\text{Raf-1}^*_\text{L}$$
$$\text{Raf-1}^*_\text{L} \stackrel{def}{=} (k5product, k_5).\text{Raf-1}^*_\text{H} + (k2react, k_2).\text{Raf-1}^*_\text{H}$$
$$+ (k13react, k_{13}).\text{Raf-1}^*_\text{H} + (k14product, k_{14}).\text{Raf-1}^*_\text{H}$$

$$\text{RKIP}_\text{H} \stackrel{def}{=} (k1react, k_1).\text{RKIP}_\text{L}$$
$$\text{RKIP}_\text{L} \stackrel{def}{=} (k11product, k_{11}).\text{RKIP}_\text{H} + (k2react, k_2).\text{RKIP}_\text{H}$$

$$\text{MEK}_\text{H} \stackrel{def}{=} (k12react, k_{12}).\text{MEK}_\text{L}$$
$$\text{MEK}_\text{L} \stackrel{def}{=} (k13react, k_{13}).\text{MEK}_\text{H} + (k15product, k_{15}).\text{MEK}_\text{H}$$

$$\text{MEK/Raf-1}^*_\text{H} \stackrel{def}{=} (k14product, k_{14}).\text{MEK/Raf-1}^*_\text{L} + (k13react, k_{13}).\text{MEK/Raf-1}^*_\text{L}$$
$$\text{MEK/Raf-1}^*_\text{L} \stackrel{def}{=} (k12react, k_{12}).\text{MEK/Raf-1}^*_\text{H}$$

$$\text{MEK-PP}_\text{H} \stackrel{def}{=} (k6react, k_6).\text{MEK-PP}_\text{L} + (k15product, k_{15}).\text{MEK-PP}_\text{L}$$
$$\text{MEK-PP}_\text{L} \stackrel{def}{=} (k8product, k_8).\text{MEK-PP}_\text{H} + (k7react, k_7).\text{MEK-PP}_\text{H}$$
$$+ (k14product, k_{14}).\text{MEK-PP}_\text{H}$$

$$\text{ERK-PP}_\text{H} \stackrel{def}{=} (k3react, k_3).\text{ERK-PP}_\text{L}$$
$$\text{ERK-PP}_\text{L} \stackrel{def}{=} (k8product, k_8).\text{ERK-PP}_\text{H} + (k4react, k_4).\text{ERK-PP}_\text{H}$$

$$\text{ERK-P}_\text{H} \stackrel{def}{=} (k6react, k_6).\text{ERK-P}_\text{L}$$
$$\text{ERK-P}_\text{L} \stackrel{def}{=} (k5product, k_5).\text{ERK-P}_\text{H} + (k7react, k_7).\text{ERK-P}_\text{H}$$

$$\text{MEK-PP/ERK}_\text{H} \stackrel{def}{=} (k8product, k_8).\text{MEK-PP/ERK}_\text{L} + (k7react, k_7).\text{MEK-PP/ERK}_\text{L}$$
$$\text{MEK-PP/ERK}_\text{L} \stackrel{def}{=} (k6react, k_6).\text{MEK-PP/ERK}_\text{H}$$

$$\text{Raf-1}^*/\text{RKIP}_\text{H} \stackrel{def}{=} (k3react, k_3).\text{Raf-1}^*/\text{RKIP}_\text{L} + (k2react, k_2).\text{Raf-1}^*/\text{RKIP}_\text{L}$$
$$\text{Raf-1}^*/\text{RKIP}_\text{L} \stackrel{def}{=} (k1react, k_1).\text{Raf-1}^*/\text{RKIP}_\text{H} + (k4react, k_4).\text{Raf-1}^*/\text{RKIP}_\text{H}$$

$$\text{Raf-1}^*/\text{RKIP/ERK-PP}_\text{H} \stackrel{def}{=} (k5product, k_5).\text{Raf-1}^*/\text{RKIP/ERK-PP}_\text{L}$$
$$+ (k4react, k_4).\text{Raf-1}^*/\text{RKIP/ERK-PP}_\text{L}$$
$$\text{Raf-1}^*/\text{RKIP/ERK-PP}_\text{L} \stackrel{def}{=} (k3react, k_3).\text{Raf-1}^*/\text{RKIP/ERK-PP}_\text{H}$$

$$\text{RKIP-P}_\text{H} \stackrel{def}{=} (k9react, k_9).\text{RKIP-P}_\text{L}$$
$$\text{RKIP-P}_\text{L} \stackrel{def}{=} (k5product, k_5).\text{RKIP-P}_\text{H} + (k10react, k_{10}).\text{RKIP-P}_\text{H}$$

$$\text{RP}_\text{H} \stackrel{def}{=} (k9react, k_9).\text{RP}_\text{L}$$
$$\text{RP}_\text{L} \stackrel{def}{=} (k11product, k_{11}).\text{RP}_\text{H} + (k10react, k_{10}).\text{RP}_\text{H}$$

$$\text{RKIP-P/RP}_\text{H} \stackrel{def}{=} (k11product, k_{11}).\text{RKIP-P/RP}_\text{L} + (k10react, k_{10}).\text{RKIP-P/RP}_\text{L}$$
$$\text{RKIP-P/RP}_\text{L} \stackrel{def}{=} (k9react, k_9).\text{RKIP-P/RP}_\text{H}$$

Fig. 2. PEPA model definitions for the reagent-centric model

cycle between high and low concentrations, there is still a choice of how to return to a high concentration (by a backwards reaction, or through a product). Most behaviours are more complex.

The equations define the possible reactions within the pathway. All of the permissible interleavings of these reactions are obtained from the (synchronised) parallel composition of these components. Figure 3 shows how these are

$$
\begin{aligned}
(\text{Raf-1}^*_H & \underset{\{k1react,k2react,k12react,k13react,k5product,k14product\}}{\bowtie} \\
(\text{RKIP}_H & \underset{\{k1react,k2react,k11product\}}{\bowtie} \\
(\text{Raf-1}^*/\text{RKIP}_L & \underset{\{k3react,k4react\}}{\bowtie} \\
(\text{Raf-1}^*/\text{RKIP}/\text{ERK-PP}_L) & \underset{\{k3react,k4react,k5product\}}{\bowtie} \\
(\text{ERK-P}_L & \underset{\{k5product,k6react,k7react\}}{\bowtie} \\
(\text{RKIP-P}_L & \underset{\{k9react,k10react\}}{\bowtie} \\
(\text{RKIP-P}/\text{RP}_L & \underset{\{k9react,k10react,k11product\}}{\bowtie} \\
(\text{RP}_H & \| \\
(\text{MEK}_L & \underset{\{k12react,k13react,k15product\}}{\bowtie} \\
(\text{MEK}/\text{Raf-1}^*_L & \underset{\{k14product\}}{\bowtie} \\
(\text{MEK-PP}_H & \underset{\{k8product,k6react,k7react\}}{\bowtie} \\
(\text{MEK-PP}/\text{ERK}_L & \underset{\{k8product\}}{\bowtie} \\
(\text{ERK-PP}_H &))))))))))))
\end{aligned}
$$

Fig. 3. PEPA model configuration for the reagent-centric model

composed in the PEPA algebra. The composition operator ($\bowtie$) is indexed by an activity set (i.e. the events whose participants must be synchronised). The left and right operands must cooperate on these activities, introducing a synchronisation point. The degenerate case of this composition operator (where the set is empty) provides the expected unrestricted parallel composition of the components, allowing all possible interleavings without synchronisation. This case is denoted by $\|$ (there is one occurrence).

The initial state of the model has high concentrations of some reagents and low concentrations of the others, as described in the previous section. Therefore, in Figure 3, proteins with an initial concentration are initially high; all others are low.

3.2 Modelling Centred on Pathways

A different view is afforded by the pathway-centric perspective. This de-emphasises reagents and emphasises sub-pathways within the signalling pathway. In this model, given in Figure 4, there are five (sub)pathways, one for each substrate with an initial concentration. Thus $Pathway_{10}$ corresponds to the pathway from RP (m_{10}), $Pathway_{20}$ to RKIP (m_2), $Pathway_{30}$ to ERK-PP (m_9), $Pathway_{40}$ to Raf-1* (m_1), and $Pathway_{50}$ to MEK-PP (m_7). Each (sub)pathway describes, in effect, how a substrate is consumed and then, eventually, replenished.

It is important to note that none of these (sub)pathways is *closed*, i.e. there are reactions with edges which are directed to/from outside of the (sub)pathway. Figure 6 gives a diagrammatic representation of the simplest pathway, $Pathway_{10}$.

$Pathway_{10} \stackrel{def}{=} (k9react, k_9).Pathway_{11}$
$Pathway_{11} \stackrel{def}{=} (k11product, k_{11}).Pathway_{10} + (k10react, k_{10}).Pathway_{10}$

$Pathway_{20} \stackrel{def}{=} (k1react, k_1).Pathway_{21}$
$Pathway_{21} \stackrel{def}{=} (k3react, k_3).Pathway_{22} + (k2react, k_2).Pathway_{20}$
$Pathway_{22} \stackrel{def}{=} (k5product, k_5).Pathway_{23} + (k4react, k_4).Pathway_{21}$
$Pathway_{23} \stackrel{def}{=} (k9react, k_9).Pathway_{24}$
$Pathway_{24} \stackrel{def}{=} (k11product, k_{11}).Pathway_{20} + (k10react, k_{10}).Pathway_{23}$

$Pathway_{30} \stackrel{def}{=} (k3react, k_3).Pathway_{31}$
$Pathway_{31} \stackrel{def}{=} (k5product, k_5).Pathway_{32} + (k4react, k_4).Pathway_{30}$
$Pathway_{32} \stackrel{def}{=} (k6react, k_6).Pathway_{33}$
$Pathway_{33} \stackrel{def}{=} (k8product, k_8).Pathway_{30} + (k7react, k_7).Pathway_{32}$

$Pathway_{40} \stackrel{def}{=} (k1react, k_1).Pathway_{41} + (k12react, k_{12}).Pathway_{43}$
$Pathway_{41} \stackrel{def}{=} (k2react, k_2).Pathway_{40} + (k3react, k_3).Pathway_{42}$
$Pathway_{42} \stackrel{def}{=} (k5product, k_5).Pathway_{40} + (k4react, k_4).Pathway_{41}$
$Pathway_{43} \stackrel{def}{=} (k13react, k_{13}).Pathway_{40} + (k14product, k_{14}).Pathway_{40}$

$Pathway_{50} \stackrel{def}{=} (k15product, k_{15}).Pathway_{51} + (k6react, k_6).Pathway_{53}$
$Pathway_{51} \stackrel{def}{=} (k12react, k_{12}).Pathway_{52}$
$Pathway_{52} \stackrel{def}{=} (k13react, k_{13}).Pathway_{51} + (k14product, k_{14}).Pathway_{50}$
$Pathway_{53} \stackrel{def}{=} (k8product, k_8).Pathway_{50} + (k7react, k_7).Pathway_{50}$

Fig. 4. PEPA model definitions for the pathway-centric model

In this case, the pathway is not closed because there are two missing edges associated with *k9react* and *k11product*.

This presentation facilitates the direct verification of simple properties of the model such as "the first observable activity is event X". For example, an initial syntactic inspection of this model would lead to the conclusion that the first activity is one of *k1react*, *k3react*, *k9react* or *k15product*. Processing the model with the PEPA Workbench [9] confirms that the initial model configuration allows only *k15product* and *k1react*, the others are not permitted because some necessary participants are not initially ready to engage in these reactions.

4   Comparison of Reagent and Pathway-Centric Models

The pathway-centric model captures longer chains of behaviour flow within the system, leading to a smaller number of component definitions. Differentiating fewer components in the pathways model leads to a simpler composition of model components, presented in Figure 5. This is not only a matter of presentation. A larger state vector representation occupies more memory so the

$$((((Pathway_{50} \underset{\{k12react,k13react,k14product\}}{\bowtie} Pathway_{40})$$
$$\underset{\{k3react,k4react,k5product,k6react,k7react,k8product\}}{\bowtie} Pathway_{30})$$
$$\underset{\{k1react,k2react,k3react,k4react,k5product\}}{\bowtie} Pathway_{20})$$
$$\underset{\{k9react,k10react,k11product\}}{\bowtie} Pathway_{10})$$

Fig. 5. PEPA model configuration for the pathway-centric model

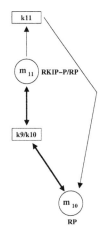

Fig. 6. $Pathway_{10}$

pathway-centric representation could potentially scale better to more detailed models of the Ras/Raf-1/MEK/ERK signalling pathway than the reagent-centric representation. But, the disadvantage of the pathway-centric representation is that it is no longer possible to read off directly concentrations of components (i.e. there is no explicit high or low concentrations). These now have to be inferred from local observations of pathways. This is relatively easy for proteins which have initial concentrations, otherwise, the inference is non-trivial.

Fortunately, the two models are observationally equivalent, that is, the two models give rise to (timing aware) bisimilar—in fact *isomorphic*—labelled multi-transition systems. We demonstrate this relationship by plotting the statespace of the two systems, see Figure 7. There are 28 states, s_1 to s_{28}, thus it is not possible in Figure 7 to give meaningful labels. In Table 2 we enumerate a few of the states. We give the name from the reagent-centric model first, followed by the name of the equivalent state from the pathway-centric model. In all cases, the synchronisation operator $\bowtie$ is removed.

We believe that for any pathway, bisimilarity holds for any pair of reagent-centric and pathway-centric models; a formal proof is beyond the scope of this paper. We restrict our attention to this pathway and the consequence of the bisimilarity result which is that the two models give rise to the same Markov

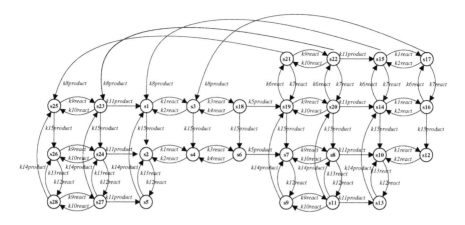

Fig. 7. The state space of the reagent and the pathway model

Table 2. Some bisimilar states

	Raf-1*	RKIP	Raf-1*/RKIP	Raf-1*/RKIP/ERK-PP	ERK-P	RKIP-P	RKIP-P/RP	RP	MEK	MEK/Raf-1*	MEK-PP	MEK-PP/ERK	ERK-PP	
s_1	$(H,$	$H,$	$L,$	$L,$	$L,$	$L,$	$L,$	$H,$	$L,$	$L,$	$H,$	$L,$	$H)$	$(Pwy_{50}, Pwy_{40}, Pwy_{30}, Pwy_{20}, Pwy_{10})$
s_2	$(H,$	$H,$	$L,$	$L,$	$L,$	$L,$	$L,$	$H,$	$H,$	$L,$	$L,$	$L,$	$H)$	$(Pwy_{51}, Pwy_{40}, Pwy_{30}, Pwy_{20}, Pwy_{10})$
s_3	$(L,$	$L,$	$H,$	$L,$	$L,$	$L,$	$L,$	$H,$	$L,$	$L,$	$H,$	$L,$	$H)$	$(Pwy_{50}, Pwy_{41}, Pwy_{30}, Pwy_{21}, Pwy_{10})$
s_4	$(L,$	$L,$	$H,$	$L,$	$L,$	$L,$	$L,$	$H,$	$H,$	$L,$	$L,$	$L,$	$H)$	$(Pwy_{51}, Pwy_{41}, Pwy_{30}, Pwy_{21}, Pwy_{10})$
s_5	$(L,$	$H,$	$L,$	$L,$	$L,$	$L,$	$L,$	$H,$	$L,$	$H,$	$L,$	$L,$	$H)$	$(Pwy_{52}, Pwy_{43}, Pwy_{30}, Pwy_{20}, Pwy_{10})$
s_6	$(L,$	$L,$	$L,$	$H,$	$L,$	$L,$	$L,$	$H,$	$H,$	$L,$	$L,$	$L,$	$L)$	$(Pwy_{51}, Pwy_{42}, Pwy_{31}, Pwy_{22}, Pwy_{10})$
s_7	$(H,$	$L,$	$L,$	$L,$	$H,$	$H,$	$L,$	$H,$	$H,$	$L,$	$L,$	$L,$	$L)$	$(Pwy_{51}, Pwy_{40}, Pwy_{32}, Pwy_{23}, Pwy_{10})$
s_8	$(H,$	$L,$	$L,$	$L,$	$H,$	$L,$	$H,$	$L,$	$H,$	$L,$	$L,$	$L,$	$L)$	$(Pwy_{51}, Pwy_{40}, Pwy_{32}, Pwy_{24}, Pwy_{11})$
s_9	$(L,$	$L,$	$L,$	$L,$	$H,$	$H,$	$L,$	$H,$	$L,$	$H,$	$L,$	$L,$	$L)$	$(Pwy_{52}, Pwy_{43}, Pwy_{32}, Pwy_{23}, Pwy_{10})$
s_{10}	$(H,$	$H,$	$L,$	$L,$	$H,$	$L,$	$L,$	$H,$	$H,$	$L,$	$L,$	$L,$	$L)$	$(Pwy_{51}, Pwy_{40}, Pwy_{32}, Pwy_{20}, Pwy_{10})$
$\vdots$				$\vdots$								$\vdots$		$\vdots$
s_{28}	$(L,$	$L,$	$L,$	$L,$	$L,$	$H,$	$L,$	$H,$	$L,$	$H,$	$L,$	$L,$	$H)$	$(Pwy_{52}, Pwy_{43}, Pwy_{30}, Pwy_{23}, Pwy_{10})$

chain representations. The Markov chain can be analysed for *transient* behaviour, or solved to find the *steady-state* (long-run) probability distribution. Here we concentrate on the latter, since it is of more interest with respect to this pathway.

In the following section we generate the steady state distribution and perform some analysis.

5   Model Analysis

We used the PEPA Workbench [9] to analyse our models. The Workbench implements the operational semantics of PEPA to generate Continuous-Time Markov Chain (CTMC) models of system descriptions, and it provides analysis tools. First, we used the Workbench to test for deadlocks in our models. Initially, there were several; this is how we discovered an incompleteness in the system description of [5], with respect to with MEK. Second, when we had deadlock-free models, we used the Workbench to generate the CTMC and analyse its long-run probability distribution. This distribution varies as the rates associated with the activities of the PEPA model are varied, so the solution of the model is relative to a particular assignment of the rates.

The steady-state probability distribution can be obtained using a number of routines from numerical linear algebra. In the case of the present model(s), we solved this using the implementation of the preconditioned biconjugate gradient method in the PEPA Workbench. This is an iterative procedure which solves systems of linear equations of moderate size very quickly.

Numerical methods based on the computation of the steady-state probability distribution for a Continuous-Time Markov Chain have wide application, but are not routinely used in computational biology. Instead biological models are often formulated as systems of first-order coupled ordinary differential equations (ODEs) and computational analysis proceeds via reaction rate equations using methods such as Runge-Kutta.

In another paper [3], we present an algorithmic procedure for generating a system of ODEs from a PEPA model of high and low component concentration. This provides a useful method of validating a process algebra model against an existing system of ODEs. In the case of the ERK pathway we have been able to recreate exactly the system of ODEs as used in [5].

Numerical integration of the ODEs gives rise to time series plots which show how the concentration of components varies over time. These tend to a steady-state equilibrium which we have found to be in good agreement with the steady-state computed by Markovian methods.

Because of this different point of view it is appropriate to say a little here about how computational analysis via CTMCs compares with analysis via ODEs.

There are two axes of comparison for numerical methods. One is numerical stability (that is, under what conditions the methods converge to an acceptable result) and the other is computational efficiency. To make both parts of the comparison between CTMCs and ODEs we consider using the Chapman-Kolmogorov differential equations to perform transient analysis of a Markov chain.

Firstly, in the seminal work on numerical solution of Markov chains Stewart [19] discourages the use of ODEs to perform transient analysis of Markov chains, pointing to poor stability properties. Thus Markovian methods have this advantage in practical application.

Secondly, although it is more informative, transient analysis has higher computational cost than steady-state analysis. This indicates a saving in computational cost because here we are considering only steady-state solutions of the reagent and pathway models.

Since the reagent and pathway models are isomorphic, the underlying steady-state probability distributions are identical. However, it is possible to make different judgements about the two models using the PEPA state-finder which allows one to search for symbolic descriptions of states. For example, in the reagent-centric model, we used the PEPA state-finder to aggregate the probabilities of all states when ERK-PP is high, or low, for a given set of rates. That is, it aggregated the probabilities of states whose (symbolic) description has the form $* \bowtie$ ERK-PP$_H$ where $*$ is a wildcard standing for any expression. We then repeated this with a different set of rates and compared results. In the

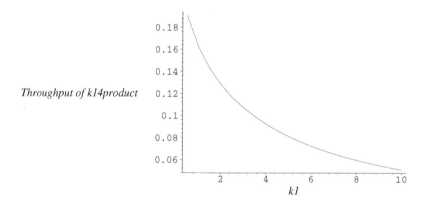

Fig. 8. Plotting the effect of $k1$ on $k14product$

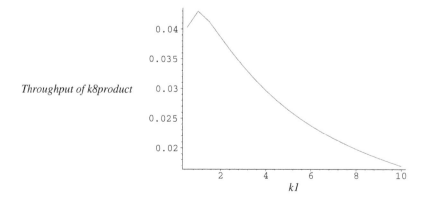

Fig. 9. Plotting the effect of $k1$ on $k8product$

reagent-centric model, we observed that the probability of being in a state with ERK-PP$_H$ *decreases* as the rate $k1$ is increased, and the converse for ERK-PP$_L$ *increases*. For example, with $k1 = 1$ and $k1 = 100$, the probability of ERK-PP$_H$ drops from .257 to .005. We can also plot throughput (rate $\times$ probability) against rate. Figures 8 and 9 shows two sub-plots which detail the effect of increasing the rate $k1$ on the $k14product$ and $k8product$ reactions – the production of (doubly) phosphorylated MEK and (doubly) phosphorylated ERK, respectively. These are obtained by solving the pathway model, taking each of the product and re-action rates to be unity and scaling $k1$ (keeping all other rates to be unity). The graphs show that increasing the rate of the binding of RKIP to Raf-1* dampens down the $k14product$ and $k8product$ reactions, and they quantify this information. The efficiency of the reduction is greater in the former case: the graph falls away more steeply. In the latter case the reduction is more gradual and the throughput of $k8product$ peaks at $k1 = 1$. Note that since $k5product$ is on the same pathway as $k8product$, both ERK-PP and ERK-P are similarly affected. Thus we conclude that the rate at which RKIP binds to Raf-1* (thus suppressing phosphorylation of MEK) affects the ERK pathway, as predicted (and observed); RKIP does indeed regulate the ERK pathway.

6   Transformation

In this section we present a set of transformations between the two styles of representation, based on an intermediate matrix representation. Thus we define an *activity matrix* M_a which captures the relationship between reagents and reactions. The matrix has one row corresponding to each reagent in the system, whilst each column corresponds to exactly one reaction. Within the matrix we quantify the impact of each reaction on each reagent in a manner analogous to the stoichiometry matrix of the chemical reaction[3]. This can be regarded as a canonical representation in the sense that there is no redundancy within it. In the example presented in this paper all reactions are deterministic and therefore entries in the activity matrix will always be between -1, 0 or $+1$.

As we will show, both reagent-centric and pathway-centric PEPA models can be readily and systematically translated into their activity matrix representation. Moreover, we will also show that for a given activity matrix a corresponding PEPA model of either form can be systematically generated. In the remainder of this section we give the algorithms for each of these transformations — from the process algebra models to the matrix, and from the matrix to each form of process algebra model.

Definition 1 (Activity Matrix). *For a system with R reactions and S reagents, the activity matrix M_a is an $S \times R$ matrix, and the entries are defined as follows.*

$$(s_i, r_j) = \begin{cases} +1 & \text{if } s_i \text{ is a consumer of } r_j \\ -1 & \text{if } s_i \text{ is a producer of } r_j \\ 0 & \text{otherwise.} \end{cases}$$

---

[3] However, we emphasise that our models do not represent individual molecules.

The relationship between the activity matrix the reagent-centric model is fairly straightforward but the relationship to the pathway model is somewhat more involved. Therefore we start by explaining the mapping from the reagent-centric model to the matrix.

Reagent-Centric Model to Activity Matrix. In the reagent centric model there are a pair of PEPA definitions corresponding to each reagent. The set of reactions that this reagent is involved in are those that appear in the definitions of these components. The impact of a reaction can be seen according to whether the reaction moves the reagent from high to low (decreasing, -1) or vice versa (increasing, $+1$). The algorithm for generating the activity matrix from a reagent-centric model is shown in Figure 10.

```
// Construct a matrix of the appropriate size
Form a matrix with one row for each pair (H,L) of components
 and a column for each activity used in the process algebra definitions

// Populate the matrix
For each H component, on the appropriate row, make a -1 entry in the
 column corresponding to each activity it enables
For each L component, on the appropriate row, make a +1 entry in the
 column corresponding to each activity it enables
```

Fig. 10. Pseudo-code for transforming a reagent-centric model to an activity matrix

Activity matrix to reagent-centric model. When forming a reagent-centric PEPA model from an activity matrix, we will generate two PEPA component definitions for each reagent/row of the matrix – one corresponding to high concentration and one corresponding to low concentrations. The reagent in high concentration will enable all those reactions which have a negative entry in the column, whilst the reagent in low concentration will enable all those reactions which have a positive entry in the column.

The algorithm for generating a reagent-centric model from an activity matrix is shown in Figure 11. There are two stages to the algorithm. First, a pair of model components are formed corresponding to each row as outlined above. Second, the components must be configured with appropriate interactions between them. We exploit the knowledge that in this style of model each component must cooperate on all its activities. Thus the model configuration is built iteratively — as each component is added it is specified to cooperate with *the rest of the model* on all its activities. Whether each reagent exhibits its high or low concentration form in the configuration depends on whether experimental data suggests it starts with initial concentration or not.

Pathway-Centric Model to Activity Matrix. The algorithm for generating the activity matrix from a pathway-centric model is shown in Figure 12. The construction of the matrix to capture the involvement of pathway model components

```
// Form the model components
For each row of the matrix assign a reactant name.
For each reactant
    make a H subscripted component based on the reactant name
    define this component to be a choice of activities as follows:
        for each -1 in the corresponding row of the activity matrix
            make an activity of the type of the appropriate column
                which results in an L subscripted component of the same name
                add this activity to the choice for the H component
    make an L subscripted component based on the reactant name
    define this component to be a choice of activities as follows:
        for each +1 in the corresponding row of the activity matrix
            make an activity of the type of the appropriate column
                which results in an H subscripted component of the same name
                add this activity to the choice for the L component

// Form the model configuration
For each reactant
    if this reagent has high initial concentration
        enter the H subscripted component
    if this reagent has low initial concentration
        enter the L subscripted component
    // build the appropriate cooperation set K
  for each non-zero entry of the corresponding row of the activity matrix
        enter the corresponding reaction/activity to the set K
    add a cooperation over the set K and "("
add one ")" for each row of the matrix
```

Fig. 11. Pseudo-code for transforming an activity matrix to a reagent-centric model

```
// Construct a matrix of the appropriate size
Form a matrix with one row for each of the components exhibited by
the
 pathways and a column for each activity used in the process algebra
 definitions

// Populate the matrix
For each component, on the appropriate row, make a -1 entry in the
 column corresponding to each activity it enables and a +1 entry in
 the same column of the resulting component.

//Reduce the matrix
Detect and remove identical rows
```

Fig. 12. Pseudo-code for transforming a pathway-centric model to an activity matrix

```
// Colour assignment
Assign a unique colour to each reagent which has initial
concentration Identify the rows of the matrix corresponding to
these reagents Colour each row accordingly

// Find minimal pathways
For each colour C
    while there are unpaired C entries in the matrix
        for each -1(resp. +1) entry in row s and column r coloured C
            find all entries in column r
                if there are more than one +1(resp. -1) entry
                    if none are already coloured C
                        provisionally colour each corresponding entry
                        record them as a row set
                if there is only one +1(resp. -1) entry, in row s' say
                    if it is not already coloured C
                        colour row s' with colour C
                        if s' was previously provisionally coloured with C
                            remove the provisional colouring from all other
                            elements of the row set

// Form the model components
For each colour C
    make an initial Pathway component
    make a Pathway component for each other row with C coloured entries
    for each C coloured Pathway component/row
        define the pathway component with one activity corresponding
        to each -1 column in the row whose resulting component will
        be the C coloured +1 entry in the same column


// Form the model configuration
For each colour C
    enter the corresponding initial Pathway component
    for each reaction r which is coloured C and another colour C'
        enter r into the cooperation set K
    add a cooperation over the set K and "("
add one ")" for each colour
```

Fig. 13. Pseudo-code for transforming an activity matrix to a pathway-centric model

in the reactions of the system is straightforward. However, this construction will result in some duplicate rows within the matrix because some compound reagents can be seen to be intermediate states of two or more pathways (e.g. RKIP-P/RP corresponds to both Pwy_{11} and Pwy_{12}). Thus the duplicates must be removed.

Activity Matrix to Pathway-Centric Model. The algorithm for generating a pathway-centric model from an activity matrix is shown in Figure 13. In the

	$k1$	$k2$	$k3$	$k4$	$k5$	$k6$	$k7$	$k8$	$k9$	$k10$	$k11$	$k12$	$k13$	$k14$	$k15$	pathways
Raf-1*	−1	+1	0	0	+1	0	0	0	0	0	0	−1	+1	+1	0	4
RKIP	−1	+1	0	0	0	0	0	0	0	0	+1	0	0	0	0	2
Raf-1*/RKIP	+1	−1	−1	+1	0	0	0	0	0	0	0	0	0	0	0	2, 4
Raf-1*/RKIP/ERK-PP	0	0	+1	−1	−1	0	0	0	0	0	0	0	0	0	0	2, 3, 4
ERK-P	0	0	0	0	+1	−1	+1	0	0	0	0	0	0	0	0	3
RKIP-P	0	0	0	0	+1	0	0	0	−1	+1	0	0	0	0	0	2
MEK-PP	0	0	0	0	0	−1	+1	+1	0	0	0	0	0	+1	−1	5
MEK-PP/ERK	0	0	0	0	0	+1	−1	−1	0	0	0	0	0	0	0	3, 5
ERK-PP	0	0	−1	+1	0	0	0	+1	0	0	0	0	0	0	0	3
RP	0	0	0	0	0	0	0	0	−1	+1	+1	0	0	0	0	1
RKIP-P/RP	0	0	0	0	0	0	0	0	+1	−1	−1	0	0	0	0	1, 2
MEK	0	0	0	0	0	0	0	0	0	0	0	−1	+1	0	+1	5
MEK/Raf-1*	0	0	0	0	0	0	0	0	0	0	0	+1	−1	−1	0	4, 5

Fig. 14. Activity matrix of the ERK pathway

activity matrix each row corresponds to a distinct reagent. In order to reconstruct the sub-pathways, we need to take into account that fact that some reagents may correspond to intermediate states in two or more pathways. Thus we introduce a notion of colouring, in which one colour is associated with each sub-pathway. A single row/reagent may have several colourings indicating which sub-pathways it participates in.

The next goal is to identify the sub-pathways. We note that for all reagents all the reactions that they participate in will be part of the same sub-pathway although it is not true that each reagent that participates in a reaction will belong to the same sub-pathway. Consequently either all the entries in a row will be coloured with some colour C or none will. However, except for the rows corresponding to initial concentrations, which are taken as the roots of our sub-pathways, any row many have any number of colours associated with it.

In order to find the sub-pathways we need to find a consumer corresponding to each producer, and vice versa, within each colour. Once such an association is made we consider the coloured matrix entry to be *paired*. The pathway is complete when all entries of that colour have been paired. In some cases there may be several candidate matrix entries for forming a pair: the corresponding rows are collected into a set of provisionally coloured rows until it becomes clear which entry completes a minimal cycle. The other rows are then discarded.

When, for each colour, all matrix entries are paired, the sub-pathway model components can be defined in a straightforward way. It remains to form the model component. Those entries which have more than one colour must be carried out in cooperation by the corresponding pathways. Thus, for a pathway component with colour C, the cooperation set is formed as those reactions corresponding to a column in the matrix in which there is an entry which is coloured C and some other colour.

As an illustration we present the activity matrix corresponding to the example presented earlier in the paper in Figure 14. This can be derived from either the reagent- or the pathway-centric model. In the far right hand column we give an indication of the colouring of the matrix to derive the pathway model shown in Figure 4 — the numbers indicate which pathway(s) each row corresponds to.

7   Further Analysis

The process algebraic approach has several tangible benefits. For example, in addition to deadlock and quantitative analysis, the compositional nature of the process algebra approach confines changes to the behaviour of a reagent to a single system component, i.e. to one or two equations. In an ODE model, such a change would be pervasive, i.e. numerous equations would have to be altered. Nevertheless, ODE models offer analysis by a wide variety of solvers. In [3] we show how an ODE model defining standard mass action kinetics can be derived automatically from the process algebra reagent-centric or pathway-centric models, via the activity matrix. A key observation is that the coarsest level of abstraction (i.e. *high* and *low*) provides sufficient information for deriving the ODE representation. In other words, it is sufficient to know which reactions increase concentration (i.e. low to high), and which ones decrease concentration (i.e. high to low). The addition of further discrete values does not add further information. Thus all the standard analysis tools available for ODEs are also available to the modeller taking the process algebraic approach with the coarsest (and simplest) discretisation of concentrations.

Further quantitative analysis is possible using probabilistic logics and probabilistic model checking. For example, we have investigated the use of the logic CSL [1] and the model checker PRISM [12]. Further analysis of a PRISM model derived from the reagent-centric model given here is reported in [4]. Examples of CSL properties (stated informally) are *"What is the probability that a concentration of a species reaches a particular value and then remains at that value thereafter?"*, and *"How does varying a reaction rate affect that probability?"*. We note that in this paradigm, the resulting probabilities depend on the granularity of discrete concentration values.

8   Related Work

The work of Regev and her co-authors has been deeply influential [16,18,15,17]. Although the exact form of the process algebra which is used in these works varies, there is some commonality in the languages and the analysis is always based on stochastic simulation. At the basis is always the fundamental mapping developed by Regev in her thesis. In this mapping a correspondence is made between molecules in the biological system and processes or agents in the process algebra.

In this paper we propose a different mapping in which a correspondence is made between a subpathway and a process in the process algebra. The most basic form of subpathway is taken to be a single species and its fluctuations in concentrations. In the paper we have demonstrated this and a larger notion of subpathway based on the notion of the possible biochemical flow of a single species. The key point is that this mapping is onto an abstract concept in the biology (the species or pathway) rather than a concrete one (the molecule). We believe that this shift to the more abstract form offers an alternative view of systems and better access to the analysis mechanisms associated with process algebras.

The work of Fisher *et al.* reported in [8] also proposes using two distinct views of the same system. However, they envisage different roles for the two views, one capturing the observations of a system which have been made experimentally (scenario-based model) and the other making an hypothesis about the mechanistic behaviour which might generate such observations (state-based model). In their terminology, both our models are state-based, seeking to give a mechanistic account for how observed behaviour may arise. It is an interesting area for future work to consider how this might be formally reconciled with experimental observations.

The pathway view of our network bears some resemblance to the *extreme pathways* (and the related concept of *elementary modes*) in the work of Papin *et al.* on metabolic pathways [14]. There the authors aim to identify and separate subpathways using linear algebra techniques applied to the stoichiometry matrix for a metabolic pathway. The exact relationship with our own work is an area for further work.

In theoretical computer science it has previously been remarked that process algebra models may be used to capture the same system in a variety of different styles e.g. [20]. We view our work as continuing in that tradition, for example our modelling styles loosely correspond to the constraint oriented style, although in a different context and considering somewhat different styles of model. As we continue to explore the relationship between our modelling styles we hope to be able to benefit from this earlier research.

9   Conclusions

We have presented two alternative PEPA models of the Raf-1/MEK/ERK module of the ERK signalling pathway and shown them to be equivalent. The reagent-based model has explicit concentrations whilst in the pathway model the concentrations are captured only implicitly via the possible activities of each sub-pathway. The pathway-based model can thus be regarded as less directly expressive, although it captures all the same behaviour. The congruence results of PEPA with respect to strong bisimulation mean that the two representations may be used interchangeably, for example within a large model. Thus we might envisage a model in which the key pathway is modelled using the reagent-style whilst peripheral pathways are modelled using the pathway-style. Or, we may have one style of model and hypothesise the other. We believe this ability to have different views is novel in the field of modelling pathways; informal discussions with biologists confirm their interest in it.

We found the multi-way synchronisation of PEPA, and the performance aspects, to be ideally suited to modelling pathway behaviour. In this example, deadlock analysis very quickly revealed an incompleteness in the published model. Once deadlock-free, one strength of models of the kind which we have used here is that they give rise to compact Markov chain representations which can be efficiently solved for different assignments to the rate variables in a series of experiments. This delivers the benefit that a thorough series of experiments can be conducted at modest computational cost.

Furthermore, we have presented transformations between the two alternative styles of representation, via an intermediate, the *activity matrix*. This means that automatic translation between representations is possible. The transformation from an activity matrix to the pathway model has some similarities with finding the minimal T-semiflows of a Petri net. Comparing our algorithm with the algorithms for T-semiflows [6], or the more general mathematical programming problem of finding the extremal directions of a cone [13], are yet to be investigated.

Process algebra opens up a host of analysis possibilities, including, in addition to Markov chain analysis, the use of ODE solvers and reasoning with probabilistic logics using probabilistic model checking. With respect to the former, we have found we require only to distinguish between high and low concentrations, further granularity adds no analytic benefit. Rather we need only model the *direction* of change (i.e. an increase or decrease of concentration). With respect to the latter, we have conducted initial investigations with the logic CSL and indicated further possibilities.

Several challenges remain. For example, we wish to derive the reagent-centric model from experimental data and model spatial aspects of pathways. We have some preliminary ideas which are the topic of future research.

Acknowledgements

Stephen Gilmore and Jane Hillston are supported by the SENSORIA (Software Engineering for Service-Oriented Overlay Computers) 6th framework Global Computing Initiative IST project funded by the European Union. Jane Hillston is funded by an Advanced Research Fellowship from the UK Engineering and Physical Sciences Research Council. Muffy Calder is supported by the DTI Beacon Bioscience Projects programme and thanks Walter Kolch, Beatson Cancer Research Centre, and Rainer Breitling, David Gilbert, Richard Orton, and Oliver Sturm from the Bioinformatics Research Centre, University of Glasgow, for helpful discussions.

References

1. A. Aziz, K. Sanwal, V. Singhal, and R. Brayton. Verifying continuous time Markov chains. In *Computer-Aided Verification*, volume 1102 of *LNCS*, pages 169–276. Springer-Verlag, 1996.

2. M. Calder, S. Gilmore, and J. Hillston. Modelling the influence of RKIP on the ERK signalling pathway using the stochastic process algebra PEPA. In *Proc. of BioConcur 2004*, pages 26–41. Danmarks Tekniske Universitet, 2004. To appear in ENTCS.
3. M. Calder, S. Gilmore, and J. Hillston. Automatically deriving ODEs from process algebra models of signalling pathways. In *Computational Methods in Systems Biology 2005*, pages 204–215. LFCS, University of Edinburgh, 2005.
4. M. Calder, V. Vyshemirsky, R. Orton, and D. Gilbert. Analysis of signalling pathways using the PRISM model checker. In *Computational Methods in Systems Biology 2005*, pages 179–190. LFCS, University of Edinburgh, 2005.
5. K.-H. Cho, S.-Y. Shin, H.-W. Kim, O. Wolkenhauer, B. McFerran, and W. Kolch. Mathematical modeling of the influence of RKIP on the ERK signaling pathway. In C. Priami, editor, *Computational Methods in Systems Biology (CSMB'03)*, volume 2602 of *LNCS*, pages 127–141. Springer-Verlag, 2003.
6. J.M. Colom and M. Silva. Convex geometry and semiflows in P/T nets. a comparative study of algorithms for computation of minimal P-semiflows. In G. Rozenberg, editor, *Advances in Petri Nets 1990*, volume 483 of *LNCS*, pages 79–112. Springer-Verlag, 1991.
7. W.H. Elliot and D.C. Elliot. *Biochemistry and Molecular Biology, 2nd edition.* Oxford University Press, 2002.
8. J. Fisher, D. Harel, E.J.A. Hubbard, N. Piterman, M.J. Stern, and N. Swerdlin. Combining state-based and scenario-based approaches in modeling biological systems. In V. Danos and V. Schachter, editors, *Computational Methods in Systems Biology 2004*, volume 3082 of *LNBI*, pages 236–241. Springer, 2005.
9. S. Gilmore and J. Hillston. The PEPA Workbench: A Tool to Support a Process Algebra-based Approach to Performance Modelling. In *Proceedings of the Seventh International Conference on Modelling Techniques and Tools for Computer Performance Evaluation*, number 794 in Lecture Notes in Computer Science, pages 353–368, Vienna, May 1994. Springer-Verlag.
10. M. Heiner and I. Koch. Petri net based model validation in systems biology. In *25th International Conference on Application and Theory of Petri Nets, Bologna, Italy*, 2004.
11. J. Hillston. *A Compositional Approach to Performance Modelling.* Cambridge University Press, 1996.
12. M. Kwiatkowska, G. Norman, and D. Parker. Probabilistic symbolic model checking with PRISM: A hybrid approach. In J.-P. Katoen and P. Stevens, editors, *Proc. 8th International Conference on Tools and Algorithms for the Construction and Analysis of Systems (TACAS'02)*, volume 2280 of *LNCS*, pages 52–66. Springer, April 2002.
13. T.H. Matheiss and D.S. Rubin. A survey and comparison of methods for finding all the vertices of convex polyhedral sets. *Mathematics of Operational Research*, 5(2):167–185, 1980.
14. J.A. Papin, N.D. Price, S.J. Wiback, D.A. Fell, and B.O. Palsson. Metabolic pathways in the post-genome era. *TRENDS in Biochemical Sciences*, 28(5):250–258, May 2003.
15. C. Priami, A. Regev, W. Silverman, and E. Shapiro. Application of a stochastic name passing calculus to representation and simulation of molecular processes. *Information Processing Letters*, 80:25–31, 2001.
16. A. Regev. *Computational Systems Biology: a Calculus for Biomolecular Knowledge.* PhD thesis, Tel Aviv University, 2002.

17. A. Regev, E.M. Panina, W. Silverman, L. Cardelli, and E. Shapiro. BioAmbients: an abstraction for biological compartments. *Theoretical Computer Science*, 325(1):141–167, 2004.
18. A. Regev, W. Silverman, and E. Shapiro. Representation and simulation of biochemical processes using the pi-calculus process algebra. In *Proceedings of the Pacific Symposium of Biocomputing (PSB2001)*, pages 459–470, 2001.
19. William Stewart. *Numerical Solution of Markov Chains*. Princeton University Press, 1994.
20. C.A. Vissers, G. Scollo, M. van Sinderen, and E. Brinksma. Specification styles in distributed systems design and verification. *Theoretical Computer Science*, 89:179–206, 1991.

A   PEPA

This appendix provides a brief introduction to PEPA in order to make the paper self-contained. It can safely be skipped by anyone who already knows the PEPA language. For a full explanation which complements the brief description presented here the reader is referred to [11].

Prefix: The basic mechanism for describing the behaviour of a system with a PEPA model is to give a component a designated first action using the prefix combinator, denoted by a full stop. For example, $(\alpha, r).S$ carries out activity (α, r), which has action type α and an exponentially distributed duration with parameter r, and it subsequently behaves as S.

Choice: The component $P + Q$ represents a system which may behave either as P or as Q. The activities of both P and Q are enabled. The first activity to complete distinguishes one of them: the other is discarded. The system will behave as the derivative resulting from the evolution of the chosen component.

Constant: It is convenient to be able to assign names to patterns of behaviour associated with components. Constants are components whose meaning is given by a defining equation. The notation for this is $X \stackrel{def}{=} E$. The name X is in scope in the expression on the right hand side meaning that, for example, $X \stackrel{def}{=} (\alpha, r).X$ performs α at rate r forever.

Hiding: The possibility to abstract away some aspects of a component's behaviour is provided by the hiding operator, denoted P/L. Here, the set L identifies those activities which are to be considered internal or private to the component and which will appear as the unknown type τ.

Cooperation: We write $P \bowtie_L Q$ to denote cooperation between P and Q over L. The set which is used as the subscript to the cooperation symbol, the *cooperation set* L, determines those activities on which the *cooperands* are forced to synchronise. For action types not in L, the components proceed independently and concurrently with their enabled activities. We write $P \parallel Q$ as an abbreviation for $P \bowtie_L Q$ when L is empty.

However, if a component enables an activity whose action type is in the cooperation set it will not be able to proceed with that activity until the other

component also enables an activity of that type. The two components then proceed together to complete the *shared activity*. The rate of the shared activity
may be altered to reflect the work carried out by both components to complete
the activity (for details see [11]).

In some cases, when an activity is known to be carried out in cooperation with
another component, a component may be *passive* with respect to that activity.
This means that the rate of the activity is left unspecified (denoted ⊤) and is
determined upon cooperation, by the rate of the activity in the other component.
All passive actions must be synchronised in the final model.

Gene Regulation in the Pi Calculus: Simulating Cooperativity at the Lambda Switch

Céline Kuttler[1] and Joachim Niehren[2]

[1] Interdisciplinary Research Institute, Lille, France[*]
[2] INRIA Futurs, Lille, France[**]

Abstract. We propose to model the dynamics of gene regulatory networks as concurrent processes in the stochastic pi calculus. As a first case study, we show how to express the control of transcription initiation at the lambda switch, a prototypical example where cooperative enhancement is crucial. This requires concurrent programming techniques that are new to systems biology, and necessitates stochastic parameters that we derive from the literature. We test all components of our model by exhaustive stochastic simulations. A comparison with previous results reported in the literature, experimental and simulation based, confirms the appropriateness of our modeling approach.

1 Introduction

In living cells, genes and proteins interact in networks of gene regulation. All cells of a multicellular organism contain the same genetic material. Nevertheless, the use made of it varies widely between different tissues. The current state of a cell is determined by the proteins it contains; it changes when new proteins are produced by decoding genetic information.

Understanding the dynamic behavior of gene regulatory systems is a challenge to computational systems biology. The molecular actors within these networks interact *nondeterministically*. Given a particular condition, one can never tell with certainty which among several thinkable reactions will follow next. What occurs strongly depends on the identities of various proteins in the cell, their interaction capabilities, quantities – and random encounters. Such effects accumulate, making it difficult to predict the behavior of a system as a whole, even if its components are well characterized.

Informal descriptions of prototypical gene regulatory networks can be found in biological textbooks [13,35]. These deal with qualitative aspects such as the possible reactions between molecular actors. They also address quantitative aspects as frequencies of such reactions, but usually remain rather vague on these. Precise quantitative parameters are more difficult to access. For well studied

---

[*] Interdisciplinary Research Institute, FRE 2963 of CNRS, in cooperation with the University of Lille 1 and supported by the Conseil Régional Nord-Pas de Calais.
[**] Mostrare Project of INRIA Futurs at the LIFL, in cooperation with the Universities of Lille 1 and 3.

C. Priami et al. (Eds.): Trans. on Comput. Syst. Biol. VII, LNBI 4230, pp. 24–55, 2006.
© Springer-Verlag Berlin Heidelberg 2006

systems they have been determined in series of experiments, and reported in the research literature.

Simulations can help understanding the dynamics of gene regulatory networks [7,19]. This particularly holds for cases in which informal qualitative descriptions exist as well as quantitative characterizations. The question that remains is whether the available knowledge suffices to correctly predict the system's behavior. This can be shown by building a mathematical model, executing it, and comparing simulation and experimental results.

In this article, we propose to formally model gene regulatory networks as *communicating stochastic processes*, to our knowledge, for the first time. We draw inspiration from previous stochastic models of gene expression [2,12,21]. We follow Regev and Shapiro [38] in applying the *stochastic π-calculus* [33] as modeling language for systems biology. This is Milner's et. al. π-calculus [29,28] – a fundamental model of concurrency – extended by stochastic control (see also [18]). Nondeterminism is inherent to concurrent computation, of which the π-calculus abstracts the essential features. Stochastic parameters control communication or *interaction* frequencies, and thus the evolution of the numbers of actors over time. Execution of stochastic π-calculus models yields *stochastic simulation* based on Gillespie's algorithm [14], using the BioSpi engine [34] or similar systems [32].

We investigate a prototypical instance of gene regulation in a bacterium, for which both qualitative and quantitative knowledge are available. As a first case study, we show how to model and simulate the control of *transcription initiation at the lambda switch* [35], a prototypical example where *cooperativity* is crucial. To be concrete, we model the molecular interactions at bacteriophage λ's right operator region, including positive control of transcription initiation and cooperativity in protein binding. This requires concurrent programming techniques that are new to systems biology:

1. we use *handshake protocols* in order to express *many-to-many communication* on same channel;
2. we use *alternative timer agents* in order to alternate stochastic rates associated to channels, this allows to express *cooperative enhancement* of the channel's activity.

We show how to compute the stochastic parameters from the literature, and integrate these parameters into our formal π-calculus models. We validate our models and parameters by running exhaustive simulation tests. One of the strengths of our approach is that we can easily simulate idealized subsystems, in order to observe distinguished phenomena independently from the system as a whole. We design a sequence of sub-models of different degrees of complexity, in order to simulate the many factors influencing transcription initiation at the λ switch. The simulation results we obtain convincingly confirm the appropriateness of our model[1].

---

[1] These simulation results are new compared to the presentation at the second international workshop on concurrent models in molecular biology (BioConcur 2004). They have permitted us to spot some flaws in the previous parameter sets.

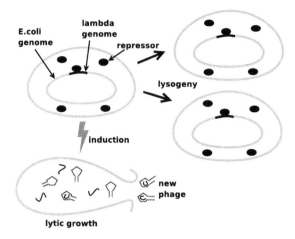

Fig. 1. Two pathways of λ infected E.coli bacterium: lysogeny and lytic growth

The general mechanisms of cooperativity we model can be observed in many other places, ranging from the assembly of protein complexes, DNA looping to regulatory mechanisms in eukaryotes. For a discussion see [36]. Note that more aspects remain to be included in our stochastic π-calculus model of the λ switch in other to reflect recent observations that lead to the revision of long established assumptions [11,40]. The modeling techniques proposed in this paper, however, should be sufficient there too.

Plan. We first describe the regulatory network at the λ switch informally (Sec. 2) and then distill the stochastic parameters from the literature (Sec. 3). We recall the stochastic π-calculus (Sec. 4) and apply it for modeling the network of the λ switch (Sec. 5). Finally, we present simulations for different scenarios obtained by implementation of our model in the BioSpi system (Sec. 6). We motivate the different set-ups with experiments or other simulations, and try to relate both to each other.

2   The λ Switch

Gene regulation at the lambda switch has remained a fruitful research area for decades [10,31,35]. It has served as a benchmark for testing simulation methods [15], and to reproduce or elucidate experimental knowledge [2,3].

2.1   Pathways

Bacteriophage λ is a virus which infects the bacterium *Escherichia coli*. Injecting its genome into the bacterial cell, two developmental pathways as illustrated in Fig. 1 are possible. Either, in *lytic growth* the viral genome uses the molecular machinery of the bacterial cell to produce new viruses and eventually burst the host. Alternatively, the viral genome gets integrated into the bacterial genome.

Note the highlighted segment within the bacterial genome in Fig. 1. The only viral protein expressed is then the λ repressor, which disables the expression of all others through binding to dedicated segments of the viral genome. The host cell is now immune against further infections. The viral genome is subsequently transmitted to further bacterial generations in a passive way. This state called *lysogeny* is extremely stable, and usually maintained for generations. Spontaneous transitions from lysogeny to the state of lytic growth would occur about once every 5000 years for a single bacterial cell [10]. Considering that it takes the bacterium no longer than hour to divide into two daughter cells, the lysogenic state is extremely stable.

But surprisingly, upon an environmental signal the phage genome can efficiently become re-activated – this is called *induction*. Now, the bacterium switches from lysogeny into the phase of lytic growth. The viral genome is extracted from the host's, and uses the cell machinery to produce a fresh crop of viruses. This unavoidably leads to the *lysis*, or destruction of the host cell. What happens during induction, as well as the maintenance of lysogeny, crucially depends on the control of transcription initiation within O_R, the right operator region of phage λ's genome. O_R is commonly referred to as *the* λ switch.

2.2   Network Controlling Transcription Initiation

The control of transcription initiation at the λ switch illustrates phenomena of *cooperativity*, which are even more important for gene regulation in higher forms of life [36]. Cooperative enhancement of a reaction between two molecular actors means that its strength is enhanced by a third, otherwise independent actor. We will see two instances of cooperative enhancement at the λ switch: *positive control* and *cooperative binding*.

Genes and promoters: The λ switch controls two *genes* cI and cro, illustrated Fig. 2. As for all other genes, transcription always starts at DNA segments called *promoters*, here P_{RM} and P_R respectively. Transcription of a gene eventually enables the production of the *protein* it encodes. RNA *polymerase* (RNAP) are molecules which can bind at promoters. Once bound to promoter P_{RM} a RNAP may initiate transcription of the cI gene, which subsequently allows for the production of new λ *repressor* proteins (Rep). An RNAP bound at P_R may start to transcribe the cro gene and thereby enables the production of Cro proteins[2].

Cro and Rep proteins appear in two forms, as *dimers* and *monomers* which can be distinguished in Fig. 3. When expressed they first appear as *monomers*. Subsequently these associate pairwise, and only in this form they can bind to DNA. Dimers are unstable, unless bound to DNA they soon dissociate back to monomers. The higher the protein concentration in the cell, the higher is the degree of dimerization.

In lysogeny, the state of the network is characterized by a high number of Rep and negligible amount of Cro proteins; these frequencies are inverted during lytic

---

[2] P_{RM} stands for *promoter for synthesis of repressor during maintenance of lysogeny*. P_R simply stands for *right promoter*.

gene	promoter	protein
cI	P_{RM}	Rep
cro	P_R	Cro

Fig. 2. A spatial view on the λ switch, a segment of phage lambda's genome. The gene cI is transcribed from the promoter P_{RM}; it encodes the regulatory protein Rep. Its antagonist protein Cro is transcribed from promoter P_R. The operator regions O_{R1} and O_{R2} lie within P_R, while P_{RM} overlaps with O_{R3}.

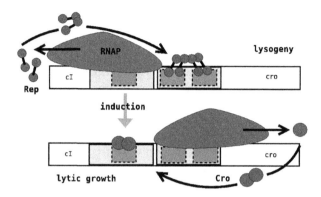

Fig. 3. Network states during lysogeny and lytic growth. In lysogeny, Rep attached to either or both of the binding sites O_{R1} and O_{R2} blocks recognition of the promoter P_R by RNAP, and thus prevents transcription of the gene *cro*. At the same time, interactions between Rep at O_{R2} and RNAP at P_{RM} stimulate transcription of the gene cI, which allows for the production of new Rep.

growth. The environmental signal upon induction leads to a massive destruction of Rep proteins. P_R then becomes activated automatically, while transcription from P_{RM} ceases. These are consequences of the network controlling transcription initiation.

Repression of promoters by steric hindrance: The regulatory proteins Rep and Cro can bind to three neighboring *operator* regions O_{R1}, O_{R2}, and O_{R3}. By doing so, they control RNAP access to the promoters. As Fig. 2 indicates O_{R1} and O_{R2} both overlap the promoter P_R, while O_{R3} lies within P_{RM}. A protein bound within a promoter blocks recognition of the promoter by RNAP. This principle is called *steric hindrance*. The typical constellations are sketched in Fig. 3. Note that all bindings are *reversible*, i.e. the proteins dissociate from the DNA strand after some time. RNAP frequently falls off a promoter without initiating transcription.

The maintenance of lysogeny depends on the presence of a sufficient amount of repressor, that is predominantly bound at O_{R1} and O_{R2}. This impedes RNAP binding to P_R. As a consequence, Cro and all other viral genes are not expressed.

Cooperative enhancement of repressor binding at O_{R2} : The intrinsic binding affinity of Rep for O_{R1} is tenfold higher than for O_{R2} and O_{R3}. Thus, Rep is likely to be found at O_{R1}. Furthermore, Rep at O_{R1} significantly favors

event	rate	name	reference
dissociation of RNAP · P$_{RM}$	0.788	Kd_RNAP_PRM	[24]
dissociation RNAP · P$_R$	0.155	Kd_RNAP_PR	[16]
dissociation of Rep · O$_{R1}$	0.155	Kd_or1_rep	[1]
dissociation of Rep · O$_{R2}$	3.99	Kd_or2_rep	[1]
dissociation of Rep · O$_{R2}$, coop.	0.155	Kd_or2_rep_coop	[41]
dissociation of Rep · O$_{R3}$	20.22	Kd_or3_rep	[22]
dissociation of Cro · O$_{R1}$	2.45	Kd_or1_cro	[41]
dissociation of Cro · O$_{R2}$	2.45	Kd_or2_cro	[41]
dissociation of Cro · O$_{R3}$	0.29	Kd_or3_cro	[41]
association of protein to operators	0.098	Ka_protein	[6]
association of RNAP to promoters	0.098	Ka_RNAP	[47]
promoted transcription from P$_{RM}$	0.086	Kf_prm_promoted	[24]
transcription from P$_{RM}$	0.005	Kf_prm	[24]
transcription from P$_R$	0.05	Kf_pr	[16]
association of repressor monomers	0.048	ka_repDimer	[8]
dissociation of repressor dimers	0.5	kd_repDimer	[8]

Fig. 4. Stochastic parameters for molecular events at the λ switch

binding of another Rep to O$_{R2}$ – this is what we call *cooperative binding*. One could say that the λ repressor at O$_{R1}$ *recruits* another to O$_{R2}$ [36].

Positive control of transcription initiation is needed for virtually all genes [36]. It refers to the fact that RNAP bound to a promoter needs the help of regulatory proteins in order to successfully initiate transcription. At P$_{RM}$, RNAP's frequency increases due to a direct contact with Rep bound at O$_{R2}$. This second instance of cooperative enhancement, called *positive control*, is decisive for maintaining the lysogenic state. Without it RNAP would rather fall off the inherently weak promoter P$_{RM}$ than start to transcribe.

The production of Rep ceases once its level allows to fill not only O$_{R1}$ and O$_{R2}$, but also the last site O$_{R3}$. At this point Rep inhibits its own production by steric hindrance of P$_{RM}$ in a negative feedback loop.

Upon *induction*, the number of repressors rapidly decreases due to an external signal, so that O$_{R1}$ and O$_{R2}$ become more and more likely to remain vacant. Now polymerases find frequent opportunities to bind to P$_R$. As P$_R$ is inherently a *strong promoter*, these bindings rapidly ensue transcription, followed by the production of Cro proteins.

3   Stochastic Parametrization

The stochastic π-calculus assumes rates that determine the speed of reactions. In this section, we discuss how to distill such rates from the literature. The resulting parameters are summarized and given mnemonic names in Figure 4.

In our system reversible binding reactions are frequent, such as by λ repressor to the operator O$_{R1}$:

$$\text{Rep} + \text{O}_{R1} \; {}_{k_d}\!\!\rightleftharpoons^{k_a} \text{Rep} \cdot \text{O}_{R1} \qquad (1)$$

This bidirectional reaction converges to an equilibrium, in which the number of reactants on both sides remains constant. The *association* constant k_a determines the speed of the association reaction. It measures the number of Rep-O_{R1}-pairs that form complexes per mol and second. For the case of regulatory proteins the *association* rate constant k_a has been experimentally determined [6,47,44]. It is given by the net rate with which a protein locates its target site on DNA:

$$k_a = \frac{10^8}{\text{mol sec}} \tag{2}$$

We assume this value for all combinations of proteins and sites [3].

The *dissociation* constant k_d specifies the speed of the de-complexation. It measures the proportion of complexes that is resolved per second. As we will see, for the case of Rep binding to O_{R1} we can assume it to be $k_d = \frac{0.155}{\text{sec}}$.

However, it is less obvious to infer such dissociation rates the literature. What is determined experimentally for such reactions is mostly *Gibbs free energy* ΔG – a notion from thermodynamics. The value of ΔG quantifies the effort necessary for decomplexation. In the concrete example of O_{R1}, Shea and Ackers [1] provide $\Delta G = -12.5 \frac{kcal}{mol}$. This energy is negative, reflecting that binding requires an effort by the environment, while unbinding happens voluntarily. Non cooperative binding of Rep at the weaker binding site O_{R2} yields a value of $\Delta G = -10.5 \frac{kcal}{mol}$, for O_{R3} we obtain $\Delta G = -9.5 \frac{kcal}{mol}$. Note that a smaller value indicates *stronger* binding, and that a difference of $1kcal$ ensues a tenfold difference in binding strength.

Gibbs free energy correlates with the equilibrium constant K_{eq} of the binding reaction, which expresses the quantities of unbound pairs Rep and O_{R1} compared to complexes Rep $\cdot$ O_{R1} in equilibrium. The relationship is expressed through the equation:

$$K_{eq} = \exp(\frac{-\Delta G}{R \cdot T}) \tag{3}$$

where $R = 1.9872 \frac{cal}{\text{mol Kelvin}}$ is the universal gas constant and $T = 310.15$ Kelvin is the absolute temperature at which the experiments were performed (it corresponds to 37 Celsius).

The equilibrium constant K_{eq} represents the ratio of association and dissociation rate constants as shows the following kinetic equation:

$$K_{eq} = \frac{k_a}{k_d} \text{ mol} \tag{4}$$

---

[3] This constant exceeds three dimensional diffusion by two orders of magnitude, and subsumes a number of mechanisms of target site location by proteins. In its search process a protein first diffuses three-dimensionally trhough the cytoplasm, hits the DNA and subsequently slides along the DNA, rapidly scanning it for its specific site. A model explaining this has been proposed in [43].

	ΔG	k_d	binding strength
O_{R1}	−12.5	0.155	strongest
O_{R2} (coop)	−12.5	0.155	
O_{R2} (isolated)	−10.5	3.99	
O_{R3}	−9.5	20.22	weakest

Fig. 5. Parameters for binding of λ repressor to the three operator regions

The experimental data on Gibbs energy together with equations (2), (3), and (4) are sufficient to compute the dissociation rate k_d by straightforward arithmetics[4].

The rate constants k_a and k_d we have met so far are *macroscopic* – as in chemical kinetics. They do not depend on the actual numbers of molecules, but on concentrations. Gillespie's algorithm, however, and thus the biochemical stochastic π-calculus use *mesoscopic* rate constants as their stochastic rates. These refer to actual numbers of molecules and are determined from their macroscopic counterparts as follows:

$$k_a^{meso} = \tfrac{k_a}{A\,V}, \qquad k_d^{meso} = k_d,$$

where $A = 6.023 \cdot 10^{23}$ is Avogadro's number – i.e. number of molecules per mole – and $V = 1.7 \cdot 10^{-15}l$ is the E. coli cell volume. We need to divide by $A \cdot V$ for reactions involving two reactants, such as binding; for reactions that transform a single reactant as unbinding, the macroscopic and mesoscopic rates coincide. Note that we assume the cell volume to be constant while ignoring cell growth. Evaluating our equation yields the following final rates for the considered example reaction between O_{R1} and Rep:

$$k_a^{meso} = 0.098/\sec \qquad k_d^{meso} = 0.155/\sec$$

We can now quantify the effects of *cooperative binding* between repressors at O_{R1} and O_{R2}. Cooperativity adds a favorable term of $-2\frac{kcal}{mol}$ to the Gibbs binding energy of Rep at O_{R2} [41] [5]. Due to the exponential relation between free energies and equilibrium constants this massively strengthens the binding: the mesoscopic dissociation rate k_d for O_{R2} decreases from 3.99 to 0.155, the same value as for O_{R1}. Figure 5 summarizes.

Finally, we need rates for transcription initiation, in which a complex of RNAP and promoter P undergoes an irreversible transition from a closed state into an

---

[4] The following set of equations determines the values of all rates for the example:

$$\Delta G = -12.5 \cdot 10^3 \text{cal/mol} \qquad K_{eq} = \exp^{-\Delta G/(R\,T)}$$
$$R = 1.9872 \text{ cal/(mol Kelvin)} \qquad k_a = 10^8/(\text{mol } sec)$$
$$T = 310.15 \text{ Kelvin} \qquad k_d = k_a/K_{eq} \text{ mol}$$

[5] Cooperativity also has a helping effect to binding at O_{R1}, however we chose to neglect this in our model as the effect at O_{R2} predominates.

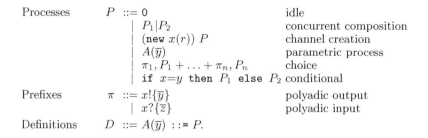

Processes	P	$::=$	0	idle
		$\mid$	$P_1 \mid P_2$	concurrent composition
		$\mid$	$(\mathbf{new}\ x(r))\ P$	channel creation
		$\mid$	$A(\bar{y})$	parametric process
		$\mid$	$\pi_1, P_1 + \ldots + \pi_n, P_n$	choice
		$\mid$	$\mathbf{if}\ x{=}y\ \mathbf{then}\ P_1\ \mathbf{else}\ P_2$	conditional
Prefixes	π	$::=$	$x!\{\bar{y}\}$	polyadic output
		$\mid$	$x?\{\bar{z}\}$	polyadic input
Definitions	D	$::=$	$A(\bar{y})\ ::= P.$	

Fig. 6. Syntax of the stochastic π-calculus, where $\bar{y} = y_1, \ldots, y_n$ and $\bar{z} = y_1, \ldots, y_n$

open one, in which the two strands of DNA have locally been separated, and after which transcription proceeds [25]:

$$\text{RNAP} + P \rightleftharpoons^{K_{eq}} (\text{RNAP} \cdot P)_{\text{closed}} \to_{k_f} (\text{RNAP} \cdot P)_{\text{open}} \qquad (5)$$

The k_f rates for the promoter P_R and P_{RM} can be found in [16,24]. *Positive control* of RNAP by repressor binding at O_{R2} increases the k_f rate of P_{RM} roughly tenfold. Note that the dissociation rate of RNAP binding at P_{RM} is not affected, which distinguishes this mechanism from cooperative binding of regulatory proteins.

Throughout this paper we assume a constant RNAP concentration of $c = 30 \cdot 10^{-9}$ mol according to [41]. This corresponds to a population of circa 30 RNAP molecules via the simple calculation $\#RNAP = c \cdot V \cdot A = 30.7$, with A and V as above.

Finally, we assume the rate at which repressor monomers associate to dimers to be $0.025\ \text{sec}^{-1}(nM)^{-1}$ while setting the dissociation rate to $0.5/\,\text{sec}$ following [8].

4   Stochastic Pi Calculus

We now recall the variant of the stochastic π-calculus [33] that is the core language underlying the *BioSpi* simulation engine [34].

Figure 6 lists the syntax of our stochastic π-calculus. The vocabulary consists of an infinite set of *channel names* x, y, z, an infinite set of *process names* A, B, C and *stochastic rates* r that are nonnegative floating point numbers. We write $\bar{y}$ for finite, possibly empty sequences of channels.

Parallel compositions $P_1 \mid \ldots \mid P_n$ are processes with parallel subprocesses P_1, $\ldots, P_n$. The composition operator is associative and commutative, so that the ordering of composition is irrelevant. The empty parallel composition where $n = 0$ is the idle process 0, the neutral element of composition. Processes $(\mathbf{new}\ x(r))P$ define a new channel x with scope P, similarly to an existential quantifier $\exists x.P$; this new channel x is associated with the stochastic rate r.

$$A(\bar{z}) \quad \rightarrow \quad P[\bar{z}/\bar{y}] \qquad \text{with respect to } A(\bar{y}) ::= P$$

$$\left.\begin{array}{l} \ldots + x?\{\bar{y}\}, P + \ldots \\ \ldots + x!\{\bar{z}\}, P' + \ldots \end{array}\right| \Big\} \quad \rightarrow \quad P[\bar{z}/\bar{y}] \mid P' \qquad \text{if } \bar{z} \text{ free for } \bar{y} \text{ in } P$$

$$\text{if } x{=}y \text{ then } P_1 \text{ else } P_2 \quad \rightarrow \quad \begin{cases} P_1 \text{ if } x = y \\ P_2 \text{ if } x \neq y \end{cases}$$

Fig. 7. Reduction rules, where $\bar{y} = y_1, \ldots, y_n$, $\bar{z} = y_1, \ldots, y_n$, and $n \geq 0$

Definitions of parametric processes $A(\bar{y})::=P$ associate the name A to a process P with free channel names $\bar{y}$, the parameters of A. Parametric definitions are universally valid for all parameter choices. They may be recursive, i.e. contain self applications. An application of a parametric process $A(\bar{z})$ calls the process named A with channels $\bar{z}$. Formally, $A(\bar{z})$ preceeds by unfolding the definition of A while substituting $\bar{z}$ for $\bar{y}$, according to the first reduction rule in Fig. 7.

A conditional[6] if $x{=}y$ then P_1 else P_2 tests for equality between channels x and y; if equality holds it reduces to P_1, otherwise to P_2. As an example, consider the definition: $A(x,y) ::= $ if $x{=}y$ then 0 else $A(y,x)$ which is valid for all channels x, y. With respect to this definition, we can reduce the process $A(z, z) \rightarrow 0$ for all z, while if $z_1 \neq z_2$ we have infinite reduction chains $A(z_1, z_2) \rightarrow A(z_2, z_1) \rightarrow A(z_1, z_2) \rightarrow \ldots$.

Choices $\pi_1, P_1 + \ldots + \pi_n, P_n$ offer synchronous communication and non-determinism. Two choices composed in parallel can communicate with each other if one of them contains an output capacity $x!\{\bar{z}\}, P'$ and the other some input capacity $x?\{\bar{y}\}, P$ for the same channel x. The result of this communication act will be $P' \mid P[\bar{z}/\bar{y}]$ where $\bar{z}$ is substituted for $\bar{y}$ in P. Communication over the channel x lets an output capacity for x send a tuple of channels $\{\bar{z}\}$ to an input capacity for x, which waits for such data to replace its tuple of formal parameters $\{\bar{y}\}$.

A complete *program* consists of a set of public channel declarations, a set of definitions, and an initial process P that is to reduced with respect to these declarations and definitions.

Let us express chemical reactions for illustration. We consider two competing reactions of type x_1 and x_2 with rates r_1 and r_2:

$$x_1 : A + B \rightarrow^{r_1} C_1$$
$$x_2 : A + B \rightarrow^{r_2} C_2$$

We encode the two rules types x_1 and x_2 as global channel with rates r_1 and r_2 and define A, B as parametric processes without parameter:

public $(x_1(r_1), x_2(r_2))$.
$A ::= x_1!\{\}, C_1 + x_2!\{\}, 0.$
$B ::= x_1?\{\}, 0 + x_2?\{\}, C_2.$

---

[6] BioSpi supports conditionals as sums of match prefixes. For better readability we adopt an alternative notation with keywords if then else.

We now compose many molecules of types A and B in parallel. Each A-B-pair can decide to react, either according to rule x_1 which reduces in the following manner:

$$A \mid A \mid B \mid B \quad \rightarrow \quad C_1 \mid A \mid 0 \mid B \quad \rightarrow \quad \ldots$$

If alternatively rule x_2 happened to be applied, one could observe:

$$A \mid A \mid B \mid B \quad \rightarrow \quad 0 \mid A \mid C_2 \mid B \quad \rightarrow \quad \ldots$$

All channels are associated with a stochastic rate, that is either introduced by `public` declaration or the `new` operator. Such rates define exponential distributions that characterise the communication activity of the channel (see [33,34]). Communications over channels with `infinite` rate are executed instantaneously, as are conditionals and channel creations. Channels with finite rates communicate only afterwards. The scheduling of communication acts over these channels is based on Gillespie's algorithm [14].

```
public (pro(ka_protein), release(kd_OR_A)).

OR_vacant  ::= pro ? {}, OR_bound.
OR_bound   ::= release ! {}, OR_vacant.
A_unbound  ::= pro ! {}, A_bound.
A_bound    ::= release ? {}, A_unbound.

System ::= OR_vacant | A_unbound | A_unbound | A_unbound.
```

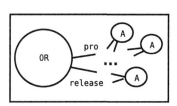 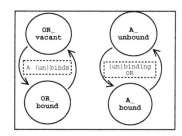

Fig. 8. An operator region and three regulatory proteins: expressing many-to-one communication over global channels. The topology of the system is shown on the left, and the state transition diagrams of molecular actors of type A and OR are given on the right.

5   Modeling the Network of Transcription Initiation

We formally model the network controlling transcription initiation at the λ switch in the stochastic π-calculus. We start with three simpler subsystems, before turning to modeling the λ switch system as described in Section 2. Following Regev and Shapiro's guidelines [39], we represent members of the biomolecular population as processes, and biomolecular events as communication.

5.1   Modeling Techniques in System Components

We start with a case of many-to-one communication, which is the simplest sub-system to model. We consider a network with a unique operator region on DNA of whatever type OR and many proteins of the same type A that can attach to it. The operator has two states vacant and bound; the possible states of the proteins are bound and unbound.

We use the four possible combinations of molecule types with their states as names of parametric processes: OR_vacant, OR_bound, A_unbound, A_bound. We introduce two global channels, pro for reactions of protein binding to the operator, and release for unbinding events. The rate of pro is the association rate ka_protein that is invariant for all types of operators and proteins. The rate of release is the dissociation rate kd_OR_A, which depends on the specificity between protein and operator. Figure 8 presents the definitions of all agents in the system in the stochastic π-calculus, the topology and state transitions.

As simple as this example may seem, it is already sufficient for simulating binding and unbinding of either Rep or Cro at *isolated* operator sites O_{R1}, O_{R2}, or O_{R3} which are then distinguished by their dissociation rates.

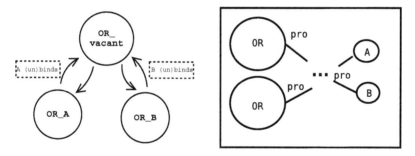

Fig. 9. Left: Operator region with distinct states when binding different proteins, right: two operator regions alongside with two proteins of different types

Many-to-many communication and handshakes: We next consider a case of many-to-many communication, for which we introduce a less simple handshake protocol. We study a system with two operators of the same type OR that can be bound by proteins of two different types A and B. We wish to design our model such that all knowledge about binding parameters is localized within operator sites. With this all proteins can bind operators in the same generic manner, only depending on their types. We thus define operators of type OR with three possible states: vacant, A, and B. Fig. 9 illustrates their state transitions. The states of proteins of types A and B remain as previously introduced: unbound and bound.

We obtain seven names for parametric processes, when building all possible pairs of molecular types with their states: A_bound, A_unbound, B_bound, B_unbound, OR_vacant, OR_A, OR_B. We again use a unique global channel pro for protein binding. The stochastic rate of pro is the association rate ka_protein

```
public (pro(ka_protein), a, b).

OR_vacant ::= pro ? {type,init},
              if type=a then (new release(kd_OR_A))
                                  init ! {release}, OR_A(release)
                            else (new release(kd_OR_B))
                                  init ! {release}, OR_B(release).
OR_A(release) ::= release ! {}, OR_vacant.
OR_B(release) ::= release ! {}, OR_vacant.

A_unbound ::= new(init(infinite))
              pro ! {a,init}, init ? {release}, A_bound(release).
B_unbound ::= new(init(infinite))
              pro ! {b,init}, init ? {release}, B_bound(release).
A_bound(release) ::= release ? {}, A_unbound.
B_bound(release) ::= release ? {}, B_unbound.

System ::= OR_vacant | OR_vacant | A_unbound | B_unbound.
```

Fig. 10. Modeling two operator regions with two proteins of different types

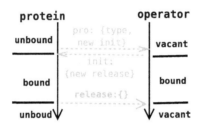

Fig. 11. Handshake protocol for protein binding to operator. Solid black arrows denote the time flow; dotted grey arrows denote communication, the annotations indicate the names of channel used and exchanged. Horizontal lines indicate the time point of state changes of corresponding molecular actor.

that is invariant for all types of proteins and operators. In addition, we introduce two channels a and b with arbitrary rates that encode the protein types.

Recall that dissociation rates are specific for each combination of proteins and operators. In addition to that, the rate of a channel is fixed upon its creation. Hence we need a dedicated release channel of appropriate rate per possible combinations of protein and operator. Furthermore, these channels should be introduced by the operators, where the knowledge on all interaction parameters is localized. The biological motivation for this is that the specificity of bindings depends on the operator's sequence. The better a protein matches this, the higher the specificity of binding. Fig. 10 presents the definitions of all agents in the system.

We deploy a handshake protocol illustrated in Fig. 11: binding is initiated by the protein, which transmits to the operator its type and a freshly created private channel of name `init`. The operator creates a new `release` channel upon each binding, that bears the suitable stochastic rate depending on the protein type - and hands it over to the protein using `init`. Subsequent dissociation occurs with the specific rate.

This generic models needs only slight generalization to apply to the interactions of multiple proteins Cro and Rep with different kinds of operator regions O_{R1}, O_{R2}, and O_{R3}. What it doesn't reflect yet are cooperative interdependencies between binding events, or mutual exclusion of binding at spatially overlapping sites.

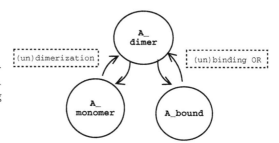

Fig. 12. State transition diagram for generic protein A with dimerization and binding

Timers: In our third case, we utilize timers as proposed by Regev [37]. Timers serve for auxiliary purposes, they don't have a biological equivalent. Their sole purpose is to trigger an activity performed by a single molecular actor. Timers wait until a partner is ready to communicate over some specific channel. Such catalysts are needed for modeling first-order reactions in the π-calculus, where all actions necessitate precisely *two* participants.

An example is to apply timers for dissociating complexes, here in the case of *dimers*. We consider a system with modified protein A. The protein B and operator site OR remain as introduced previously. We distinguish between A monomers and A dimers, and enable only dimers to bind to OR. Proteins of type A hence have states `monomer`, `dimer`, and `bound`, Fig. 12 illustrates the transitions between these. Operator regions of type OR are either `vacant` or in bound states A or B as previously. The definition of the system is given in Fig. 13.

For every type of protein A we use two global channels `dimerize_A` and `undimerize_A`. Every A monomer has the choice to read or write on the channel `dimerize_A`. We have chosen somehow arbitrarily that the writer continues as a dimer, while the reader dies. In order to undimerize, a dimer of type A interacts with `Timer(undimerize_A)`, and dissociates back into two monomers of type A.

5.2 Modeling the λ Switch

The molecular population is summarized in Fig. 14. In a λ infected E. coli cell, we assume precisely one copy of each P_{RM}, P_R, O_{R1}, O_{R2}, and O_{R3}, disregarding

```
public (pro(ka_protein),
        dimerize_A(ka_A_Dimer), undimerize_A(kd_A_Dimer))).

A_monomer ::= dimerize_A ! {}, A_dimer
            + dimerize_A ? {}, 0.
A_dimer   ::= (new init(infinite))
                pro ! {a,init}, init ? {release}, A_bound(release)
            + undimerize_A ? {}, A_monomer | A_monomer.
A_bound(release) ::=  release ? {}, A_dimer.

OR_vacant ::= pro ? ... # rules for OR_A, OR_B as before

Timer(c) ::= c ! {}, Timer(c).

System := Timer(undimerize_A) |
          A_monomer | A_monomer | A_monomer | OR_vacant.
```

Fig. 13. Modified system with timer for dissociation of dimers into monomers

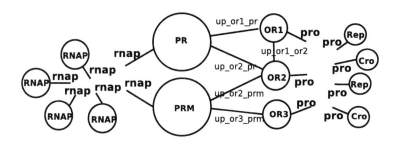

Fig. 14. The molecular population with its communications channels

```
public (rnap(Ka_RNAP), pro(Ka_protein),
        up_or1_pr(infinite), up_or2_pr(infinite),
        up_or2_prm(infinite), up_or3_prm(infinite),
        up_or1_or2(infinite),
        vacant, blocked, inhibited, cro, rep, polymerase).
```

Fig. 15. Public channels with their stochastic rates

replication. Alongside with these reside a large number of RNAP, and variable numbers of the regulatory proteins Rep and Cro.

Molecular actors are connected by public channels in Fig. 14 that are declared and assigned stochastic rates in Fig. 15. The channel **rnap** is used both for RNAP docking to P_{RM} and P_R, and is assigned the rate Ka_RNAP. Regulatory proteins establish connections to operator regions over the channel **pro** with

P_{RM}	P_R	O_{R1}, O_{R3}	O_{R2}	Rep, Cro	RNAP
vacant	vacant	vacant	vacant	unbound	unbound
rnap_high	rnap	cro	cro	bound	bound
rnap_low	inhibited	rep	rep_high	monomer	
inhibited		blocked	rep_low		
			blocked		

Fig. 16. States of molecular actors

association rate Ka_protein. Since both interactions are of many-to-many type, all establishment of bindings follow our handshake protocol.

The possible *states of molecular actors* are listed in Fig. 16. Particular channels are used to communicate *state updates*. We declare these update channels up_A_B with rate infinite. They will be used to transmit *state update messages*, whose names indicate the new state the sender is switching to: vacant, blocked, and alike. These last are encoded by channels of arbitrary rates.

We use update channels for synchronization purposes, modeling cooperativity for instance between O_{R1} and O_{R2}, as well as for implementing mutual inhibition. Consider P_R, where binding is mutually exclusive with O_{R2}. The frequency of transcription initiation at P_{RM} depends on O_{R2}'s state - Rep present there exerts positive control on it. Binding of Rep to O_{R2} in turn can be cooperatively strengthened, which depends on whether another Rep is bound to O_{R1}.

Handshake and state updates at O_{R3}: The model for the generic operator region from Fig. 10 was sufficient for a first interaction with Rep and Cro. However, we need specializations in order to appropriately reflect any of the actual operator regions at the λ switch.

Consider the operator site O_{R3}. It can be either vacant, blocked by a RNAP at P_R, occupied by a Cro protein (state cro), or Rep. Figure 17 illustrates O_{R3}'s transitions. Note the introduction of a second category of annotations, not yet present in former examples: transitions to and from inhibited are triggered by events at P_{RM}. Recall that bindings of RNAP to P_{RM} and regulatory proteins at O_{R3} mutually exclude each other. We thus keep the states of O_{R3} and P_{RM} consistent by instantaneous state updates, for which we reserve a dedicated *update channel* up_or3_prm.

The π-calculus implementation of O_{R3} is given in Fig. 18. Besides being one of the possible counterparts for protein binding and implementing the handshake protocol, the code comprises state updates: when OR3 releases a bound protein and is about to depart from either of its states rep or cro, it notifies PRM (which is currently in state inhibited) via up_or3_prm, and only after this continues as OR3_vacant. In analogy upon protein docking, OR3_vacant again updates P_{RM}. Alternatively, as soon as PRM gets docked by a polymerase and communicates this up_or3_prm, OR3_vacant switches to OR3_blocked.

Cooperative repressor binding at O_{R2} necessitates more sophisticated control than seen so far. Recall that we assigned it to the operator the task to determine the unbinding time point. In cases without cooperativity, the operator simply associates the appropriate dissociation rate to the release channel upon

Fig. 17. State transitions of O_{R3}. Transitions can be caused locally, or follow as side effects of events at other molecular actors.

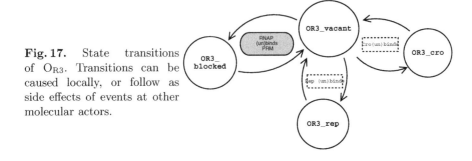

```
OR3_rep(release) ::= release ? {}, up_or3_prm ! {vacant}, OR3_vacant.
OR3_cro(release) ::= release ? {}, up_or3_prm ! {vacant}, OR3_vacant.
OR3_blocked    ::=  up_or3_prm ? {new_prm}, OR3_vacant.
OR3_vacant ::=
pro ? {type,init},
      if type=rep then (new release(Kd_or3_rep))
          init ! {release}, up_or3_prm ! {rep}, OR3_rep(release)
      else           (new release(Kd_or3_cro))
          init ! {release}, up_or3_prm ! {cro}, OR3_cro(release)
+ up_or3_prm ? {new_prm},
      if new_prm=polymerase then OR3_blocked else OR3_vacant.
```

Fig. 18. Specification of O_{R3} module

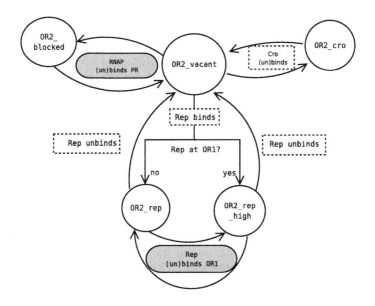

Fig. 19. State transitions of the O_{R2} model

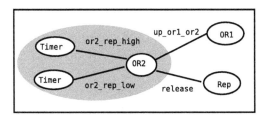

Fig. 20. OR2 with auxiliary timers for the adjustment of binding strength for repressor, depending on OR1's state as notified over up_or1_or2

creation. For the case of cooperative repressor binding to OR2, we delay the reading offer on the **release** channel. This is performed by associating an **infinite** rate to **release**. OR2 applies a delay determined differentially for cases with or without cooperativity. For this, OR2 makes use of *two alternative timer processes*. When repressor binding is cooperative and OR2 thus is in state **rep_high**, dissociation is triggered over channel **or2_rep_high**. Otherwise, it is determined by channel **or2_rep_low**, both bear a distinct rates determined in Sec. 3. OR2 works by selecting appropriate states and switching between these as necessary. Figure 19 shows OR2's state transitions, Fig. 20 illustrates the topology, for the full π-calculus specification see Fig. 21.

Positive control at P_{RM}: switchable timers. We now come to modeling cooperative enhancement of transcription initiation of RNAP bound to P_{RM} by repressors at O_{R2}. The technique introduced at O_{R2} is useful again. This time, we model variation of the rate of transcription initiation with the help of switchable timers. We use two auxiliary timer processes communicating with P_{RM} over public channels **prm_high** and **prm_low** with rates from Figure 4.

    public(prm_high(Kf_prm_promoted),prm_low(Kf_prm)).

Fig. 22 illustrates our idea. For the full specification of the P_{RM} module see Fig. 23. Let us highlight the last paragraph, which defines the P_{RM} module as the concurrent composition of four processes: two timers, the promoter and the gene it controls.

    Module ::=
    Timer(prm_high) | Timer(prm_low) | Gene_cI | PRM_vacant(vacant).

Assume polymerase being docked to P_{RM} in our model. Transcription is then triggered over the instantaneous channel **transcribe_now**. Depending on the occupancy of OR2, PRM switches to one of two states representing the complex with RNAP. In the first, **PRM_rnap_low**, there is no **Rep** at OR2 and P_{RM} hence works only at basal rate. This is indicated by waiting for the **prm_low** timer to shoot. Alternatively PRM is in state **PRM_rnap_high** and listens to **prm_high** in order to trigger transcription initiation. Switching between both timers follows instantaneously upon update from OR2. In either case, the polymerase may also unbind.

RNAP: To conclude we give our π-calculus model of RNAP in Fig.24. We introduce only two states, **bound** and **unbound**. Note that the handshake protocol deployed for RNAP binding to promoters slightly differs from that for regulatory proteins. This is the case because RNAP needs a channel **release** for simple unbinding, another **transcribe_now** for transcription to be kicked off, and **toGene**

```
public(or2_rep_high(Kd_or2_rep_coop),
    or2_rep_low(Kd_or2_or2)).

OR2_vacant(or1) ::=
  pro ? {id,init},
  if   id=cro
  then up_or2_prm ! {cro}, up_or2_pr ! {cro},
       (new release(Kd_or2_cro)) init ! {release},
       OR2_cro(or1,release)
  else up_or2_prm ! {rep}, up_or2_pr ! {rep},
       (new release(infinite)), init ! {release},
       if or1=rep
       then OR2_rep_high(release)
       else OR2_rep_low(or1,release)
+ up_or1_or2 ? {new_or1},
       OR2_vacant(new_or1)
+ up_or2_pr ? {new_pr},
       if new_pr=polymerase
       then up_or2_prm ! {blocked}, OR2_blocked
       else OR2_vacant(or1).

OR2_cro(or1,release) ::=
  release ? {},
       up_or2_prm ! {vacant},
       up_or2_pr ! {vacant},
       OR2_vacant(or1)
+ up_or1_or2 ? {new_or1},
       OR2_cro(new_or1, release).


OR2_rep_high(release) ::=
  or2_rep_high ? {},
       release ? {},
       up_or2_prm ! {vacant},
       up_or2_pr ! {vacant},
       OR2_vacant(rep)
+ up_or1_or2 ? {new_or1},
       OR2_rep_low(new_or1, release).

OR2_rep_low(or1,release) ::=
  or2_rep_low ? {},
       release ? {},
       up_or2_prm ! {vacant},
       up_or2_pr ! {vacant},
       OR2_vacant(or1)
+ up_or1_or2 ? {new_or1},
       if   new_or1=rep
       then OR2_rep_high(release)
       else OR2_rep_low(new_or1, release).

OR2_blocked ::= up_or2_pr ? {c}, OR2_vacant(vacant).

Module ::= Timer(or2_rep_low)
         |   Timer(or2_rep_high)
         |   OR2_vacant(vacant).
```

Fig. 21. Specification of the O_{R2} module

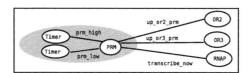

Fig. 22. Module abstracting P$_{RM}$ with its two auxiliary timer processes. The frequency of transcription initiation by RNAP is controlled by channel prm_high for PRM_rnap_high; or via prm_low for state PRM_rnap_low. Transitions between these two states in turn depend on changes of state of OR2, and are synchronized over up_or2_prm.

to be pointed at the right gene to transcribe. The behavior of RNAP as sketched here is simplified. For RNAP's behavior beyond the initiation of transcription, which is out of this present paper's scope, the model needs to be extended (see [23]). The same holds for the specification of the genes, e.g. the process Gene_cI within the PRM module needs to be replaced in order to obtain an appropriate model of transcription.

6   Stochastic Simulation

We next validate our π-calculus model of the dynamics at the λ switch by exhaustive stochastic simulation. These are performed by execution with the BioSpi system [34].

We use a sequence of models of distinguished subsystems in order to evaluate the different components independently. Given its complexity, it does not make sense to directly start with the complete system. From the software engineering perspective, this is necessary for debugging reasons. From the biological standpoint, it is a current practice to isolate subsystems in order to observe their aspects as independently as possibly. The π-calculus programming approach is advantageous in that perspective, in that it allows to freely design and compose subsystems of interest.

6.1   Simulating Components

We thus perform simulations of subsystems that can be compared against existing knowledge, either experimental or from established other simulation studies. Our strategy is incremental and bottom up. First we present simulations of repressor dimerization. We then move over binding of Rep to DNA, and the impact of dimerization on binding patterns to that of cooperative interaction between Rep *on* DNA. Finally we investigate interactions between RNAP, DNA, and Rep's positive control thereof. The control of transcription initiation from P$_{RM}$ is highly relevant; it has been subject to a number of theoretical and experimental studies [4,5,24,41].

Dimerization: The essential point to remind about repressor dimerization was the concentration dependent equilibrium [35]; we can observe this in simulations. Figure 25 visualizes the dynamics of the dimerization process starting with different numbers of monomers. As an example, for the case of three

```
public(prm_high(Kf_prm_promoted),
       prm_low (Kf_prm),
       gene_cI(infinite).

PRM_vacant(or2) ::=
  rnap ? {init},
    if    or2=rep
    then (new transcribe_now(infinite), release(Kd_rnap_prm))
         init ! {transcribe_now, release, gene_cI},
         up_or3_prm ! {polymerase},
         PRM_rnap_high(transcribe_now,release)
    else (new transcribe_now(infinite), release(Kd_rnap_prm))
         init ! {transcribe_now, release, gene_cI},
         up_or3_prm ! {polymerase},
         PRM_rnap_low(transcribe_now,release,or2)
+ up_or2_prm ? {new_or2},
         PRM_vacant(new_or2)
+ up_or3_prm ? {new_or3},
         PRM_inhibited(or2) .

PRM_rnap_low(transcribe_now,release,or2) ::=
  prm_low ? {},
       transcribe_now ! {},
       up_or3_prm ! {vacant},
       PRM_vacant(or2)
+ up_or2_prm ? {new_or2},
       if new_or2=rep
       then PRM_rnap_high(transcribe_now, release)
       else PRM_rnap_low(transcribe_now, release, new_or2)
+ release ? {}, up_or3_prm ! {vacant}, PRM_vacant(or2).

PRM_rnap_high(transcribe_now,release) ::=
  prm_high ? {},
       transcribe_now ! {},  up_or3_prm ! {vacant},
       PRM_vacant(rep)
+ up_or2_prm ? {new_or2},
       PRM_rnap_low(transcribe_now, release, new_or2)
+ release ? {},
       up_or3_prm ! {vacant},
       PRM_vacant(rep).

PRM_inhibited(or2) ::=
  up_or2_prm ? {new_or2}, PRM_inhibited(new_or2)
+ up_or3_prm ? {new_or3}, PRM_vacant(or2).

Gene_cI ::= gene_cI ? {},
       mRNA_cI | Gene_cI.

Timer(c) ::= c ! {}, Timer(c).

Module ::=  Timer(prm_high)
        |     Timer(prm_low)
        |     Gene_cI
        |     PRM_vacant(vacant).
```

Fig. 23. Specification of P_{RM} module with cI gene

```
RNAP_unbound ::=
  (new init(infinite)) rnap ! {init},
  init ? {transcribe_now, release, toGene},
  RNAP_bound(transcribe_now, release, toGene).

RNAP_bound(transcribe_now, release, toGene) ::=
  transcribe_now ? {}, toGene ! {}, RNAP_unbound
+ release ! {}, RNAP_unbound.
```

Fig. 24. Specification of RNAP

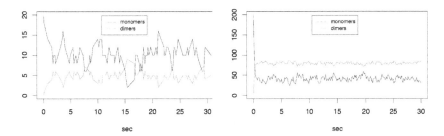

Fig. 25. Dynamics of formation and breakage of λ repressor dimers over 30 simulated seconds. Initiation with 20 monomers (left) or 200 monomers (right).

monomers the starting point would be the parallel composition of three instances of Rep_monomer with a timer for dimer dissociation:

```
System ::= (new rep_undimerize(kd_repDimer),
            rep_dimerize(ka_repDimer))
           Timer(rep_undimerize) |
           Rep_monomer | Rep_monomer | Rep_monomer.
```

When launched with 20 monomers, such a system tends towards a mean setting in which around around half the total repressors can be found as monomers, while the others are present as dimers. Note that in this case, one observes strong fluctuations (see Fig.25 left). Only a rough quarter of initially 200 monomers are present as such in average, while around 75% are dimer-bound - with less important fluctuations. The *shift* of the equilibrium towards dimers becomes more obvious as we plot the average ratio of repressors present as monomers to that of dimer-bound ones over a long time range for various levels of repressors, see Fig. 26.

6.2   Repressor Binding to DNA

We now consider the binding of repressor dimers to operator sites on DNA. The following set up allows to simulate site O_{R1} and three repressor dimers that can reversibly attach to it, or dissociate back to monomers:

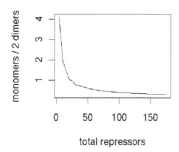

Fig. 26. Shift of concentration dependent equilibrium between monomers and dimers

Fig. 27. Binding to isolated operator sites, assuming 100 repressor monomers.

	ΔG	mean sojourn	bound
O_{R1}	−12.5	6.4	96 %
O_{R2}	−10.5	0.25	46 %
O_{R3}	−9.5	0.05	15 %

```
System ::= (new dimerize(ka_repDimer), rep_undimerize(kd_repDimer),
            bind(Ka_protein), release(Kd_or1_rep))
            OR | Timer(rep_undimerize) |
            Rep_unbound | Rep_unbound | Rep_unbound .
```

By adjustment of the rate for channel **release**, we can simulate binding to the *isolated* sites O_{R1}, O_{R2} and O_{R3}. Figure 27 summarizes corresponding simulations, emphasizing the impact of different binding site site affinities. Recall from Sec. 3 that a smaller value of the Gibbs free energy ΔG indicates a stronger binding.

We make two corresponding observations. The complex of repressor and operator site is most stable at O_{R1}, where we observe an average sojourn time of Rep of 6.4 seconds (this value is the mean of an exponential distribution not shown here). This is consistent with [35], reporting that binding of repressor to O_{R1} persists in the order of up to 10 seconds. For O_{R2} and O_{R3} less favorable ΔGs lead to drastic drops of complex stability.

The efect is also visible when considering not individual binding events, but average behaviour. For a given concentration and a long time scale, O_{R1} is better saturated with repressor than any of the other sites. The last column in Tab. 27 reports the fraction of time the respecitve sites are bound when 100 Rep are included and dimerization activated.

Binding of repressor to the right operator O_R: Figure 28 shows the saturation of sites O_{R1}, O_{R2} and O_{R3} as they arise in our simulations of the λ switch when both repressor dimerization and cooperative repressor binding between O_{R1} and O_{R2} are enabled. Each of the curves summarize a series of

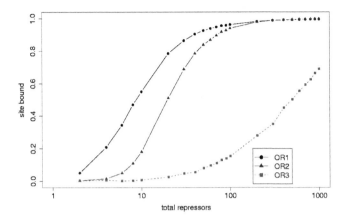

Fig. 28. Occupancy of sites O_{R1}, O_{R2} and O_{R3} in the presence of dimerization and cooperative binding. Each point represents the relative occupancy of a site over 5000 simulated seconds, for a given number of total repressors. In a lysogen, one can expect 100-200 total repressors.

experiments for varying Rep levels. Before discussing the full system, we will investigate the underlying components and mechanisms one by one.

Dimerization sharpens response at O_{R1}: Figure 29 (left) illustrates the saturation of O_{R1} as a function of repressor level. Each of the two curves summarizes a series of experiments. For the solid line dimerization is enabled, i.e. only part of the total repressors are present as dimers and thus able to bind the operator. The dashed line assumes that dimers are stable at all concentrations, meaning that 100% of total repressors are found as dimers regardless of the concentration. The x axis indicates the number of total repressors on a logarithmic scale, while the y axis gives the relative occupancy of O_{R1}. Each data point represents the relative occupancy of O_{R1} for an experiment simulating the full dynamics of docking to DNA with or without dimerization over 5000 seconds.

Over this time scale, we can compare our results based on a stochastic discrete event approach against other's from deterministic continuous models, which compute only averages: one sees both qualitative and quantitative agreement with results from [35] reproduced in Fig. 29 (right). Dimerization has the effect to change the shape of the binding curve, namely to give a sharper response in terms of site occupancy as the amount of repressor increases.

Superimposing dimerization and cooperative binding at O_{R2}: Figure 30 summarizes how the second operator site fills with Rep for three scenarios. The dashed curve illustrates binding to O_{R2} in presence of O_{R1} and dimerization. We contrast this with binding to the isolated O_{R2} with and without dimerization. Note that the effect of *dimerization* is far less pronounced at an isolated O_{R2} than it was O_{R1}, where dimerization lead to a sharp increase of

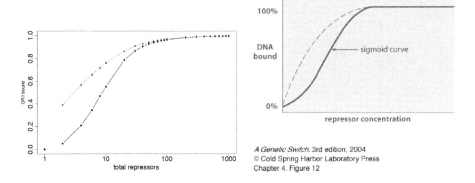

Fig. 29. Occupancy of operator region O_{R1} as a function of repressor concentration and dimerization. Our results (left), benchmark from Ptashne's book [35] (right). Dashed lines: all repressors are found as dimers regardless of concentration. Solid lines: dimerization of repressors is included, hence the concentration-dependent equilibrium affects the binding curve.

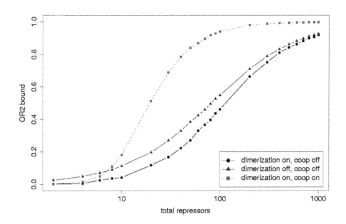

Fig. 30. Occupancy of site O_{R2}, as a function of repressor level, dimerization and cooperativity. We consider *isolated* O_{R2} for the curves 'with'/'without' dimerization, and a system comprising both O_{R1} and O_{R2} for the curve 'O_{R2}, coop and dimerization'. Because at very low concentrations, binding occurs mainly at O_{R1}, the cooperative advantage only becomes visible at a certain level.

sensitivity in the lower concentration range. This can be explained because the isolated weaker O_{R2} only fills notably at higher Rep concentrations, when the equilibrium is heavily biased toward dimers. However, now the *combined effect of cooperativity and dimerization* becomes prominent. Recall that binding at O_{R2} is cooperatively strengthened as O_{R1} is placed next to it. As can be seen from the dashed curve in Fig. 30 the predominant cause of O_{R2}'s saturation at lysogenic repressor concentration levels is cooperative binding with O_{R1}. This cooperativity propagates O_{R1}'s stronger sensitivity to O_{R2}.

Negative auto-regulation of Rep at O_{R3}: Our results on Rep binding to the third operator O_{R3} are included in Fig. 28. The binding curve is again based on the observation of the isolated operator, under variation of repressor level while disregarding interfering traffic between RNAP and P_{RM}. The most striking effect when comparing the binding curve with the other operators' is that the site fills to a significantly lower degree. It reaches around 30% when 200 repressors are included in the simulation. Even with an amount of 1000 repressors the isolated O_{R3} remains unsaturated. As we will report later the saturation further decreases to 4% as RNAP docking to P_{RM} interferes.

These results agree with recent experimental findings. Dodd and co-workers have demonstrated that an *additional layer of cooperativity* is needed for effective repression of P_{RM} [9] at lysogenic repressor concentrations. Revet and co-workers first observed a long-range DNA loop between the right operator and another distal region in λ's genome [40]. As was subsequently understood, this loop is stabilized by an assembly of eight repressor proteins, in which the two repressor dimers cooperatively bound to O_{R1} and O_{R2} participate. They cooperatively interact with another repressor tetramer bound to λ's *left operator* region O_L - while looping the DNA between the two regions. The large assembly further stabilizes all participants. More importantly, it juxtaposes O_{R3} with a third site at the left operator, O_{L3}. This allows for cooperative binding of repressor at O_{R3} and O_{L3}.

This additional level of cooperativity is a recent finding and not, as yet, fully characterized. However its importance is clearly seen [46]. It allows to repress P_{RM} and maintain a low level of Rep, that is not yet ensured by binding to O_{R3} alone. Thus in a bacterium hosting phage λ, the lysogenic repressor concentration never surpasses a range allowing to return to the level in which O_{R1} and O_{R2} can be vacated. This is the key to induction back from lysogeny to the state of lytic growth [11].

6.3 RNAP Binding and Transcription Initiation

We further increase the scope of the model, by adding P_{RM} and RNAP to the three operator sites and repressors simulated so far. We study this system over 20 minutes simulated time, comparable with the life span of an individual bacterium. This allows to observe the occupancy patterns of both P_{RM} and the operators, as well as the initiation of transcription for the cI gene. We first consider the impact of varying repressor levels in a model including the essential cooperative features - dimerization, cooperative repressor binding and positive control of transcription initiation. Next we perturb our model and study the consequences.

Figure 31 summarizes a series of simulations. For each set-up we indicate the number of repressors included, and whether cooperative binding and positive

coop	pos. control	repressors	transcription initiations from P_{RM}	RNAP at P_{RM} (sec)	P_{RM} repressed (sec)	P_{RM} vacant (sec)	Rep at O_{R2} (sec)
on	on	100	58	873	46	280	1111
			76	870	46	279	1120
			71	873	46	279	1120
			58	889	44	266	1110
			74	903	43	253	1111
		50	67	901	19	281	990
			69	921	14	265	985
			70	899	18	283	972
		25	46	917	5	278	728
			52	929	5	266	730
			51	922	5	273	727
		10	19	927	< 1	272	305
			26	932	< 1	267	323
			28	922	< 1	277	300
off	on	100	38	886	41	273	570
			35	867	45	285	587
			31	890	43	267	575
on	off	100	5	899	41	260	1108
			6	915	39	246	1118
			4	898	44	258	1101

Fig. 31. Simulations over 1200 seconds: P_{RM} activity (absolute number of transcription initiations). Values are in units of simulated seconds for the following columns: P_{RM} repression, P_{RM} vacancy, and occupancy of O_{R2} by Rep. First block: results for varied repressor levels when both cooperative repressor binding and positive control are enabled. Second and third block: simulation results under elimination of either of the two mechanisms, for a level of 100 repressors.

control are enabled. Each line of the table summarizes one simulation run, for which we report the following quantities:

- absolute number of transcription initiations from P_{RM} observed. This should be related to the theoretical upper bound of 103, estimated form P_{RM}'s maximal rate of 0.086 initiations per second and the simulated time of 1200 seconds.
- absolute time that RNAP is bound to P_{RM} (in sec),
- absolute time P_{RM} is repressed as a consequence of Rep binding to O_{R3} (in sec),
- vacancy of P_{RM} (in sec),
- occupancy of O_{R2} by repressor (in sec).

To begin with, we mimic the system's behavior under *lysogenic repressor concentrations* with 100 repressors. The first block in Tab. 31 summarizes five executions of our model. For all runs P_{RM} is bound by RNAP in approximately

70 % of the time, P_{RM} is inhibited via competing Rep binding to O_{R3} for 4 % of the time, and otherwise vacant. The second operator site O_{R2} is bound by Rep around 92 % of the time for all five runs. The numbers of transcription initiations range between 58 and 76. Note that the variability of this figure is significantly higher than that of any other considered.

The actual number of transcript initiations from P_{RM} in a single lysogenic bacterium is difficult to determine experimentally. In the past, a precise level was deemed necessary for the maintenance of lysogeny [20]. This was rectified by recent experiments showing that repressor levels varies widely from cell to cell [4]. This phenomenon is known as *transcriptional noise*. Our result are in agreement with an estimated average number of transcripts per cell cycle of 70.

Reactions to partial and near-total Rep depletion: Our next step is to preserve the system's essential characteristics - dimerization, positive control and cooperative binding - but to thin out the repressor pool. In the remainder of Figure 31's first block we report the outcomes of each three simulations with 50, 25 and 10 total repressors.

The primary effect is that saturation of O_{R2} drops nonlinearly. This has important secondary effects on transcription initiation from P_{RM}. A first reduction to 50 repressors de-represses P_{RM} and seems to favor initiation, at least in these runs. As a reaction to further depletion transcription visibly reduces, while the actual P_{RM} saturation by RNAP increases: in the presence of 10 repressors, initiations drop to around a third of those seen with 50 repressors. This should be related to the increasing vacancy of O_{R2}. It gives a first impression of how the system of positive auto-regulation breaks down.

Examining this question in detail seems promising for two reasons. First, the λ switch is known to be extremely robust. It needs to cope with transient fluctuations of Rep level. Nevertheless, *induction* relies on the system's ability to escape from the lysogenic state when repressor falls below a critical threshold. Recall that as both O_{R1} and O_{R2} are vacated, P_{RM}'s antagonist P_R becomes likely to take over. A detailed investigation remains beyond the current paper's scope.

The impact of cooperative repressor binding on P_{RM} activity is another point of interest. After we have observed its immediate impact at O_{R2}, we move on to a larger perspective. We perturb our π-calculus model by lowering the cooperative dissociation rate of Rep at O_{R2} to the basal one. This lowers O_{R2}'s saturation to half the previous amount, see Figure 31 (second block, last column). And it has consequences for RNAP at P_{RM}. The binding itself is not lowered - our simulations even indicate a slightly higher promoter saturation. Nevertheless, the number of transcription initiations drops to half that of the wild type.

Impact of positive control: We last eliminated the positive control of transcription initiation in our model. This is reached by lowering the parameter for promoted transcription the basal one, i.e. by manipulating the stochastic parameters of the channels illustrated in Fig. 22. Our resulting in silico experiments are summarized in the last block in Figure 31. The number of initiations in presence of 100 total repressors dramatically decreases from an average of 67 in the

	our prediction	reference value	
P_{RM} activity, (full system)	67 initiations in 1200 sec	estimate: 70 per cell cycle	[4]
P_{RM} activity, (pos. control off)	> 90% reduced	observation: positive control can be eliminated, but this needs to be compensated by up-regulation of basal rate in order to maintain system functional	[27]
P_R repressed (> 45 Rep)	> 98.1 %	98.5 %	[26]
O_{R1}-O_{R2} cooperativity	(reproduced)	necessary to repress P_R efficiently	[35]
P_{RM} repression at lysogenic Rep levels, considering O_R only	4%	repression is ineffective; transcription initiations lowered 5-20% as a consequence of O_{R3} binding	[26,9]

Fig. 32. Overview of our predictions and results from other studies

initial system to an average of 5. All the while, immediate RNAP bindings as well as all other features are not affected, when compared to the original setting. This underlines the importance of positive control.

This simulation scenario was motivated by wet lab experiments with modified λ repressors. These mutants bind cooperatively but fail to stimulate transcription. As [17] reported the λ switch was no longer functional. Our simulation outcomes seem in rough agreement with this, even though we can not directly compare the results. Most recently Michalowski and Little [27] suggested that positive auto-regulation may be a dispensable feature altogether. They experimentally observed that the λ switch remains functional if positive control is eliminated, but at the same time P_{RM}'s intrinsic initiation rate k_f increased.

7   Conclusion and Future Work

We have presented a detailed model for the mechanism of transcription initiation control at the λ switch in the stochastic π-calculus. We have distilled the stochastic parameters from the literature, implemented the model in the BioSpi system, and obtained confirming simulation results. Figure 32 summarizes our simulations.

In follow up work we have already extended our approach to modeling the dynamics of transcript elongation itself [23]. Work on translation is under way, again the most subtle aspects include appropriate parameter choices [7]. This will permit us to close the complex feedback loops at the λ switch.

---

[7] The parameter set for cI translation in [2] and adopted by several others should be revised in order to reflect newer findings [30,42].

We aim to obtain a simulation of *induction*. Recent experiments suggest a new ambiguity for Cro's role. The common assumption that its presence at intermediate repressor levels rapidly leads to induction has been falsified. DNA looping between the right and left operator region seems to render the switch insensitive to the presence of Cro [45]. Therefore, we also plan to refine our approach in order to account for long-distance cooperativity in repressor binding. The techniques developed in this paper should be helpful.

Finally, we plan to study more effects of parameter variation systematically.

Acknowledgments. Our view of the λ switch has been sharpened in discussions with Erik Aurell, Isabella Moll, and Mark Ptashne. We thank Keith Shearwin for feed-back on the manuscript, and Denys Duchier, Cédric Lhoussaine, and Bernard Vandenbunder for discussions. This work was partly carried out during a research visit of CK to the *Linnaeus Centre for Bioinformatics* in Uppsala (Sweden), enabled through a European Commission grant HPRI-CT-2001-00153. Last but not least, she gratefully acknowledges the LIFL for its hospitality.

References

1. Gary K. Ackers, Alexander D. Johnson, and Madeline A. Shea. Quantitative model for gene regulation by λ phage repressor. *Proceedings of the National Academy of Sciences USA*, 79(4):1129–1133, February 1982.
2. Adam Arkin, John Ross, and Harley H. McAdams. Stochastic kinetic analysis of developmental pathway bifurcation in phage λ-infected Escherichia coli cells. *Genetics*, 149:1633–1648, 1998.
3. Erik Aurell, Stanley Brown, Johan Johanson, and Kim Sneppen. Stability puzzles in phage λ. *Physical Review E*, 65:051914, 2002.
4. Kristoffer Baek, Sine Svenningsen, Harvey Eisen, Kim Sneppen, and Stanley Brown. Single-cell analysis of λ immunity regulation. *Journal of Molecular Biology*, 334(3):363–372, 2003.
5. Audun Bakk. Transcriptional activation mechanisms of the P_{RM} promoter of λ phage. *Biophysical Chemistry*, 114(2–3):229–234, 2005.
6. Otto G. Berg, Robert B. Winter, and Peter H. von Hippel. Diffusion-driven mechanisms of protein translocation on nucleic acids: 1 - models and theory. *Biochemistry*, 20:6929–6948, 1981.
7. J. M. Bower and H. Bolouri, editors. *Computational Modeling of Genetic and Biochemical Networks*. MIT Press, 2001.
8. Ralf Bundschuh, F. Hayot, and C. Jayaprakash. The role of dimerization in noise reduction of simple genetic networks. *Journal of Theoretical Biology*, 220:261–269, 2003.
9. Ian B. Dodd, A.J. Perkins, D. Tsemitsidis, and J.B. Egan. Octamerization of CI repressor is needed for effective repression of P_{RM} and efficient switching from lysogeny. *Genes & Development*, 15:3013–3022, 2001.
10. Ian B Dodd, Keith E Shearwin, and J Barry Egan. Revisited gene regulation in bacteriophage λ. *Current Opinion in Genetics & Development*, 15(2):145–152, 2005.
11. Ian B. Dodd, Keith E. Shearwin, Alison J. Perkins, Tom Burr, Ann Hochschild, and J. Barry Egan. Cooperativity in long-range gene regulation by the lambda CI repressor. *Genes Dev.*, 18(3):344–354, 2004.

12. Johan Elf and Mans Ehrenberg. What makes ribosome-mediated trascriptional attenuation sensitive to amino acid limitation? *PLoS Computational Biology*, 1(1):14–23, 2005.

13. Harley Lodish et al. *Molecular Cell Biology*. Freeman, 2003.

14. Daniel T. Gillespie. A general method for numerically simulating the stochastic time evolution of coupled chemical reactions. *Journal of Computational Physics*, 22:403–434, 1976.

15. Jeff Hasty, David McMillen, Farren Isaacs, and James J. Collins. Computational studies of gene regulatory networks: In numero molecular biology. *Nature Reviews Genetics*, 2:268–279, 2001.

16. DK Hawley, AD Johnson, and WR McClure. Functional and physical characterization of transcription initiation complexes in the bacteriophage lambda O_R region. *J. Biol. Chem.*, 260(14):8618–8626, 1985.

17. D.K. Hawley and W.R. McClure. The effect of a lambda repressor mutation on the activation of transcription initiation from the lambda P_{RM} promoter. *Cell*, 32:327–333, 1983.

18. Jane Hillston. *A Compositional Approach to Performance Modelling*. PhD thesis, University of Edinburgh, 1995. Distinguished Dissertations Series. Cambridge University Press, 1996.

19. T. Ideker, T. Galitski, and L. Hood. A new approach to decoding life: systems biology. *Annual Review of Genomics and Human Genetics*, 2(343), 2001.

20. A D Johnson, A R Poteete, G Lauer, R T Sauer, G K Ackers, and M Ptashne. λ repressor and Cro – components of an efficient molecular switch. *Nature*, 294(5838):217–223, 1981.

21. Andrzej M. Kierzek, Jolanta Zaim, and P. Zielenkiewicz. The effect of transcription and translation initiation frequencies on the stochastic fluctuations in prokaryotic gene expression. *Journal of Biological Chemistry*, 276:8165–8172, 2001.

22. Kenneth S. Koblan and Gary K. Ackers. Site-specific enthalpic regulation of DNA transcription at bacteriophage λ O_R. *Biochemistry*, 31:57–65, 1992.

23. Céline Kuttler. Bacterial transcription in the pi calculus. In *3rd International Workshop on Computational Methods in Systems Biology*, 2005.

24. Mei Li, W.R. McClure, and M. M. Susskind. Changing the mechanism of transcriptional activation by phage λ repressor. *Proceedings of the National Academy of Sciences USA*, 94:3691–3696, 1997.

25. William R. McClure. Mechanism and control of transcription initiation in prokaryotes. *Annual Review Biochemistry*, 54:171–204, 1985.

26. B. Meyer and M. Ptashne. Gene regulation at the right operator O_R of bacteriophage lamba. I. O_{R3} and autegeneous negative control by repressor. *J. Mol. Biol.*, pages 19–205, 1980.

27. Christine B. Michalowski and John W. Little. Postitive autoregulation of cI is a dispensable feature of the phage λ gene regulatory circuitry. *J. Bacteriol.*, 187(18):6430–6442, 2005.

28. Robin Milner. *Communicating and Mobile Systems: the π-calculus*. Cambridge University Press, 1999.

29. Robin Milner, Joachim Parrow, and David Walker. A calculus of mobile processes (I and II). *Information and Computation*, 100:1–77, 1992.

30. Isabella Moll, Go Hirokawa, Michael C. Kiel, Akira Kaji, and Udo Bläsi. Translation initiation with 70S ribosomes: an alternative pathway for leaderless mRNAs. *Nucl. Acids Res.*, 32(11):3354–3363, 2004.

31. Amos B. Oppenheim, Oren Kobiler, Joel Stavans, Donald L. Court, and Sankar Adhya. Switches in bacteriophage lambda development. *Annual Reviews Genetics*, 39:409–429, 2005.

32. Andrew Phillips and Luca Cardelli. A correct abstract machine for the stochastic pi-calculus. *Transactions on Computational Systems Biology*, 2005. to appear.

33. Corrado Priami. Stochastic π-calculus. *Computer Journal*, 6:578–589, 1995.

34. Corrado Priami, Aviv Regev, Ehud Shapiro, and William Silverman. Application of a stochastic name-passing calculus to representation and simulation of molecular processes. *Information Processing Letters*, 80:25–31, 2001.

35. Mark Ptashne. *A Genetic Switch: Phage Lambda Revisited*. Cold Spring Harbor Laboratory Press, 3rd edition, 2004.

36. Mark Ptashne and Alexander Gann. *Genes and Signals*. Cold Spring Harbor Laboratory Press, 2002.

37. Aviv Regev. *Computational Systems Biology: A Calculus for Biomolecular Knowledge*. Tel Aviv University, 2002. PhD thesis.

38. Aviv Regev and Ehud Shapiro. Cells as computation. *Nature*, 419:343, 2002.

39. Aviv Regev and Ehud Shapiro. The π-calculus as an abstraction for biomolecular systems. In Gabriel Ciobanu and Grzegorz Rozenberg, editors, *Modelling in Molecular Biology*. Springer, 2004.

40. Bernard Révet, Brigitte von Wilcken-Bergmann, Heike Bessert, Andrew Barker, and Benno Müller-Hill. Four dimers of lambda repressor bound to two suitably spaced pairs of lambda operators form octamers and DNA loops over large distances. *Current Biology*, 9(3):151–154, 1999.

41. Madeline Shea and Gary K. Ackers. The O_R control system of bacteriophage lambda: A physical-chemical model for gene regulation. *Molecular Biology*, 181:211–230, 1985.

42. C. S. Shean and M. E. Gottesman. Translation of the prophage λ cI transcript. *Cell*, 70(3):513–522, 1992.

43. Michael Slutsky and Leonid A. Mirny. Kinetics of protein-DNA interaction: Facilitated target location in sequence-dependent potential. *Biophys. J.*, 87(6):4021–4035, 2004.

44. Kim Sneppen and Giovanni Zocchi. *Physics in Molecular Biology*. Cambridge University Press, 2005.

45. Sine L. Svenningsen, Nina Costantino, Donald L. Court, and Sankar Adhya. On the role of Cro in λ prophage induction. *Proceedings of the National Academy of Sciences USA*, 102(12):4465–4469, 2005.

46. Jose MG Vilar and Leonor Saiz. DNA looping in gene regulation: from the assembly of macromolecular complexes to the control of transcriptional noise. *Current Opinion in Genetics & Development*, 15:1–9, 2005.

47. Rolf Wagner. *Transcription Regulation in Prokaryotes*. Oxford University Press, 2000.

From Logical Regulatory Graphs to Standard Petri Nets: Dynamical Roles and Functionality of Feedback Circuits

Elisabeth Remy[1], Paul Ruet[1], Luis Mendoza[2], Denis Thieffry[3], and Claudine Chaouiya[3]

[1] IML, Campus de Luminy
13288 Marseille Cedex 9, France
{remy, ruet}@iml.univ-mrs.fr
[2] Serono Pharmacological Research Institute
Geneva, Switzerland
Luis.Mendoza@serono.com
[3] LGPD, Campus de Luminy
13288 Marseille Cedex 9, France
{chaouiya, thieffry}@ibdm.univ-mrs.fr

Abstract. Logical modelling and Petri nets constitute two complementary approaches for the dynamical modelling of biological regulatory networks. Leaning on a translation of logical models into standard Petri nets, we propose a formalisation of the notion of circuit functionality in the Petri net framework. This approach is illustrated with the modelling and analysis of a molecular regulatory network involved in the control of Th-lymphocyte differentiation.

Keywords: genetic regulatory graphs, Petri nets, feedback circuit, discrete dynamics, qualitative analysis.

1 Introduction

Regulatory networks are found at the core of all biological functions, from biochemical pathways, to gene regulation mechanisms, and intercellular communication processes. Their complexity often defies the intuition of the biologist and calls for the development of proper mathematical methods to model their structure and simulate their dynamical behaviour. The modelling of biological regulatory networks has been addressed using a large variety of formal approaches, from ordinary or partial differential systems, to sets of stochastic equations (for a recent review, see [10]). However, as precise, quantitative information about the shape of regulatory functions, or the values of involved parameters is generally lacking, qualitative approaches are usually more easily deployed.

Our work relies on a qualitative approach which consists in modelling regulatory networks in terms of logical equations, using either Boolean or multi-level variables (see [12], [33] and references therein). The development of logical models for various biological networks has already led to interesting insight into the

C. Priami et al. (Eds.): Trans. on Comput. Syst. Biol. VII, LNBI 4230, pp. 56–72, 2006.
© Springer-Verlag Berlin Heidelberg 2006

relationships between the regulatory network structure (*i.e.*, presence of regulatory feedback circuits) and the corresponding dynamical properties [33]. The generalised logical approach of R. Thomas has been recently implemented in a software tool, GINsim, which enables the biologist to specify a regulatory model and check the qualitative evolution of the system for given initial states [9,19,38]. However, as the number of qualitative states grows exponentially with the number of elements involved in the regulatory network, there is a need for proper mathematical methods to cope with the analysis of larger regulatory networks.

At this stage, it appears interesting to articulate the logical approach with another qualitative approach, namely the Petri net modelling [22,28]. Indeed, Petri nets (PN) offer a mathematical framework to model, analyse and simulate the dynamical behaviour of large systems. As a first step in this direction, we have recently proposed a translation of logical regulatory models into specific *regulatory Petri nets*, focusing on the Boolean case [8]; this has been extended to the multilevel case in [7]. This bridge between the two formalisms should help us to simultaneously exploit the corresponding analytical and simulation tools.

Petri nets have been successfully applied to the modelling and the analysis of metabolic networks [24,16,18,15]. As emphasised in [36], one can draw extensive relationships between the traditional biochemical modelling and Petri net theory. In particular, the stoichiometry matrix of a metabolic network corresponds to the Petri net incidence matrix. One can identify clear correspondences between qualitative properties of the dynamics of biological networks and classical PN behavioural properties. For example, a dead marking represents a stable state of the system, while transition invariants correspond to cyclical trajectories.

Although the kinetic parameters are generally not precisely accessible, most of the works related to Petri net approaches for the modelling of biological networks concentrate on quantitative aspects. Leaning on simulations, these works refer to several extensions of Petri nets, including hybrid PN, where places and transitions are either discrete, or continuous [2,13,6,20,11].

In the case of genetic regulatory networks, the PN representation is not so natural because the semantics associated with the interactions between components varies. Furthermore, regulators are usually not consumed during the regulatory processes (while reactants are transformed into products by chemical reactions). In this paper, regulatory interactions are considered at a qualitative abstraction level, where the details of the regulation processes are not taken into account.

Amid the promising applications of Petri net theory to biological systems, we have proposed a systematic rewriting of Boolean regulatory graphs into a Petri net formalism in [8], and then extended this procedure to the multivalued case in [7].

The paper is organised as follows. First, we define the *Boolean Regulatory Petri Nets* (BRPN) which correspond to Boolean regulatory models. Then, after recalling the properties of isolated regulatory circuits, we introduce a formal definition of the notion of regulatory feedback circuit functionality. Next, these definitions are applied to a regulatory network involved in the control of Th-lymphocyte differentiation. Finally, conclusions and prospects are proposed.

2   Boolean Regulatory Petri Nets

In this section, we recall the definition of the Petri net corresponding to a Boolean regulatory graph, *i.e.*, the PN whose dynamics simulates the dynamical behaviour of the underlying genetic regulatory network (for further detail, see [8]).

First, we briefly describe logical regulatory graphs in the Boolean case: a gene can be ON or OFF (for more details on the formalism in the multivalued case, see [9]).

A *regulatory graph* is a directed graph representing interactions between genes $g_1, \ldots g_n$. Each interaction involves two genes (or other kinds of molecular components), the source and the target. As one gene can be the target of several interactions, we define, for each gene g_i, the set $\mathcal{I}(i)$, called *input of g_i*, which contains the source genes of all interactions targeting g_i. For each gene g_i, a *parameter $K_i(X)$* is defined for each subset X of $\mathcal{I}(i)$. The value of this parameter gives the level to which g_i tends when X is the set of the sources of the incoming interactions which are operating (we consider that an interaction is operating when its source gene is ON). In the Boolean case, these parameters take their values in $\{0, 1\}$.

More formally, a regulatory graph is a triple $(\mathcal{G}, \mathcal{A}, \mathcal{K})$ which consists in:

- a set of nodes $\mathcal{G} = \{g_1, \ldots, g_n\}$,
- a set of arcs $\mathcal{A}$, which leads to the specification of the sets $\mathcal{I}(i)$, defining the sources of interactions towards g_i, $\forall i \in \{1, \ldots, n\}$,
- a set of parameters $\mathcal{K} = \{K_i(X), i = 1, \ldots, n, X \subseteq \mathcal{I}(i)\}$.

For a given regulatory graph of n genes, we can now address its dynamical behaviour. A *state* of the system is defined as the n-dimensional vector of the expression levels of the n genes. We further define a *state transition graph* where nodes represent states and arcs represent transitions between states. For a specific initial state, the corresponding state transition graph defines all the possible trajectories of the system from the selected initial conditions. We can also consider the *whole* state transition graph consisting of all the 2^n states. We thus face a classical combinatorial explosion problem: the size of the whole state transition graph exponentially increases with the number of genes.

In the sequel, we briefly describe our translatation of Boolean regulatory graphs into standard Petri nets.

Basic Definitions and Properties: Consider a Boolean regulatory graph $\mathcal{R} = (\mathcal{G}, \mathcal{A}, \mathcal{K})$. We shall define the corresponding Petri net with the following properties:

- To each gene correspond two places g_i, $\overline{g_i}$, $i \in \{1, \ldots, n\}$, such that the sum of tokens in places g_i and $\overline{g_i}$ equals 1 (they are then complementary). The position of the token in g_i or $\overline{g_i}$ indicates whether the gene is ON or OFF. The set of places P thus contains $2\,n$ elements: $P = \mathcal{G} \cup \overline{\mathcal{G}}$, with $\overline{\mathcal{G}} \stackrel{\triangle}{=} \{\overline{g_1}, \ldots, \overline{g_n}\}$.
- To each parameter $K_i(X)$, where $i \in \{1, \ldots, n\}, X \subseteq \mathcal{I}(i)$, corresponds a transition t_X^i. The transition t_X^i is enabled as soon as all places of the set X

AND all complementary places of the set $\mathcal{I}(i) \setminus X$, the complementary set of X in $\mathcal{I}(i)$, are marked.

Definition 1. *Given a Boolean regulatory graph, $\mathcal{R} = (\mathcal{G}, \mathcal{A}, \mathcal{K})$, the associated Boolean regulatory Petri net (BRPN) $\mathbf{N}(\mathcal{R}) = (P, T, Pre, Post)$ is defined as follows:*

- $P = \mathcal{G} \cup \overline{\mathcal{G}} = \{g_1, \overline{g_1}, \ldots, g_n, \overline{g_n}\}$ *is the set of places.*
- $T = \{t_X^i, \ i = 1, \ldots, n, \ X \subseteq \mathcal{I}(i)\}$ *is the set of transitions.*
- $Pre : P \times T \to \{0, 1\}$ *is the mapping defining arcs between places and transitions (*Pre-conditions*).*
- $Post : T \times P \to \{0, 1\}$ *is the mapping defining arcs between transitions and places (*Post-conditions*).*

The functions Pre and Post are defined as follows:

1. *Case $g_i \notin \mathcal{I}(i)$ (g_i is not a self-regulator). For a given transition t_X^i, the only terms to be defined (i.e., all other terms equal zero) are:*

$$Pre(g_i, t_X^i) = Post(t_X^i, \overline{g_i}) = 1 - K_i(X), \tag{1}$$

$$Pre(\overline{g_i}, t_X^i) = Post(t_X^i, g_i) = K_i(X), \tag{2}$$

$$Pre(g_j, t_X^i) = Post(t_X^i, g_j) = 1 \qquad \forall g_j \in X, \tag{3}$$

$$Pre(\overline{g_j}, t_X^i) = Post(t_X^i, \overline{g_j}) = 1 \qquad \forall g_j \in \mathcal{I}(i) \setminus X. \tag{4}$$

2. *Case $g_i \in \mathcal{I}(i)$ (g_i is a self-regulator). For a given transition t_X^i,*
   - *if $g_i \in X$, the only case to be considered is $K_i(X) = 0$ (cf Remark 1). Therefore, the only terms to be defined are:*

$$Pre(g_i, t_X^i) = Post(t_X^i, \overline{g_i}) = 1, \tag{5}$$

$$Pre(g_j, t_X^i) = Post(t_X^i, g_j) = 1 \qquad \forall g_j \in X, g_j \neq g_i, \tag{6}$$

$$Pre(\overline{g_j}, t_X^i) = Post(t_X^i, \overline{g_j}) = 1 \qquad \forall g_j \in \mathcal{I}(i) \setminus X. \tag{7}$$

   - *if $g_i \notin X$, the only case to be considered is $K_i(X) = 1$. Therefore, the only terms to be defined are:*

$$Pre(\overline{g_i}, t_X^i) = Post(t_X^i, g_i) = 1, \tag{8}$$

$$Pre(g_j, t_X^i) = Post(t_X^i, g_j) = 1 \qquad \forall g_j \in X, \tag{9}$$

$$Pre(\overline{g_j}, t_X^i) = Post(t_X^i, \overline{g_j}) = 1 \qquad \forall g_j \in \mathcal{I}(i) \setminus X, g_j \neq g_i. \tag{10}$$

Equations (1)-(2) state that if the parameter $K_i(X)$ equals 1, g_i is an input and $\overline{g_i}$ an output of the corresponding transition t_X^i. In other words, there can be a decrease of the level of g_i if it is already present. Symmetrically, if $K_i(X) = 0$, then $\overline{g_i}$ is an input and g_i is an output of the corresponding transition t_X^i. Equations (3)-(4), (6)-(7) and (9)-(10) state that the elements contributing to the combination of interactions involved in $K_i(X)$ (*i.e.*, which are in X) constitute "side conditions" of the corresponding transitions (represented by "test arcs").

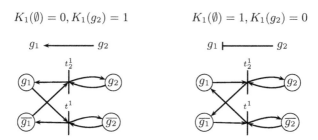

$$K_1(\emptyset) = 0, K_1(g_2) = 1 \qquad\qquad K_1(\emptyset) = 1, K_1(g_2) = 0$$

Fig. 1. Modelling of the activation of g_1 by g_2 (left) and of the inhibition of g_1 by g_2 (right). Top: regulatory graph representation and logical parameters (K's) for each type of regulation. $K_1(\emptyset)$ represents the basal expression of gene g_1, *i.e.*, in the absence of the regulatory product of gene g_2, whereas $K_1(g_2)$ represents the expression of g_1 in the presence of the regulatory product. Bottom: corresponding Petri net representation, with two places for each gene. Transition t^1 corresponds to parameter $K_1(\emptyset)$, while t_2^1 corresponds to $K_1(g_2)$.

As an illustration, let us consider the simplest case where a gene g_2 regulates a gene g_1. The two interesting situations occur when a change of the level of g_2 leads to a change of the level of g_1; this interaction is called *activation* if the presence of g_2 implies the presence of g_1 and conversely the absence of g_2 implies the absence of g_1. The opposite situation corresponds to an *inhibition*.

Figure 1 illustrates the BRPNs corresponding to an activation (left) and to an inhibition (right) between two genes, respectively (to simplify the notation, we have denoted $K_i(\{g_j\})$ by $K_i(g_j)$ and $t_{\{g_j,\ldots,g_k\}}^i$ by $t_{j,\ldots,k}^i$).

Given a regulatory graph involving n genes, the corresponding BRPN has exactly $2n$ places and up to $\sum_{i=1,\ldots n} 2^{|\mathcal{I}(i)|}$ transitions. This number of transitions can be lowered applying two kinds of reductions. Remark 1 deals with the first reduction related to self-regulations, already considered in Definition 1, case 2. The second class of reductions regards the possible simplification of the logical formulæ associated to each gene (see Remark 2).

Remark 1. Let g_i be a self-regulator; there should be one transition t_X^i for each parameter $K_i(X)$. But two cases do not lead to any change on g_i: when $g_i \notin X$ (*i.e.*, g_i is absent) and $K_i(X) = 0$, and when $g_i \in X$ (*i.e.*, g_i is present) and $K_i(X) = 1$. The resulting transitions are never enabled and are therefore omitted.

Remark 2. Each set $X \subseteq \mathcal{I}(i), i = 1, \ldots, n$ defines a logical formula which is a conjunction of literals $[x_j = 1]$ for all $g_j \in \mathcal{I}(i)$ and $\neg [x_j = 1]$ for all $g_j \notin \mathcal{I}(i)$. Now, for a given gene g_i, consider all the logical parameters having the same value x (0 or 1). They define a disjunction of conditions (the corresponding sets $X \in \mathcal{I}(i)$) under which g_i should tend to its level x. This formula is a disjunctive normal form (DNF, *i.e.*, a disjunction of conjunctions of literals). Such DNF can often be simplified, resulting in a reduction of the number of transitions to consider in the corresponding Petri net. One approach to simplify DNF uses ordered binary decision diagrams as introduced in [5]. An illustration of this type of reduction is provided in Section 4.

Although the graphical representation of a BRPN is more complex than the corresponding regulatory graph (indeed the BRPN represents the regulatory graph together with its parameterisation), several analytical tools available for the standard PN framework should be usefull in our context.

Let us introduce the following notations for all $i \in \{1, \ldots n\}$:

- $\widehat{K}_i(X) \stackrel{\triangle}{=} 2\,K_i(X) - 1$,;
- d_i the number of transitions for g_i $(d_i \leqslant 2^{\#\mathcal{I}(i)})$.
- X_i^j the jth subset of $\mathcal{I}(i)$ (for an arbitrary numbering).

Then, the *incidence matrix* $C \stackrel{\triangle}{=} Post^T - Pre$ is a $2n \times \left(\sum_{i=1,\ldots,n} d_i\right)$ matrix. Its components take their values in $\{-1, 0, 1\}$, and C has the following structure:

$$C = \begin{pmatrix} \boxed{D_1} & 0 & \ldots & 0 \\ 0 & \boxed{D_2} & \ldots & 0 \\ \ldots & \ldots & \ldots & \ldots \\ \ldots & \ldots & \ldots & \ldots \\ 0 & 0 & \ldots & \boxed{D_n} \end{pmatrix} \quad \text{with} \quad D_i \stackrel{\triangle}{=} \begin{pmatrix} \widehat{K}_i(X_i^1) & \ldots & \widehat{K}_i(X_i^{d_i}) \\ -\widehat{K}_i(X_i^1) & \ldots & -\widehat{K}_i(X_i^{d_i}) \end{pmatrix}.$$

Note that matrix C does not totally reflect the incidence relations of the BRPN which is not pure (it contains a number of test arcs).

Definition 2. *Given a regulatory Petri net* $\mathbf{N}(\mathcal{R}) = (P, T, Pre, Post)$, *a* **valid marking** $M : P \to \{0, 1\}$ *corresponds to a state of the Boolean regulatory graph* $\mathcal{R}$ *which verifies:* $\forall g_i \in \mathcal{G}, M(g_i) = 1 - M(\overline{g_i})$.

In the sequel, we will only consider valid markings.

The *Boolean state transition graph* is isomorphic to the *reachability graph* of the corresponding BRPN. Given a regulatory graph with n nodes, a state S in the state transition graph is a n-dimensional vector giving the state of each gene (expressed or not), while a valid marking in the corresponding BRPN is a $2n$-dimensional vector.

There exists an edge from state S_1 to state S_2 in the whole state transition graph related to a Boolean regulatory graph $\mathcal{R} = (\mathcal{G}, \mathcal{A}, \mathcal{K})$, iff there exists an enabled transition t in the associated BRPN such that M_1 verifies $M_1[t\rangle M_2$ (t is enabled by M_1 and its firing leads to the marking M_2) with, for all $i = 1, \ldots n$,

$$M_1(g_i) = S_1(i) \quad M_1(\overline{g_i}) = 1 - S_1(i)\,,$$
$$M_2(g_i) = S_2(i) \quad M_2(\overline{g_i}) = 1 - S_2(i)\,.$$

Note that usually, in the PN formalism, the (reachability) marking graph is defined for a specific initial marking. Here, we consider the *whole* marking graph of a Petri net corresponding to the whole state transition graph associated to a regulatory graph (containing all possible states).

3 Dynamical Role of Regulatory Circuits

For complex regulatory networks, R. Thomas has enounced rules binding the dynamical behaviour to the presence of specific types of circuits. More precisely, he has conjectured that a necessary condition for multistationarity is the presence of a positive circuit (*i.e.*, containing an even number of inhibitions), whereas a necessary condition for homeostasis and/or sustained, stable oscillations is the presence of a negative circuit (with an odd number of inhibitions) (cf. [33] and references therein). These rules have already been formally stated and partly demonstrated whithin different formalisms [32,14,30,3,31,26,27].

In what follows, we first derive a general Petri net formulation for these two classes of isolated circuits and check that their dynamical properties depend on their signs (section 3.1). Then, we focus on the notion of functionality of circuits (section 3.2). Indeed, the presence of a circuit is not sufficient to give rise to the corresponding dynamical property, it has to be moreover *functional*. We propose here a formal definition of this notion (which has been introduced in [29] in the multilevel degenerated case), and an algorithm to test if a circuit is functional in specific regions of the Boolean state space.

3.1 Isolated Regulatory Circuits

In the case of isolated regulatory circuits, each gene g_i is the target of a unique interaction exerted by g_{i-1}, and is the source of a unique interaction towards g_{i+1} (here and in the sequel, indices are considered *modulo n*, the length of the circuit, *i.e.*, $i + n = i$).

Let $\mathcal{C} = (\mathcal{G}, \mathcal{K})$ be a regulatory circuit, with $\mathcal{G} = \{g_1, \ldots, g_n\}$ and $\mathcal{K} = \{K_i(\emptyset), K_i(g_{i-1})\}_{i=1,\ldots,n}$, recalling that $\mathcal{I}(i) = \{g_{i-1}\}$ (cf. [25] for more details). In this simpler context, when we consider the interaction from g_i to g_{i+1}, the values of parameters for which the circuit is *functional* (see Section 3.2) are $K_{i+1}(\emptyset) = 0$ and $K_{i+1}(g_i) = 1$ (we say that this interaction is an activation), or $K_{i+1}(\emptyset) = 1$ and $K_{i+1}(g_i) = 0$ (the interaction is an inhibition).

The corresponding regulatory Petri nets $\mathbf{N}(\mathcal{C})$ have a well defined structure, see Figure 2.

In [25], we have proved that an isolated functional positive circuit generates two stable states, which are *mirroring* each other (a component is ON in one state iff it is OFF in the other state), and that an isolated functional negative circuit leads to a dynamical graph where all states feed a specific dynamical circuit of length twice the number of elements in the circuit. These results can be restated in the Petri net formalism (see [8]):

Property 1. – Let $\mathbf{N}(\mathcal{R})$ be a regulatory Petri net corresponding to an isolated (functional) positive regulatory circuit, then there are exactly two dead valid markings M_d^1 and M_d^2 which are mirroring each other. Each of these two markings is reachable from any other valid marking.

– Let $\mathbf{N}(\mathcal{R})$ be a regulatory Petri net corresponding to a (functional) negative regulatory circuit and E be the set of all valid markings which enable exactly one transition.

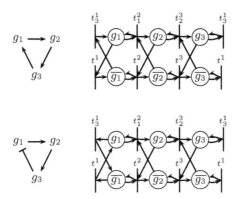

Fig. 2. Three-element regulatory circuits and the corresponding Petri nets. Upper row: positive circuit. Lower row: negative circuit. Note that transitions t^1 and t_3^1 are repeated, illustrating the ring structure of the net.

1. Any valid marking of the net is not dead.
2. E has $2n$ elements and is organised as a cycle (defining a livelock).
3. Each marking in E is reachable from any valid marking.

3.2   Functionality of Regulatory Circuits

Thomas' conjectures only refer to necessary conditions. Indeed, in many cases, although circuits do exist in the regulatory graph, we do not observe the expected dynamical properties, or at least not everywhere in the phase space.

Consider the following example:

$\mathcal{R} = (\mathcal{G}, \mathcal{A}, \mathcal{K})$ with $\mathcal{G} = \{x, y, z\}$, $\mathcal{A} = \{(x, y), (y, x), (z, y)\}$, and

$$\mathcal{K} = \{K_x(\emptyset) = 0,\ K_x(y) = 1,\ K_y(\emptyset) = 0,\ K_y(x) = K_y(z) = K_y(x, z) = 1\}.$$

The circuit $x \rightleftharpoons y$ could be embedded in a larger graph, but, for the sake of conciseness, we represent the external influence upon this circuit by the input variable z, which acts here only on y (cf. Figure 3).

For the parameter values selected, when the variable z is set to 0, multistationarity appears, but when z is set to 1, the dynamical behaviour is degenerated (see Figure 3). Indeed, when z is present, the state of x (its presence or absence) has no influence on y ($K_y(z) = K_y(x, z)$). We say that the interaction $x \rightarrow y$ is not functional when z is present (and, *a fortiori*, the circuit $x \rightleftharpoons y$ is not functional).

In the sequel, we present a formal definition of the notion of functionality, for one interaction and, more generally, for a circuit. This definition is local, *i.e.*, functionality is defined *within a specific context*, since the functionality of a circuit embedded in a more complex regulatory network may depend on the effect of some combination of incoming interactions. These definitions are proposed here in the Petri net framework, but they easily translate into other discrete modelling frameworks.

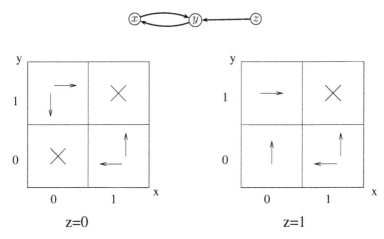

Fig. 3. Top: Two-element regulatory circuit $x \leftrightarrows y$ submitted to an external influence represented by node z. Bottom: Dynamical behaviour of the regulatory circuit depending on the value of the input z. When z is OFF (left), the system reaches two stable states (boxes [00] and [11]); when z is ON (right), the system exhibits a unique stable state (box [11]).

Definition 3. Functionality of an interaction *Let* $\mathcal{R} = (\mathcal{G}, \mathcal{A}, \mathcal{K})$ *be a Boolean regulatory graph, and* $\mathbf{N}(\mathcal{R}) = (P, T, Pre, Post)$ *its associated Boolean regulatory Petri net. Let us consider an interaction* $A : g_i \longrightarrow g_j$ *of the graph* $\mathcal{R}$, *and* (X, X') *a partition of* $\mathcal{I}(j) \setminus \{g_i\}$ *into two sets, possibly empty, of* g_j *regulators. When*

$$Post(t_X^j, g_j) \neq Post(t_{X \cup \{g_i\}}^j, g_j),$$

we say that A *is* **functional in the context** (X, X'). *Then, its* **functionality marking set** *is denoted* $\mathcal{S}_A \subseteq \{M : P \to \{0, 1\}\}$, *and contains all the valid markings for which* A *is functionnal:*

$$\mathcal{S}_A = \bigcup_{(X, X')} \{M : P \to \{0, 1\} \mid M(g) = 1 \ \forall g \in X, \ and \ M(g) = 0 \ \forall g \in X'\},$$

where the union is taken over all the partitions (X, X') *of* $\mathcal{I}(j) \setminus \{g_i\}$.

Therefore, an interaction is said to be functional within some context if the modification of the level of expression of its source leads to a change of the level of its target. The functionality of a circuit thus depends on the existence of a context for which all the transitions of this circuit are functional.

Definition 4. Functionality of a circuit *A marking* M *belongs to the functionality marking set of a circuit* $\mathcal{C}$ *if it belongs to the intersection* $\mathcal{S}_\mathcal{C}$ *of the functionality marking sets of all interactions of* $\mathcal{C}$.

If such a marking exists $(\mathcal{S}_\mathcal{C} \neq \emptyset)$, *then* $\mathcal{S}_\mathcal{C}$ *is the functionality marking set of the circuit* $\mathcal{C}$.

Note that if $\mathcal{S}_\mathcal{C} = \emptyset$, we say that the circuit is not functional.

We propose hereafter an algorithm to determine the functionality marking set of a given circuit $\mathcal{C}$ embedded in a Boolean regulatory graph $\mathcal{R}$.

Let $\mathbf{N}(\mathcal{R}) = (P, T, Pre, Post)$ be the BRPN associated to $\mathcal{R}$. Assume that $\mathcal{C}$ consists in p interactions $I^i : g_i \rightarrow g_{i+1}$, for $i = 1, \dots, p$ (notation *modulo p*). For each i, apply the following procedure:

1. Determine $\mathrm{Trans}(g_{i+1})$, the set of all transitions t_X^{i+1}, for all $X \subseteq \mathcal{I}(i+1)$: $\mathrm{Trans}(g_{i+1}) = \{t \in T, C(g_{i+1}, t) = 1 \text{ or } C(\overline{g_{i+1}}, t) = 1\}$, where C is the incidence matrix of $\mathbf{N}(\mathcal{R})$.
2. Determine the pairs of transitions $(t, t') \in \mathrm{Trans}(g_{i+1})$ such that: $Pre(g_i, t) \neq Pre(g_i, t')$, and for all g different from g_i and g_{i+1}, $Pre(g, t) = Pre(g, t')$.
3. For each such pair (t, t'), test whether the interaction is functional, *i.e.*, $Post(t, g_{i+1}) \neq Post(t', g_{i+1})$. In this case,
   - The context of functionality (X, X') is given by:
   $$X = \{g \in \mathcal{I}(i+1) \setminus \{g_i\} \text{ s.t. } Pre(g, t) = Pre(g, t') = 1\}$$
   $$X' = \{g \in \mathcal{I}(i+1) \setminus \{g_i\} \text{ s.t. } Pre(g, t) = Pre(g, t') = 0\}.$$
   - We define the set $\mathcal{S}_{t,t'}$ of markings M such that for each $g \in X$, $M(g) = 1$ and for each $g \in X'$, $M(g) = 0$.
4. Define $\mathcal{S}_i$ to be the union of all the $\mathcal{S}_{t,t'}$.

Finally, the functionality marking set of $\mathcal{C}$ is the intersection of the functionality marking sets $\mathcal{S}_i$, $i = 1, \dots, p$.

In conclusion, the functionality of a circuit has to be considered for all different possible contexts. This relates to the notion of "local graph" derived from the Jacobian matrix in the case of ODE systems (see [31] and [26] for the Boolean case).

4 Application to the Modelling of Th-Lymphocyte Differentiation

4.1 Introducing Th-Cell Differentiation

The vertebrate immune system contains diverse cell populations, like antigen presenting cells, natural killer cells, and B and T lymphocytes. Among the latter, CD4+ T helper lymphocytes (Th), upon receiving an appropriate antigenic stimulus, can further differentiate into T-helper 1 (Th1) or Th2 cells, which enable cell mediated immunity and humoral responses, respectively. Th1 and Th2 cells can be distinguished according to their pattern of cytokine secretion. Immune responses biased towards the Th1 phenotype may result in autoimmune diseases, while enhanced Th2 responses can lead to allergic reactions [1,23]. Various mathematical models have been proposed for the differentiation, activation and proliferation of Th-lymphocytes, but most of these models focus on interactions between immunological cell populations at a macroscopic level [4,35]. Other model analyses aim at understanding the mechanism of the generation of antibody and T-cell receptors diversity, as well as the dynamical properties of the large networks defined by the interactions between cytokines [17] or between immunoglobulins (see *e.g.* [34]).

The Boolean model considered hereafter is a simplification of the multi-valued logical model defined and analysed in [21], where the biological justification of

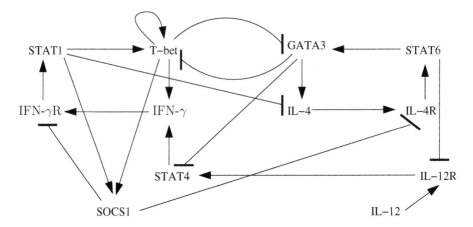

Fig. 4. Regulatory graph of the network controlling Th lymphocyte differentiation. The nodes represent transcription regulatory factors (T-bet, GATA-3), signaling transduction factors (STAT1, STAT4, STAT6, SOCS-1), lymphokines (IFN-γ, IL-4, IL-12) and receptors (IFN-γR, IL-4R, IL-12R), whereas the edges represent activations (arrows) or inhibitions (blunt arrows) between these components.

the set of interactions is given, accompanied with an extensive list of references to the immunological literature.

Here, we focus on the delineation of the multi-stability properties of the network as a result of the functionality of specific positive regulatory circuits found in the corresponding regulatory graph. Furthermore, we show that this type of feedback circuit analysis can be processed directly in the context of the Petri net formalism, relying on the sole analysis of the *Pre* and *Post* matrices.

Given the regulatory graph in Figure 4, and the set of parameters in Table 1, we construct the associated BRPN $(P, T, Pre, Post)$ with:

- the set of places $P = \{g_1, \overline{g_1}, \ldots g_{12}, \overline{g_{12}}\}$ (the numbering of the places is defined in Table 1),
- the set of transitions $T = \{t_X^i, i = 1 \ldots 12, X \subset \mathcal{I}(i)\}$ (where t_X^i denotes the transition corresponding to parameter $K_i(X)$).

The complete definition of the BRPN corresponding to the regulatory graph is defined through the matrices Pre (of size (24×39)) and $Post$ (of size (39×24)) (not shown). Applying the reduction rules described in Remark 1 and Remark 2, the number of transitions can be reduced to 31. To illustrate the simplication of the resulting BRPN, let consider the case of IFN-γ, we have $K_1(9) = K_1(11) = K_1(9, 11) = 1$. These parameters lead to the definition of 3 transitions. In this case, it is easy to simplify the Boolean function: IFN-γ is called to increase if one of its activator is present, whatever the state of the other regulator; therefore, 2 transitions can account for this situation. Let now consider the case of T-bet, which is a self-regulator and have 2 other regulators, namely STAT1 and GATA3. As T-bet is subject to 3 interactions, $8 (= 2^3)$ parameters are to be defined, 5 of them are zero (see Table 1). First, applying Remark 1 for the non-zero

Table 1. For each gene of the regulatory graph presented in Figure 4: the non-zero parameters and the corresponding expression level in each stable state (S_1, S_2, S_3). As $IL-12$ acts as an input, the only parameter to be defined is its *base value* ($K_{12}(\emptyset)$ which is set to 0).

Genes		Non-zero parameters	Stable states		
			S_1	S_2	S_3
IFN-γ	(1)	$K_1(9)$ $K_1(11)$ $K_1(9,11)$	0	0	1
IL-4	(2)	$K_2(12)$	0	1	0
IL-12	(3)		0	0	0
IFN-γR	(4)	$K_4(1)$	0	0	0
IL-4R	(5)	$K_5(2)$	0	1	0
IL-12R	(6)	$K_6(3)$	0	0	0
STAT1	(7)	$K_7(4)$	0	0	0
STAT6	(8)	$K_8(5)$	0	1	0
STAT4	(9)	$K_9(6)$	0	0	0
SOCS1	(10)	$K_{10}(7)$ $K_{10}(11)$ $K_{10}(7,11)$	0	0	1
T-bet	(11)	$K_{11}(7)$ $K_{11}(11)$ $K_{11}(7,11)$	0	0	1
GATA-3	(12)	$K_{12}(8)$	0	1	0

parameters, we can dismiss t_{11}^{11} and $t_{7,11}^{11}$. Then, for the situations conducing to a decrease of the level of T-bet, again, we can dismiss all transitions corresponding to conditions where T-bet is absent (Remark 1).

The regulatory graph of Figure 4 contains 18 regulatory circuits (15 positive, three negative), involving from one to ten elements. Using the logical formalism, it can be shown that nine of these circuits (seven positive, two negative) are functional. Still in the context of the logical approach, three stable states are found. In what follows, we show that these three stable states actually correspond to "dead markings" in the corresponding BRPN, and we apply the procedure described in Section 3.2 to one particular circuit.

4.2   Stable States and Their Biological Interpretation

Using the logical approach, it can be shown that the system encompasses the three stable states included in Table 1. The first stable state (S_1) corresponds to the virgin Th cells, whereas the second and third stable states correspond to Th2 and Th1 differentiated lymphocytes, respectively. We can easily check that these stable states correspond to dead markings for the corresponding BRPN, verifying that: $\forall t \in T, \exists p \in P$ s.t. $Pre(p,t) = 1$ and $M(p) = 0$. We will only give here some hint of the proof:

- For S_1, where all genes are OFF ($S_1(g_i) = 0$, $i = 1, \ldots 12$), it is clear that no transition is enabled because of the matrix Pre which verifies: $\forall t \in T, \exists g$ s.t. $Pre(g,t) = 1$.
- For S_2, $S_2(g_2) = S_2(g_4) = S_2(g_8) = S_2(g_{12}) = 1$ whereas $S_2(g_i) = 0$ for the other genes. $S_2(g_2) = 1$ could enable t^2, t_7^2, $t_{7,12}^2$, t_2^5 and $t_{2,10}^5$, but:

$Pre(\overline{g_{12}}, t^2) = Pre(\overline{g_{12}}, t_7^2) = 1$ and $S_2(g_{12}) = 1 \ (\Leftrightarrow S_2(\overline{g_{12}}) = 0)$,
$Pre(g_7, t_7^2) = 1$ and $S_2(g_7) = 0$,
$Pre(g_5, t_2^5) = 1$ and $S_2(g_5) = 0$,
$Pre(g_{10}, t_{2,10}^5) = 1$ and $S_2(g_{10}) = 0$.

Consequently, no transition is enabled under the marking S_2.

– A similar reasoning can be developed for S_3.

The logical approach is well suited to determine the set of stable states of a regulatory network (generating the "whole" state transitions graph when it is feasible, or using a constraint-programming approach). In the PN framework, we may be also able to determine the set of dead markings, independently of the initial conditions, using model-checking or pure algebraic approaches.

Once, the dead markings are determined, it is necessary to check their reachability from specific initial conditions. We have performed such analyses with INA (Integrated Net Analyzer [37] and obtained meaningful trajectories (see [21]). From an initial marking corresponding to a virgin cell state (S_1) but with IL-4 present (simulating the effect of adding IL4 to the extracellular medium), the resulting marking graph contains 14 markings including the two reachable dead markings S_1 and S_3. Now, with an initial state corresponding to a virgin cell state but with IFN-γ present, the marking graph contains 24 markings, including the two reachable dead markings S_1 and S_2.

4.3   Regulatory Circuits: Dynamical Roles and Functionality Constraints

To illustrate the procedure defined in Section 3.2, let us consider the following positive circuit: $\mathcal{C}=$ [IL-4, IL-4R, STAT6, GATA-3]. In order to determine the functionality marking set of this circuit, we perform the first step of the procedure, on each of the four interactions defining $\mathcal{C}$, successively. This leads to the selection of the following submatrices of Pre (Table 2) and $Post$ (Table 3).

Note that the set of genes to be considered encompasses not only the four genes of $\mathcal{C}$ (IL-4, IL-4R, STAT6, GATA-3), but also the genes exerting inputs on these genes (STAT1, SOCS1, T-bet).

Following the procedure, we now need to apply steps 1-4 to each interaction of the circuit $\mathcal{C}$ (we denote $\mathcal{S}_i$ the functionality marking set of the interaction targeting the node i). We limit ourselves here to their applications to the interaction from IL-4 (2) to IL-4R (5). Step 1 of the procedure leads to the definition of the set $\text{Trans}(IL - 4R) = \{t^5, t_2^5, t_{10}^5, t_{2,10}^5\}$. Then, step 2 results in the selection of the pairs (t^5, t_2^5) and $(t_{10}^5, t_{2,10}^5)$. Proceeding with steps 3 and 4:

– For the pair (t^5, t_2^5), we have $Post(t^5, g_5) \neq Post(t_2^5, g_5)$, and the interaction is thus functional in the context $X = \emptyset$ and $X' = \{g_{10}\}$. The corresponding functionality marking set is $\mathcal{S}_2 = \{M : P \rightarrow \{0, 1\}$ s.t. $M(g_{10}) = 0\}$.
– For the second pair, we have $Post(t_{10}^5, g_5) = Post(t_{2,10}^5, g_5)$. Consequently, these transitions add no further marking to the current functionality marking set.

Table 2. Sub-matrix *Pre* for the circuit $\mathcal{C}$ =[IL-4, IL-4R, STAT6, GATA-3] and its inputs

	t^2	t^2_7	t^2_{12}	$t^2_{7,12}$	t^5	t^5_2	t^5_{10}	$t^5_{2,10}$	t^8	t^8_5	t^{12}	t^{12}_8	t^{12}_{11}	$t^{12}_{8,11}$
IL-4 (2)	1	1	0	1	0	1	0	1	0	0	0	0	0	0
	0	0	1	0	1	0	1	0	0	0	0	0	0	0
IL-4R (5)	0	0	0	0	1	0	1	1	0	1	0	0	0	0
	0	0	0	0	0	1	0	0	1	0	0	0	0	0
STAT1 (7)	0	1	0	1	0	0	0	0	0	0	0	0	0	0
	1	0	1	0	0	0	0	0	0	0	0	0	0	0
STAT6 (8)	0	0	0	0	0	0	0	0	1	0	0	1	0	1
	0	0	0	0	0	0	0	0	0	1	1	0	1	0
SOCS1 (10)	0	0	0	0	0	0	1	1	0	0	0	0	0	0
	0	0	0	0	1	1	0	0	0	0	0	0	0	0
T-bet (11)	0	0	0	0	0	0	0	0	0	0	0	0	1	1
	0	0	0	0	0	0	0	0	0	0	1	1	0	0
GATA-3 (12)	0	0	1	1	0	0	0	0	0	0	1	0	1	1
	1	1	0	0	0	0	0	0	0	0	0	1	0	0

Table 3. Sub-matrix $Post^T$ for the circuit $\mathcal{C}$ =[IL-4, IL-4R, STAT6, GATA-3] and its inputs

	t^2	t^2_7	t^2_{12}	$t^2_{7,12}$	t^5	t^5_2	t^5_{10}	$t^5_{2,10}$	t^8	t^8_5	t^{12}	t^{12}_8	t^{12}_{11}	$t^{12}_{8,11}$
IL-4 (2)	0	0	1	0	0	1	0	1	0	0	0	0	0	0
	1	1	0	1	1	0	1	0	0	0	0	0	0	0
IL-4R (5)	0	0	0	0	0	1	0	0	0	1	0	0	0	0
	0	0	0	0	1	0	1	1	1	0	0	0	0	0
STAT1 (7)	0	1	0	1	0	0	0	0	0	0	0	0	0	0
	1	0	1	0	0	0	0	0	0	0	0	0	0	0
STAT6 (8)	0	0	0	0	0	0	0	0	0	1	0	1	0	1
	0	0	0	0	0	0	0	0	1	0	1	0	1	0
SOCS1 (10)	0	0	0	0	0	0	1	1	0	0	0	0	0	0
	0	0	0	0	1	1	0	0	0	0	0	0	0	0
T-bet (11)	0	0	0	0	0	0	0	0	0	0	0	0	1	1
	0	0	0	0	0	0	0	0	0	0	1	1	0	0
GATA-3 (12)	0	0	1	1	0	0	0	0	0	0	0	1	0	0
	1	1	0	0	0	0	0	0	0	0	1	0	1	1

The same reasoning can be followed for the three other interactions of the circuit $\mathcal{C}$, leading to: $\mathcal{S}_5 = \{M : P \to \{0,1\}\}$ (all possible valid markings), $\mathcal{S}_8 = \{M : P \to \{0,1\}$ s.t. $M(g_{11}) = 0\}$, and $\mathcal{S}_{12} = \{M : P \to \{0,1\}$ s.t. $M(g_7) = 0\}$.

Finally, the functionality marking set of the circuit $\mathcal{C}$ is the intersection of the four resulting marking sets: $\mathcal{S}_\mathcal{C} = \mathcal{S}_2 \cap \mathcal{S}_5 \cap \mathcal{S}_8 \cap \mathcal{S}_{12} = \{M : P \to \{0,1\}$ s.t. $M(g_7) = M(g_{10}) = M(g_{11}) = 0\}$.

In conclusion, the positive circuit $\mathcal{C}$ is functional provided that the products STAT1 (g_7), SOCS1 (g_{10}) and T-bet (g_{11}) are absent. It is interesting to note that, if we switch the value of the parameter $K_2\{12\}$ to zero, this positive circuit looses its functionality. This loss of functionality results in the loss of the stable state Th2 (S_2).

5   Conclusions and Prospects

In this paper, we have described a systematic way to translate Boolean models of genetic regulatory networks into standard Petri nets (see also [8]). We have particularly focused on the delineation of a procedure to determine the marking sets insuring the functionality of the feedback circuits found in genetic regulatory graphs. This procedure leads to interesting insights into the temporal behaviour of the modelled system, as it is well established that regulatory circuits are found at the origin of fundamental dynamical properties, such as multistability or homeostasis. The functionality marking set of a circuit defines the sub-region of the phase space where this circuit generates the corresponding dynamical property (*e.g.* the presence of a separatrix in the positive circuit case).

To illustrate our approach, we have delineated the Petri net translation of a Boolean model for the molecular regulatory network controlling Th-lymphocyte differentiation [21]. On the basis of this translation, we have shown that all three logical stable states correspond to dead markings in the Petri net model. These states represent specific lymphocyte populations: the virgin Th population, and the differentiated Th1 *versus* Th2 populations, corresponding respectively to the enhancement of cellular *versus* humoral immune response. Focusing on one functional positive circuit, we have further illustrated how our formal procedure can be applied to the Th-lymphocyte network model in order to delineate the corresponding functionality marking set. Moreover, we have shown that the contradiction of the functionality constraints (*e.g.* by changing the value of a logical parameter in the logical formalism, or the incidence matrix in the Petri net model) leads to the loss of one of the stable states.

To cover the full expression power of the generalised logical formalism [33], we have recently proposed a generalisation of our rewriting rules to encompass multilevel logical models in [7]. However, the feedback circuit analysis presented in Section 3. has still to be generalised to the resulting *Multilevel Regulatory Petri Nets* (MRPN).

Along with theoretical studies, our aim is to provide an integrated software suite which allows the biologist to specify regulatory networks, develop tentative models, and obtain qualitative results. We have already developed a software which implements our logical modelling approach (GINsim, [38]). We are currently developing a module to automate the translation of logical regulatory networks into Petri nets, allowing the analysis of the reachability graph using existing tools such as INA (Integrated Net Analyzer, [37]). Furthermore, as many of the crucial qualitative dynamical properties can be expressed in temporal logic (*e.g.* CTL), we are looking forward the application of model-checking techniques developped in the Petri nets framework.

Finally, we are considering the use of colored Petri nets to generate graphically simpler and more readable nets. The BRPN would then constitute the reference unfolding to perform different types of analysis.

Logical modelling and Petri nets constitute two complementary approaches for the dynamical modelling of biological regulatory networks. Their combination opens new prospects for the analysis of complex regulatory networks. In particular, our rewriting rules for genetic regulatory interactions should ease the modelling and analysis of mixed metabolic-genetic networks. The PN translation of logical regulatory models further constitutes a promising intermediate step for the development of more quantitative models, e.g. using hybrid or stochastic extensions of PN framework.

References

1. Agnello D., C.S.R. Lankford, J. Bream, A. Morinobu, M. Gadina, J. O'Shea and D.M. Frucht, *Cytokines and transcription factors that regulate T helper cell differentiation: new players and new insights*, J. Clin. Immunol. **23** (2003), 147-161.
2. Alla H. and R. David, *Continuous and hybrid petri nets*, Journal of Circuits, Systems, and Computers **8-1** (1998), 159–188.
3. Aracena J., "Modèles mathématiques discrets associés à des systèmes biologiques. Application aux réseaux de régulation génétiques," Thèse de Doctorat Spécialité Mathématiques Appliquées, Université Joseph Fourier, Grenoble, 2001.
4. Bergmann C., J.L. Van Hemmen and L.A. Segel, *Th1 or Th2: how an appropriate T helper response can be made*, Bull. Math. Biol. **63** (2001), 405–430.
5. Bryant R., *Graph-Based Algorithms for Boolean Function Manipulation*, IEEE Trans on Computers, **C-35**, 8:677-691 (1986).
6. Chen M. and R. Hofestaedt., *Quantitative Petri net model of gene regulated metabolic networks in the cell*, In Silico Biology **3**, 0029 (2003).
7. Chaouiya C., E. Remy, and D. Thieffry, *Petri Net Modelling of Biological Regulatory Networks*, IML Research report 2005-20, (2005). Accessible at `http://iml.univ-mrs.fr/editions/preprint2005/preprint2005.html`.
8. Chaouiya C., E. Remy, P. Ruet and D. Thieffry, *Qualitative Modelling of Genetic Networks: From Logical Regulatory Graphs to Standard Petri Nets*, ICATPN04, J. Cortadella and W. Reisig (Eds), LNCS **3099** (2004), 137–156.
9. Chaouiya C., E. Remy, B. Mossé and D. Thieffry, *Qualitative analysis of regulatory graphs: a computational tool based on a discrete formal framework*, L. Benvenuti, A. De Santis, L. Farina (Eds), POSTA03, LNCIS **294** (2003), 119–126.
10. de Jong H., *Modeling and Simulation of Genetic Regulatory Systems: A Literature Review*, J. Comp. Biol. **9** (2002), 67–103.
11. Doi A., S. Fujita, H. Matsuno, M. Nagasaki and S. Miyano, *Constructing biological pathway models with hybrid functional Petri nets*, In Silico Biology **4**, 0023 (2004).
12. Glass L. and S.A. Kauffman, *The logical analysis of continuous, non-linear biochemical control networks*, J.Theor.Biol. **39** (1973), 103–129.
13. Goss P.J.E. and J. Peccoud, *Quantitative modeling of stochastic systems in molecular biology by using stochastic Petri nets*, Proc. Natl. Acad. Sci. USA. **95** (1998), 6750–6755.
14. Gouzé J.L., *Positive and negative circuits in dynamical systems*, J. Biol. Syst. **6** (1998): 11–15.
15. Heiner M. and I. Koch, *Petri Net Based Model Validation in Systems Biology*, J. Cortadella and W. Reisig (Eds), ICATPN04, LNCS **3099** (2004), 216–237.

16. Hofestädt R. and S. Thelen, *Quantitative Modeling of Biochemical Networks*, In Silico Biology **1** (1998), 39-53.
17. Krueger G.R.H., G.R. Marshall, U. Junker, H. Schroeder, L.M. Buja and G. Wang, *Growth factors, cytokines, chemokines and neuropeptides in the modeling of T-cells*, In vivo **16** (2002), 365-386.
18. Küffner R., R. Zimmer and T. Lengauer, *Pathway analysis in metabolic databases via differential metabolic display (DMD)*, Bioinformatics **9** (2000), 925-936.
19. Larrinaga A., A. Naldi, L. Sánchez, D. Thieffry, C. Chaouiya, *GINsim: a software suite for the qualitative modelling, simulation and analysis of regulatory networks*, BioSystems, *in press*.
20. Matsuno H., Y. Tanaka, H. Aoshima, A. Doi, M. Matsui and S. Miyano, *Biopathways representation and simulation on hybrid functional Petri net*, In Silico Biology **3** (2003), 0032.
21. Mendoza L., *A network model for the control of the differentiation process in Th cells*, BioSystems, *in press*.
22. Murata T., *Petri Nets: Properties, Analysis and Applications*, Proceedings of the IEEE **77** (1989), 541–580.
23. Murphy K.M. and S.L. Reiner, *The lineage decisions on helper T cells*, Nat. Rev. Immunol. **2** (2002), 933-944.
24. Reddy V.N., M.N. Liebman and M.L. Mavrovouniotis, *Qualitative analysis of biochemical reaction systems*, Comput. Biol. Med. **26** (1996), 9-24.
25. Remy E., B. Mossé, C. Chaouiya and D. Thieffry, *A description of dynamical graphs associated to elementary regulatory circuits*, Bioinformatics **19** (2003), ii172–178.
26. E. Remy, P. Ruet and D. Thieffry, *Graphic requirement for multistability and attractive cycles in a Boolean dynamical framework*, IML Research report 2005-08, (2005). Accessible at `http://iml.univ-mrs.fr/~ruet/papiers.html`.
27. E. Remy and P. Ruet, *On differentiation and homeostatic behaviours of Boolean dynamical systems*, BioConcur 2005 (2005).
28. Reisig W., Petri Nets, Springer-Verlag (1985).
29. Snoussi, E. H. and Thomas, R. (1993). Logical identification of all steady states : the concept of feedback loop characteristic states, Bul. Math. Biol. 55: 973-991.
30. Snoussi E.H., *Necessary conditions for multistationatity and stable periodicity*, J. Biol. Syst. **6** (1998),3–9
31. Soulé C., *Graphic requirements for multistationarity*, ComPlexUs **1** (2003),123-133.
32. Thomas, R., 1994. The role of feedback circuits: positive feedback circuits are a necessary conditions for positive eigenvalues of the Jacobian matrix. Ber. Besenges. Phys. Chem. 98, 1148-1151.
33. Thomas R., D. Thieffry and M. Kaufman, *Dynamical behaviour of biological regulatory networks–I. Biological role of feedback loops and practical use of the concept of the loop-characteristic state*, Bull. Math. Biol. **57** (1995), 247–276.
34. Weisbuch G., R.J. De Boer, A.S. Perelson, *Localized memories in idiotypic networks*, J. theor. Biol. **146** (1990), 483–499.
35. Yates A., C. Bergman, J.L. Van Hemmen, J. Stark and, R. Callard, *Cytokinemediated regulation of helper T cell populations*, J. theor. Biol. **206** (2000), 539–560.
36. Zevedei-Oancea I. and S. Schuster, *Topological analysis of metabolic networks based on Petri net theory*, In Silico Biology **3** (2003), 0029.
37. INA: Integrated Net Analyzer
    URL: `http://www.informatik.hu-berlin.de/lehrstuehle/automaten/ina/`
38. GINsim: Gene Interaction Network simulation
    URL: `http://www.esil.univ-mrs.fr/~{}chaouiya/GINsim`

Translating SBML Models into the Stochastic π-Calculus for Stochastic Simulation

Claudio Eccher[1,2] and Paola Lecca[1]

[1] Dept. of Information and Communication Technologies
University of Trento, Italy
{eccher, lecca}@dit.unitn.it
[2] ITC-irst Center for Scientific and Technological Research
Povo (Trento), Italy

Abstract. This paper addresses the translation of Systems Biology Mark-Up Language (SBML) Level 2 models of network of biochemical reactions into the Biochemical Stochastic π-calculus (SPI). SBML is XML-based formalism for systems biology, while SPI can describe the concurrency of the different interactions occurring in a network of biochemical stochastic reactions. SPI models can be used for simulation by available computer packages. We present the approach followed in designing a software tool for working biologists that parses an SBML model and performs the unsupervised translation into the process algebra model. To test the correctness of the translation process we present the results obtained by performing simulations of a translated simplified circadian clock model, comparing our results with that obtained with the original differential equation model.

1 Introduction

The essence of a biological system lies in its dynamics and it cannot be described merely by enumerating its components. Systems biology is an emergent field that has grown rapidly over the last few years [1]. It aims at system-level understanding of biological systems. A promising research field is the application of IT techniques to systems biology for understanding of structure of systems and their dynamics, both quantitatively and qualitatively. Considerable attention has been paid in the literature to the development of methods for bio-pathway representation and simulation, with which it is possible to model the dynamic causal interactions of complex biochemical entities [2],[3],[4],[5]. Exchange languages have been recently developed to promote the integration of models and tools from various sources [6],[7]. The Systems Biology Mark-up Language (SBML) is an XML-based model representation formalism for systems biology [8],[9] oriented towards describing Ordinary Differential Equation (ODE) models of biochemical reactions (metabolic networks, cell-signalling pathways, biochemical reactions, gene regulation, etc.). SBML stemmed from the necessity of the systems biology community for information standards in order to allow sharing, evaluation, and cooperative development of large models. Several

C. Priami et al. (Eds.): Trans. on Comput. Syst. Biol. VII, LNBI 4230, pp. 73–88, 2006.
© Springer-Verlag Berlin Heidelberg 2006

software utilities and tools have been developed for converting existing pathway files from genome databases into the SBML representation. For instance, KEGG2SBML is an available tool to convert pathways from Kyoto Encyclopedia of Genes and Genomes [10] into SBML.

On the other hand, process calculi, traditionally used as theoretical frameworks for the study of concurrent computation, are adapted for applications in systems biology, where concurrent processes are the norm. In this application domain, process calculi do not represent a paradigm, but tools for a direct description of the system. In particular, the stochastic π-calculus [11] formalism has been used for the specification of molecular mechanisms governing the biochemistry of different biological systems and phenomena. Moreover, the availability of simulators for the stochastic π-calculus, such as BioSpi [12] and the more recent SPIM [13], made it possible to obtain from the models' specifications also quantitative simulation results. The recent literature reports examples of π-calculus modeling and simulation of cell cycle control [14], gene regulation expression [15], λ-phage switch [16], lymphocyte recruitment in inflamed brain micro-vessels [17]. These results emphasize the advantages of the use of the new formalism in comparison to the more traditional mathematical approaches, such as the ordinary differential equations based models. Unlike the ODE approach, the stochastic π-calculus has the property of compositionality, which is also the main feature of a network of biochemical interactions. It means that complex systems are composed of independent parts. This feature is quite hard to be expressed by a set of interdependent differential equations.

However, the translation from SBML of large molecular networks and their specification into process algebra requires a level of encoding detail that deters biologists not trained in formal methods from performing this conversion. Thus the motivation for the present work is the development of a tool for working biologists allowing them to convert SBML models into the π-calculus formalism for feeding available stochastic π-calculus simulators. Although SBML is supported by more than 80 software systems, to our knowledge no tool exists for converting models into process calculi for subsequent simulation. Since biologists hardly have the knowledge to intervene in intermediate steps of the translation, this process has to be fully automatic.

In this paper we present an automatic translation tool and the methods followed in developing it. The challenges we approached in this task were the definition of techniques for the unsupervised extraction of specifications into process calculi from the possibly incomplete information in the SBML description. This paper is structured as follows: the next section briefly recalls the basics of the SBML formalism and of the biochemical stochastic π-calculus; Sections 3 and 4 contain the assumptions on which the translation is based and a description of the algorithm and of the tool implemented. In Section 5 we show a case study on which we tested the proposed translation method and the results obtained by performing simulation with SPIM (Version 0.02) on the translated model. Finally, in Section 6 we present some conclusions and final remarks.

2   Background

2.1   Brief SBML Description

The Systems Biology Markup Language is a machine-readable model definition language, based upon XML (the eXtensible Markup Language), for systems biology, oriented toward describing systems of biochemical reactions: cell signalling pathways, metabolic pathways, biochemical reactions, gene regulations, etc. The current SBML release is Level 2. The following is an example of a simple network of biochemical reactions that can be represented:

$$S_1 \xrightarrow{k_1} S_2$$
$$S_3 \xrightarrow{k_2} S_3 + S_4$$

where S_i are species and the k_i are arbitrarily complex reaction rates, expressed in mathML format, involving parameters and species concentrations. Reactions in SBML are defined primarily in terms of the participating reactants and products (and their corresponding stoichiometries), along with optional modifier species, an optional kinetic law describing the rate at which the reaction takes place, and optional parameters entering into the kinetic law. The model contains a number of components: reactant species, products species, reactions, rate laws, and parameters in the rate laws. The SBML model consents to define lists of *Function definitions*, *Unit definitions*, *Compartments*, *Species*, *Parameters*, *Rules*, *Reactions*, and *Events*.

A *Function definition* is a named mathematical function that can be used in rate equations and other formulas; a *Unit definition* is a name for a unit used in expression of quantities; a *Compartment* is a container of finite volume for a species; a *Species* is a substance or entity, located in a compartment, that takes part in a reaction; a *Parameter* is a quantity with a symbolic name; a *Rule* is a mathematical expression added to the equations constructed on the set of reactions, used to set parameter values, establishes constraints between variables, etc.; a *Reaction* is the description of some transformation, transport or binding process that can change the amount of some species, given in terms of reactants, products, modifiers and a kinetic law; an *Event* is a statement describing an instantaneous, discontinuous change in a set of variables when a triggering condition is satisfied. Detailed information about the SBML components can be found in the specifications available at [8].

The SBML formalism allows models of arbitrary complexity to be represented. Each type of component in a model is described using a specific type of data structure that organizes the relevant information. Figure 1 shows a fragment of the SBML file of a minimal model for circadian oscillations available in the SBML model database [18].

2.2   The Biochemical Stochastic π-Calculus

In this section we briefly recall the biochemical stochastic π-calculus [11], a stochastic extension of the π-calculus [19][20] for modeling biological concurrent

```
<listOfCompartments>
  <compartment id="deterministicOscillator"/>
</listOfCompartments>
<listOfSpecies>
  <species id="EmptySet" compartment= "deterministicOscillator"
    initialAmount="0" boundaryCondition="true"/>
  <species id="A" compartment="deterministicOscillator"
    initialAmount="0"/>
  <species id="C" compartment="deterministicOscillator"
    initialAmount="0"/>
  <species id="R" compartment="deterministicOscillator"
    initialAmount="0"/>
    ...
</listOfSpecies>
<listOfReactions>
  <reaction id="Reaction1" reversible="false">
    <listOfReactants>
      <speciesReference species="A"/>
      <speciesReference species="R"/>
    </listOfReactants>
    <listOfProducts>
      <speciesReference species="C"/>
    </listOfProducts>
    <kineticLaw>
      <math xmlns="http://www.w3.org/1998/Math/MathML">
        <apply>
          <times/>
            <ci> A </ci>
            <ci> R </ci>
            <ci> gammaC </ci>
        </apply>
      </math>
      <listOfParameters>
        <parameter id="gammaC" value="2"/>
      </listOfParameters>
    </kineticLaw>
  </reaction>
  ...
</listOfReactions>
```

Fig. 1. A fragment of the SBML file of the Vilar minimal circadian clock model

processes. The processes are selected according to a suitable probability distribution in order to quantitatively accommodate the rates and the times at which the reactions occur. At the microscopic scale, biological processes are carried out by networks of interacting molecules, each composed of several distinct independent structural parts, called domains. The interaction between molecules causes their biochemical modification. These modifications affect the potential of the modified molecules to interact with other molecules. The biochemical stochastic π-calculus represents the molecules as computational processes and the network of interacting molecules as a mobile concurrent system. This kind of systems are composed of a community of co-existing computational processes that communicate with each other and change their interconnection structure at execution time. Each computational process is defined by its potential communication activity. The communication between processes, namely the abstraction of the chemical interaction, occurs via channels, denoted by their names (ranged over by $x, y, \dots$). The basic communication primitives are *input* and *output* actions, denoted respectively by $x(y)$ and $\overline{x}\langle z \rangle$. Two concurrent processes can communicate only if they share a common channel name. Executing the input $x(y)$ means being ready to receive a name for y along the channel x, and executing $\overline{x}\langle z \rangle$ stays for being able to send the name z along channel x. In what follows, when the parameter of the communication is not relevant, we shortly denote an output action and an input action on channel x by $\overline{x}$ and x, respectively.

Processes (ranged over by capital letters $P, Q, \dots$) are given by the following BNF-like syntax:

$$P ::= \mathbf{0} \mid (\pi, r).P \mid (\nu y)P \mid P|P \mid P + P \mid A(y_1, \dots, y_n).$$

where $\pi ::= x(y) \mid \overline{x}\langle z \rangle$.

The simplest process is the empty process $\mathbf{0}$ that can do nothing. A process P may be prefixed by (π, r) where π is the first atomic action (either an input or output action) that the process $(\pi, r).P$ can perform and r is the single parameter of an exponential distribution that characterizes the stochastic behavior of the activity corresponding to the prefix π. If π is the input action $x(y)$, then it is a binder for the name y with scope P. The restriction operator (νy) in $(\nu y)P$ is another binder for y with scope P: it declares that y is a private resource of P, as opposed to a global (or public) name. An occurrence of a name in a process is free if it is not within the scope of a binder for that name. The infix operator $\mid$ denotes the parallel composition of the two processes, and $+$ the choice between the possible actions of the two operands. Finally, $A(y_1, .., y_n)$ is a constant definition. The dynamic behavior of a process is driven by a Gillespie algorithm for the exact simulation of coupled chemical reactions [21]. Given a mixture of N chemical species interacting through M reaction channels, the algorithm proceeds iteratively by selecting at each iteration a reaction μ ($\mu = 1 \dots, M$) at a time step τ, changing the number of the molecules to reflect the execution of the selected reaction μ and advancing the time according to the selected time step τ. The process is repeated until some threshold time is reached. The algorithm makes time steps of variable length, based on the reaction rate constants and population size of each chemical species. In each iteration one random number is used to determine when the next reaction will occur, and another random number determines which reaction it will be. The random numbers are taken from the exponential distribution as this is the only distribution which has the memoryless property. This means that the probability of a reaction is independent of the elapsed time, given that the possible reactions remain the same.

2.3   The Stochastic Pi Machine

In the Stochastic Pi Machine (SPIM) [22] a given process P is encoded in a corresponding simulator term V, consisting of a list of summations with a number of top-level private names:

$$\nu x_1 \nu x_2 \ldots \nu x_N \left(\sum\nolimits_1 :: \sum\nolimits_2 \cdots :: \sum\nolimits_M :: [] \right)$$

The simulation of a summation list is performed in two steps: firstly an interaction channel x and the corresponding interaction time τ are stochastically chosen by using the Gillespie algorithm. Then the simulator randomly selects a summation $x(m).P + \sum$, containing an input on channel x and a second summation $x\langle n \rangle.Q + \sum'$ containing an output on x. The selected components synchronize on channel x and the value n is sent over x and substituted to m in process P (written as $P\{n/m\}$). After the interaction, the unused choices $\sum$ and $\sum'$ are discarded and the processes $P\{n/m\}$ and Q are added to the rest of the list to be simulated.

3   Assumptions

Not all the components of a SBML Level 2 model can be translated into a stochastic π-calculus model. In the following we give a brief list of the most important components for the description of network of reactions found in models, along with their use in the translation process.

Species
Species in SBML Level 1 and 2 are treated as simple, indivisible biochemical entities having only one possible state [9]. The possible different internal states of a biological entity or its sub-components are represented as a separately-named chemical species.

The consequence of representing each different state as a species is the loss of compositionality, which, on the contrary, is the main feature of the π-calculus formalism. The absence of compositionality in a biological model can lead in many cases to hide or even to neglect relevant information. Let us consider, for example, the series of events described by the following two reactions:

$$S_1 + S_2 \xrightarrow{k_1} S_3$$
$$S_3 \xrightarrow{k_2} S_4$$

In SBML S_1, S_2, S_3 and S_4 have to be modeled as separately-named species and it is not possible to formalize further knowledge about the internal structure of S_3 and S_4: whether S_3 is a physical binding of S_1 and S_2 or something else, or whether S_4 is also a complex or not. Although the π-calculus can express this kind of biological information, the automatic translation can only reproduce the same level of abstraction, and thus the same content of knowledge, of the original SBML model. In fact, an automatic system cannot retrieve from the SBML model any non-explicitly expressed information about both the internal structure of species and the chemical dynamics of the reaction. For this reasons we consider species as monolithic entities and adopt a literal translation of the SBML model.

Reactions

A reaction is described in terms of reactants and products with their stoichiometries, modifiers and an optional kinetic law. The SBML specification does not impose any restriction on the number of reactants and products in a reaction. Reactions with more than two reactants should be factorized in binary interactions that can be translated into pairwise communications of stochastic π-calculus. However, the available information in the SBML model is not sufficient to allow the application of this procedure. Various reasons motivate this assertion. In general the dynamic of the intermediate binary interactions may be not known: the lack of information can regard simply the values of the rates of each reaction step, or the causality of the events. But there is a more serious reason. Even in the simple case of a third order reaction, it appears fairly hard to represent the simultaneity of the 3-body process into process algebra through an appropriate factorization. Consider, for example, a third order reaction where each reactant is modeled as a process. It could be factored in two second order steps. The first step consumes two reactants to produce an intermediate process. In the second step the intermediate process reacts with the third reactant. However, if the third reactant process is not available, the overall result is to consume two reactants for creating deadlock intermediate processes. For these reasons the current work is limited to the translation of SBML models containing at most second order reactions.

The limitation of the translation to first and second order reactions also imposes constraints on the stoichiometry values that can be associated to reactants. For first order reactions, the reactant stoichiometry can be at most two. For second order reactions the stoichiometry of each reactant can be only one. On the contrary, the stoichiometry of a product can be any integer.

The kinetic law associated to a reaction, expressed in MathML, can be an arbitrarily complex mathematical expression, involving constants as well as concentrations of species. A species acting as catalyst or inhibitor of a reaction is modeled as a modifier that is neither created or destroyed in that reaction, although it can be the product of other reactions. The effect of the modifier is taken into account by using its concentration in the expression of the kinetic rate. The Gillespie's theory of stochastic chemical kinetics does not deal with complex rates depending on time or catalysts' concentrations, and the translation of reaction with catalysts is still an open problem. Thus, at the moment, the conversion process does not take in account the presence of modifiers. Moreover, in SBML Level 1 and 2 there is no information that indicates whether the given rates are the deterministic rates or the stochastic ones. For these reasons the correct rates cannot be automatically read by the SBML model, but have to be introduced in the translated model by the user.

Compartments

Compartments are defined as bounded spaces in which species are located. In fact, the compartment is an attribute of the species, not of the reaction. This means that it is not necessary to use process algebra mechanisms (such as chan-nel restrictions) for isolating a reaction in a given compartment. If the value of the initial concentration of a species and the size attribute of its compartment are both present, they can be used to set the initial instances' number of the process corresponding to the species.

Rules and events
Rules are mathematical expressions to set parameters, establish constraints be-tween quantities, etc, whereas events are mathematical formulas evaluated at specified moments in the time evolution of the system. It is not obvious how to force the number of processes to depend on trigger events or on constraints that cannot be expressed using reactions. Thus the current work is limited to the translation of models in which these entities are not present.

4   Translation

The algorithm implemented allows the tool to automatically translate first and second order reactions with an arbitrary number of products. For each reactant species S we define a process P of the form:

$$P = \sum_{i=1}^{m} P_i$$

where m is the number of reactions in which S takes part as reactant. Each P_i is a prefix process of the form $(\pi_i, r_i).Q_i$, where π_i is an input (output) globally fresh name and r_i is the channel communication rate. The form of Q_i depends on the occurrence of the reactant species only as reactant or as product as well. The form of Q_i is also determined by two boolean SBML species attributes that specify possible constraints on the concentration of a given species: namely the `constant` and `boundaryCondition` fields (see [8]). The combination of these fields' values indicates whether the species concentration has to remain constant, or can be changed either by the set of reactions or by the rules. In the latter case, since we do not consider models with rules, we treat the concentration as constant.

In the following we give the rules for determining the form of the concurrent processes distinguishing between first and second order reactions.

4.1   First Order Reactions

The i-th member of the summation P determined by the reaction $R_i : S \xrightarrow{k_i} \sum_j n_j S_j$, where $j = 1, \ldots, l$, l is the number of the product species, and n_j is the stoichiometry of the j-th product, is of the form:

$$P_i = (a_i, r_i).Q_i \tag{1}$$

where a_i is an input channel and the stochastic communication rate r_i is pro-portional to the kinetic reaction rate. The algorithm distinguishes two cases:

(i) the reaction changes the reactant concentration and (ii) the reaction cannot change the reactant concentration. The latter case occurs when the concentration value is constrained to remain constant by the values of the species attributes `constant` and `boundaryCondition`.

If the reactant concentration does not change the process Q_i is defined as:

$$Q_i = P| \prod_{j=1}^{l'} V_j \tag{2a}$$

where V_j is given by:

$$V_j = \overbrace{W_j| \ldots |W_j}^{n_j - times} \tag{2b}$$

The set of the W_j indexed by $\{1, \ldots, l'\}$ contains each process corresponding to a product species S_j (with stoichiometry n_j) whose concentration can be changed by the set of reactions, but does not contain the process P.

If the reaction can change the reactant concentration, the process Q_i is given by:

$$Q_i = \prod_{j} V_j \tag{2c}$$

where V_j is as in (2b), but now the set of the W_j contains P if the reactant appears as product as well. If the set of the W_j is empty the process Q_i is set to the null process.

Since communications in π-calculus are pairwise, a special process $CLOCK_i$ is created for allowing the reaction to proceed. The process $CLOCK_i$ is given by:

$$CLOCK_i = (\overline{a_i}, r_i).CLOCK \tag{3a}$$

where CLOCK is:

$$CLOCK = \sum_{k=1}^{q} CLOCK_k \tag{3b}$$

and q is the number of first order reactions in the network.

4.2 Second Order Reactions

Given a second order reaction $R_i : S_1 + S_2 \xrightarrow{k_i} \sum_j n_j S_j, j = 1, \ldots, l$, the reactant species S_1 and S_2 are abstracted by the processes $P_1 = \sum_i P_{1i}$ and $P_2 = \sum_i P_{2i}$ where:

$$P_{1i} = (a_i, r_i).Q_{1i}$$
$$P_{2i} = (\overline{a_i}, r_i).Q_{2i}$$

If the concentration of the species S_1 cannot be changed by the set of reactions, the expression of Q_{1i} is:

$$Q_{1i} = P_1| \prod_{j=1}^{l'} V_j \tag{4a}$$

where the set of the V_j is as in (2) and $P_1 \notin \{W_j\}$, otherwise:

$$Q_{1i} = \prod_j V_j \qquad (4b)$$

and P_1 can be in $\{W_j\}$. If $\{W_j\}$ is empty Q_{1i} is set to the null process.
  The process Q_{2i} is defined by:

$$Q_{2i} = P_2|0 \qquad (5a)$$

if the concentration of the species S_2 cannot be changed by the set of reactions, otherwise:

$$Q_{2i} = 0 \qquad (5b)$$

A special case is represented by first order reactions in which the reactant S has a stoichiometry of two. In this case the reaction is a homodimerization and is treated as a second order reaction where the two reactant processes are the same component of the summation P with complementary channels.

4.3 An Example

Let us consider the translation of the reaction network composed by the following four reactions:

$$
\begin{array}{ll}
R_0: & S0 \xrightarrow{k_0} S0 + S1 \\
R_1: & S1 + S2 \xrightarrow{k_1} S3 \\
R_2: & S3 \xrightarrow{k_2} S4 \\
R_3: & S3 + S5 \xrightarrow{k_3} S6 \\
R_4: & S4 \xrightarrow{k_4} S7 + S8
\end{array}
$$

where no species concentration is constrained to remain constant by the respective attributes' values. The set of species $\{S0, \ldots, S8\}$ is translated into the set of processes $\{P0, \ldots, P8\}$:

$$
\begin{array}{lll}
P0 = (chan\_R_0, r_0).(P0|P1) & \text{using (2c)} \\
P1 = (chan\_R_1, r_1).P3 & \text{using (4b)} \\
P2 = \overline{(chan\_R_1, r_1)}.0 & \text{using (5b)} \\
P3 = (chan\_R_2, r_2).P4 + (chan\_R_3, r_3).P6 & \text{using (2c) and (4b)} \\
P4 = (chan\_R_4, r_4).(P7|P8) & \text{using (2c)} \\
P5 = \overline{(chan\_R_3, r_3)}.0 & \text{using (5b)}
\end{array}
$$

and, finally, using (3a) and (3b):

$$
CLOCK = \overline{(chan\_R_0, r_0)}.CLOCK + \overline{(chan\_R_2, r_2)}.CLOCK + \\
+ \overline{(chan\_R_4, r_4)}.CLOCK
$$

4.4   The Implementation

The translation tool is implemented in Java. In this section we briefly describe the main steps performed by the translator.

Step1: Parsing the SBML file and classifying the reactions
The program starts parsing the XML files chosen by the user for reading the reactions, the species and their roles in each reaction and creates an internal representation of these objects. The algorithm classifies the reactions as first or second order reactions, according to the number of reactants. Also the algorithm determines if the reaction changes the concentration of each participating species. At this step the reaction network is graphically represented in the user interface to give user a more friendly representation of the SBML model.

Step2: Solving the reaction network
At this step the tool solves each reaction of the network and creates the processes associated to each species and the process $CLOCK$ according to the rules given above.

A particular case can occur when no reactants or products are specified in a reaction (this description is permitted by the SBML specification). Biologically, this specification corresponds to a creation and a degradation of one or more species, respectively. The creation reaction is treated as a first order reaction, in which a fictitious species with constant concentration is substituted to the missing reactant. Degradation is treated similarly by creating a constant concentration product species abstracted by the null process.

Step3: Composing the system
At this step the whole system is composed according to the SPIM syntax to obtain the process calculus model. The system definition starts with the definition of the global channels, followed by the parallel composition of the concurrent processes associated to the species, and by the set of instructions necessary to set the initial amount of each process. The stochastic π-calculus model is displayed in the user interface. An input form allows user to insert in the model the stochastic communication rates and the initial number of each process. Then the model is saved on the disk for the subsequent simulation.

5   Case Study

To test the translation process some stochastic π models available in the SBML repository were feed as input to the SPi-Machine. As a case study we show here the results of the simulation obtained upon translation of a minimal model of genomically based oscillations originally described in [23] as a simplified circadian clock model. The model, shown in Figure 2, involves two mutually interacting genes, an activator A and a repressor R, which are transcribed into mRNA and subsequently translated into protein. The activator A binds to the A and R promoters increasing their transcription rates; the repressor R binds to A to

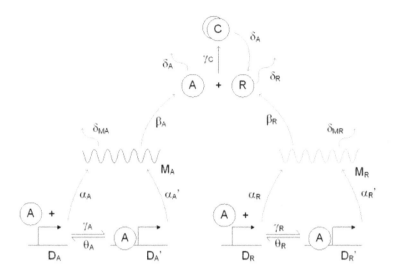

Fig. 2. Biochemical network of the circadian oscillator model taken from [23]

Table 1. The set of the reactions and the respective stochastic rates represented in the SBML model of the Vilar circadian clock. Reactions with the species "EmptySet" as product are degradations; this is expressed in the model by the value "true" of the attribute `boundaryCondition`, which does not allow the set of reactions to change the EmptySet's concentration (see Paragraph 4).

Name	Reaction	Rate constant
Reaction1	A + R → C	$\gamma_C = 2$
Reaction2	A → EmptySet	$\delta_A = 1$
Reaction3	C → R	$\delta_A = 1$
Reaction4	R → EmptySet	$\delta_R = 0.2$
Reaction5	A + DA → DAp	$\gamma_A = 1$
Reaction6	DAp → A + DA	$\theta_A = 50$
Reaction7	DA → DA + MA	$\alpha_A = 50$
Reaction8	DAp → DAp + MA	$\alpha_{Ap} = 500$
Reaction9	MA → EmptySet	$\delta_{MA} = 10$
Reaction10	MA → A + MA	$\beta_A = 50$
Reaction11	A + DR → DRp	$\gamma_R = 1$
Reaction12	DRp → A + DR	$\theta_R = 100$
Reaction13	DR → DR + MR	$\alpha_R = 0.01$
Reaction14	DRp → DRp + MR	$\alpha_{Rp} = 50$
Reaction15	MR → EmptySet	$\delta_{MR} = 0.5$
Reaction16	MR → MR + R	$\beta_R = 5$

form the inactive complex C. Thus positive feedback is provided by the activator protein A, while negative feedback is provided by the repressor protein R.

The original model was generated in SBML by Shapiro using Cellerator, a Mathematica package designed to facilitate biological modeling via automated equation generation [24],[25]. The network of reactions represented in the SBML model is shown in Table 1. A and R are the activator and repressor proteins; DA is the activator gene; DAp denotes the activator gene bound to A; DR and DRp refer similarly to the repressor promoter; MA and MR denote mRNA of A and R, respectively; C is the inactivated complex formed by A and R.

The model in SPIM syntax (Version 0.02) generated by processing the SBML file is shown in the following. The initial amount of each process is the number between angle brackets in the last set of channels (with the species names prefixed by Init_). At the beginning of the simulation one single copy of the activator gene and one of the repressor gene are present. The stochastic rates, provided by the paper of Vilar, are those given in Table 1 and are inserted in the directives **new** of the SPIM file.

Spim program listing of the Vilar circadian rhythm model

```
new chan_Reaction5:1.0:<> (*A, DA*)
new chan_Reaction11:1.0:<> (*A, DR*)
new chan_Reaction1:2.0:<> (*A, R*)
new chan_Reaction2:1.0:<> (*A, CLOCK*)
new chan_Reaction3:1.0:<> (*C, CLOCK*)
new chan_Reaction8:500.0:<> (*DAP, CLOCK*)
new chan_Reaction9:10.0:<> (*MA, CLOCK*)
new chan_Reaction6:50.0:<> (*DAP, CLOCK*)
new chan_Reaction7:50.0:<> (*DA, CLOCK*)
new chan_Reaction10:50.0:<> (*MA, CLOCK*)
new chan_Reaction14:50.0:<> (*DRP, CLOCK*)
new chan_Reaction12:100.0:<> (*DRP, CLOCK*)
new chan_Reaction13:0.01:<> (*DR, CLOCK*)
new chan_Reaction16:5.0:<> (*MR, CLOCK*)
new chan_Reaction4:0.2:<> (*R, CLOCK*)
new chan_Reaction15:0.5:<> (*MR, CLOCK*)
(*EOGAC*)
new Init_A:<int>
new A:<>
new Init_C:<int>
new C:<>
new Init_DA:<int>
new DA:<>
new Init_DAP:<int>
new DAP:<>
new Init_DR:<int>
new DR:<>
new Init_DRP:<int>
new DRP:<>
new Init_MA:<int>
new MA:<>
new Init_MR:<int>
new MR:<>
new Init_R:<int>
new R:<>
new Init_CLOCK:<int>
new CLOCK:<>

(
    !A();(chan_Reaction5();DAP<> + chan_Reaction11();DRP<> + chan_Reaction1();C<> +
        chan_Reaction2();())
  | !C();chan_Reaction3();R<> | !DA();(chan_Reaction5<>;() + chan_Reaction7();(MA<> | DA<>))
  | !DAP();(chan_Reaction8();(MA<> | DAP<>) + chan_Reaction6();(A<> | DA<>))
```

```
|  !DR();(chan_Reaction11<>;() + chan_Reaction13();(MR<> | DR<>))
|  !DRP();(chan_Reaction14();(MR<> | DRP<>) + chan_Reaction12();(A<> | DR<>))
|  !MA();(chan_Reaction10();(A<> | MA<>) + chan_Reaction9();())
|  !MR();(chan_Reaction16();(R<> | MR<>) + chan_Reaction15();())
|  !R();(chan_Reaction1<>;() + chan_Reaction4();())
|  !CLOCK();(chan_Reaction8<>;CLOCK<> + chan_Reaction10<>;CLOCK<> +
             chan_Reaction14<>;CLOCK<> + chan_Reaction12<>;CLOCK<> +
             chan_Reaction13<>;CLOCK<> + chan_Reaction16<>;CLOCK<> +
             chan_Reaction4<>;CLOCK<> + chan_Reaction15<>;CLOCK<> +
             chan_Reaction2<>;CLOCK<> + chan_Reaction9<>;CLOCK<> +
             chan_Reaction6<>;CLOCK<> + chan_Reaction7<>;CLOCK<> +
             chan_Reaction3<>;CLOCK<>)
|  !Init_A(n); if n>0 then (A<>|Init_A<n-1>)
|  !Init_C(n); if n>0 then (C<>|Init_C<n-1>)
|  !Init_DA(n); if n>0 then (DA<>|Init_DA<n-1>)
|  !Init_DAP(n); if n>0 then (DAP<>|Init_DAP<n-1>)
|  !Init_DR(n); if n>0 then (DR<>|Init_DR<n-1>)
|  !Init_DRP(n); if n>0 then (DRP<>|Init_DRP<n-1>)
|  !Init_MA(n); if n>0 then (MA<>|Init_MA<n-1>)
|  !Init_MR(n); if n>0 then (MR<>|Init_MR<n-1>)
|  !Init_R(n); if n>0 then (R<>|Init_R<n-1>)
|  !Init_CLOCK(n); if n>0 then (CLOCK<>|Init_CLOCK<n-1>)
|  Init_A<0>
|  Init_C<0>
|  Init_DA<1>
|  Init_DAP<0>
|  Init_DR<1>
|  Init_DRP<0>
|  Init_MA<0>
|  Init_MR<0>
|  Init_R<0>
|  Init_CLOCK<1>
)
```

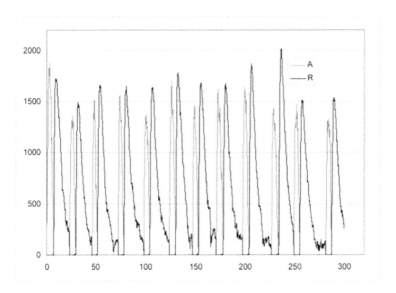

Fig. 3. The behavior of the activator A and repressor R proteins in terms of number of processes versus time (in hours) resulting from the simulation performed on the translated minimal circadian oscillator model

The results of the simulation with SPIM of the Vilar model are shown in Figure 3. The diagram reports the number of processes representing the activator A and the repressor R versus time in hours. As expected, activator A and repressor R show the out-of-phase oscillatory behavior with a period of about 24 hours characteristic of the circadian rhythm. Our results are in excellent agreement with that obtained in the original paper, both in the period of oscillations and in the number of molecules of each species.

6 Discussion and Conclusions

The theoretical approach to the translation from SBML into the π-calculus and the implemented algorithm yielded to develop a usable and valuable tool. The simulation results of the stochastic π-calculus model generated by the tool are in agreement with those showed in the original paper. Furthermore, the translation is completely automatic hiding the complexity of both the formalisms from the biologists. Since SBML is a standard widely supported by the systems biology community, this tool can allow to perform simulation on a great number of biological models available in the SBML repository.

A set of problems remains open and further investigation is needed. The problem related to the lack of structure and internal states of species can be addressed when the SBML Level 3 extension, currently under development, will be available. As regards the role of modifiers, the translation procedure presented here can also be applied to simple reactions with one modifier, one reactant and a constant rate. In general, complex dynamic rates involving modifiers may be accounted for by adding modifier processes producing (for catalysts that augment the reaction rate) or consuming (for catalysts slowing down the reaction) reactant processes. However, the relation between the amount of the modifier processes and the given kinetic law has to be deeply investigated.

References

1. Kitano, H.: Systems biology: a brief overview. Science **295** (2002) 1662–1664
2. Matsuno, H., Tanaka, Y., Aoshima, H., Doi, A., Matsui, M., Miyano, S.: Biopathways representation and simulation on hybrid functional petri net. Silico Biol. **3** (2003) 389–404
3. Kam, N., Cohen, I., Harel, D.: The immune system as a reactive system: Modeling t cell activation with statecharts. In: Proc. Symposia on Human-Centric Computing Languages and Environments, IEEE Computer Society Press (2001) 15–22
4. Kahn, S., Makkena, R., McGeary, F., Decker, K., Gillis, W., Schmidt, C.: A multiagent system for the quantitative simulation of biological networks. In: Proceedings of the AAMAS '03, Melbourne, Australia (2003) 385–392
5. Peleg, M., Yeh, I., Altman, R.B.: Modeling biological processes using workflow and petri net models. Bioinformatics **18** (2002) 825–837
6. Winter, A., Kullbach, B., Riediger, V.: An overview of the gxl graph exchange language. In Diehl, S., ed.: Software Visualization - International Seminar Dagstuhl Castle, Revised Lectures, Germany, Springer Verlag (2001)

7. The Bioinformatic Sequence Markup Language: `http://www.bsml.org`.
8. Finney, A., Hucka, M.: Systems biology markup language (sbml) level 2: Structures and facilities for model definitions. (Available at `http://www.sbml.org`)
9. Hucka, M., Finney, A., Bornstein, B.J., Keating, S.M., Shapiro, B.E., Matthews, J., Kovitz, B.L., Schilstra, M.J., Funahashi, A., Doyle, J.C., Kitano, H.: Evolving a lingua franca and associated software infrastructure for computational systems biology: The systems biology markup language (sbml) project. Systems Biology **1** (2004) 41–53
10. Kaneisha, M., Goto, S.: Kegg: Kyoto encyclopaedia of genes and genomes. Nucleic Acid Res. **28** (2000) 27–30
11. Priami, C., Regev, A., Shapiro, E., Silvermann, W.: Application of a stochastic name-passing calculus to representation and simulation of molecular processes. Information processing letters **80** (2001) 25–31
12. The BioSpi project: `http://www.wisdom.weizmann.ac.il/~biospi`.
13. Phillips, A., Cardelli, L.: A correct abstract machine for the stochastic pi-calculus. In: Proceedings of BioConcur 2004. (2004)
14. Lecca, P., Priami, C.: Cell cycle control in eukaryotes: a biospi model. Technical Report DIT-03-045, University of Trento (2003)
15. Regev, A., Silverman, W., Shapiro, B.E.: Representation and simulation of biochemical processes using the pi-calculus process algebra. In: Proceedings of the Pacific Symposium of Biocomputing (PSB2001). Volume 6. (2001) 459–470
16. Kuttler, C., Niehren, J., Blossey, R.: Gene regulation in the pi calculus: Simulating cooperativity at the lambda switch. In: Proceedings of BioConcur. (2004) 459–470
17. Lecca, P., Priami, C., Quaglia, P., Rossi, B., Laudanna, C., Costantin, G.: A stochastic process algebra approach to simulation of autoreactive lymphocyte recruitment. SIMULATION: Transactions of the society for modelling and simulation international **80** (2004) 273–288
18. The SBML BioModels Database: `http://sbml.org/models.html`,.
19. Milner, R.: Communicating and Mobile Systems: the π-calculus. Cambridge University Press (1999)
20. Priami, C.: Stochastic π-calculus. The Computer Journal **38** (1995) 578–589
21. Gillespie, D.T.: Exact stochastic simulation of coupled chemical reactions. J. Phys. Chem. **81** (1977) 2340–2361
22. Blossey, R., Cardelli, L., Phillips, A.: A compositional approach to the stochastic dynamics of gene networks. Available at `http://www.luca.demon.co.uk/` (2005)
23. Vilar, J.M.G., Kueh, H.Y., Barkai, N., Leibler, S.: Mechanisms of noise resistance in genetic oscillators. PNAS **99** (2002) 5998–5992
24. The Cellerator Web Site: `http://www.cellerator.info/`.
25. Shapiro, B.E., Mjolsness, E.D.: Developmental simulations with cellerator. In Yi, T., Hucka, M., Morohashi, M., Kitano, H., eds.: Proceedings of the Second International Conference on Systems Biology (ICSB2001), Omnipress (2001)

Graph Theory for Rule-Based Modeling of Biochemical Networks

Michael L. Blinov, Jin Yang, James R. Faeder, and William S. Hlavacek

Theoretical Biology and Biophysics Group, Theoretical Division, Los Alamos
National Laboratory, Los Alamos, NM 87545, USA
{mblinov, jyang, faeder, wish}@lanl.gov

Abstract. We introduce a graph-theoretic formalism suitable for modeling biochemical networks marked by combinatorial complexity, such as signal-transduction systems, in which protein-protein interactions play a prominent role. This development extends earlier work by allowing for explicit representation of the connectivity of a protein complex. Within the formalism, typed attributed graphs are used to represent proteins and their functional components, complexes, conformations, and states of post-translational covalent modification. Graph transformation rules are used to represent protein-protein interactions and their effects. Each rule defines a generalized reaction, i.e., a class of potential reactions that are logically consistent with knowledge or assumptions about the represented biomolecular interaction. A model is specified by defining 1) molecular-entity graphs, which delimit the molecular entities and material components of a system and their possible states, 2) graph transformation rules, and 3) a seed set of graphs representing chemical species, such as the initial species present before introduction of a signal. A reaction network is generated iteratively through application of the graph transformation rules. The rules are first applied to the seed graphs and then to any and all new graphs that subsequently arise as a result of graph transformation. This procedure continues until no new graphs are generated or a specified termination condition is satisfied. The formalism supports the generation of a list of reactions in a system, which can be used to derive different types of physicochemical models, which can be simulated and analyzed in different ways. The processes of generating and simulating the network may be combined so that species are generated only as needed.

1 Introduction

A common feature of biochemical networks, especially those comprising protein-protein interactions, is combinatorial complexity [15,7,29,26], which is present whenever a relatively small number of biomolecular interactions have the potential to generate a much larger number of distinct chemical species and reactions. For a system marked by combinatorial complexity, the conventional approach of manually specifying each term of a mathematical model is often impossible if the

C. Priami et al. (Eds.): Trans. on Comput. Syst. Biol. VII, LNBI 4230, pp. 89–106, 2006.
© Springer-Verlag Berlin Heidelberg 2006

model is intended to account comprehensively for the consequences of biomolecular interactions. Thousands of reactions may arise from the interactions of only a few proteins, as in cases we have studied [25,19,5]. A solution to this problem is to specify a rule for each biomolecular interaction and its effects, and then use the rules to automatically generate a logically consistent reaction network and corresponding models, which may take diverse forms. This approach has been used, typically ad hoc, to model a number of signal-transduction systems (for examples, see [47,28,36]). These systems, in which combinatorial complexity is ubiquitous, regulate cellular responses to environmental stimuli through protein-protein interactions and play important roles in many diseases. The complexity of models can be reduced in certain circumstances [8,18,6], but methods for treating combinatorial complexity are still needed.

Recently, several frameworks and software tools have been developed for modeling biochemical networks through formalized descriptions of biomolecular interactions. These frameworks include visualization tools and visual languages [34,12,32,1], process algebras [43,10], and different types of rewrite systems [9,48,20,4,17]. Software tools that allow specification of a kinetic model via rules for biomolecular interactions include BioNetGen [4,17] and BIOCHAM [20]. In both cases, rules are expressed in a rudimentary but general-purpose language and interpreted through procedures of pattern matching and string rewriting. Another tool that can be used to obtain a kinetic model, Moleculizer, provides a set of modules for model specification [37]. Each module functions as a reaction generator for a particular type of reaction. Related work is discussed in more detail later.

Here, we provide a theoretical framework for extending the BioNetGen language to include graph transformation rules [2]. This report formalizes the diagrammatic conventions proposed in [16] for representing proteins and protein complexes as graphs and introduces new details about the graphical procedures for model specification and generation. The motivation for this extension is a desire to be able to explicitly track and account for the connectivity of a protein complex, which is important, for example, when the reactivity of a complex depends on its configuration, which is common. The graph-theoretic formalism is tailored to the problem of building physicochemical models of biochemical networks, particularly protein-protein interaction networks. It allows for the abstraction of proteins, functional components of proteins, and protein complexes, including multimeric proteins that function as a unit. Throughout the text, we will illustrate concepts using cartoon diagrams of [16]. Most of these diagrams pertain to the model of [19] for membrane-proximal events in FcεRI-mediated signal transduction.

2   Model Specification

A model specification necessarily includes a definition of the material parts of a system and all of the internal states of these parts to be considered. An example of an internal state, which might be associated with a tyrosine residue (as a convenient abstraction), is phosphorylation status. The two possible states of such a protein component might be labeled 'phosphorylated' and 'not phosphorylated.' Another example is the three-dimensional conformation of a protein. If consideration of two conformations is adequate for modeling purposes, these states might be labeled 'open' and 'closed.' A specification also includes a definition of the chemical transformations that can potentially take place in a system. Some transformations may change the connectivity of molecular parts, as when two proteins form a complex. Other transformations may change the internal states of molecular parts, as when a protein tyrosine kinase (PTK) catalyzes a phosphorylation reaction or when binding of a ligand induces a conformational change of an allosteric enzyme. A reaction network is obtained by applying reaction rules for chemical transformations to a seed set of chemical species. Ensemble functions corresponding to readouts of interest, such as conserved quantities or observables, can be used to specify model outputs. Graphs for elements of a model specification are defined in detail below.

2.1   Molecular Entities, Components, and Complexes

Most molecular entities of interest, such as polypeptide chains, are structured units of a biochemical network. Proteins involved in signal transduction, for example, typically contain multiple functional components and interactions are mediated by such components. Examples include sites of modification (amino acid residues), protein motifs, catalytic subunits, and protein interaction domains [41].

Definition 1. *A Molecular-entity Graph is a triple $M = (V, E, A_M)$, where V is a set of labeled attributed vertices and E is a set of undirected edges. Vertices represent components. Vertex labels need not be unique; multiple vertices with the same label indicate components considered to be equivalent and may give rise to structural symmetry. Edges represent intra- or intermolecular bonds between components. A molecular-entity graph has a unique label and may have an optional set of attributes A_M.*

Molecular-entity graphs for the four proteins considered in the FcεRI model are shown in Fig. 1(a). Note that edges are not included, even though the components of the molecules are physically connected. Consideration of these connections would not affect the behavior of this particular model. Molecular-entity graphs reflect the level of abstraction in a model and largely define the model's scope. Additional definition of the problem domain comes from typing of the components and edges in molecular-entity graphs, which is discussed later. Briefly, typing defines which attributes of a vertex are variable and which are fixed. Typing also defines the possible values of the variable attributes. Fixed attributes might include sequence, molecular weight, links to annotation sources, etc. Molecular weight is one example of a fixed attribute that might affect reactivity [37,17]. An example of a variable attribute is phosphorylation status, which often affects binding activity.

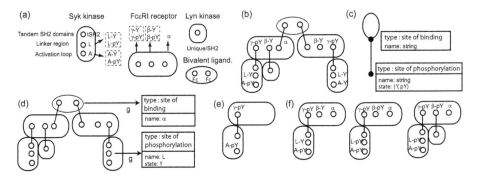

Fig. 1. Graphs of the FcεRI model. (a) Graph representations of molecular entities in the model of [19] according to conventions proposed in [16], with minor deviations. Vertices within the PTK Syk represent three components: tandem SH2 phosphotyrosine binding domains, linker region (*L*) and activation loop (*A*). Components *L* and *A* have a 'state' attribute that can take two values: Y and pY, corresponding to 'not phosphorylated' and 'phosphorylated'. The bivalent ligand is comprised of two identical binding domains (Fc). The PTK Lyn includes a single component that lumps the unique and SH2 domains of this protein. The multichain FcεRI receptor consists of three components representing the α, β and dimeric γ chains of the receptor. The β and γ components have phosphorylation state attributes like *A* and *L* above. (b) A chemical species graph. (c) Component-level type graph (CTG) corresponding to this model. (d) The chemical species in (b) typed over CTG by the typing mapping g. (e) A pattern graph. (f) Members of an ensemble of chemical species matched by the pattern graph.

In the future, it may be desirable to extend the concept of molecular entity to embrace recursion, such that a molecular entity may be comprised of molecular entities. In the meantime, we treat a complex of molecular entities as a special case.

Definition 2. *A* Complex Graph M_Σ *is a connected set of molecular-entity graphs. A complex graph may be associated with an alphanumeric label, if desired, and an optional set of attributes.*

In the model of [19], 300 out of 354 potential chemical species contain a receptor dimer, which can be represented as a complex graph. It is important to consider complexes, because complexes can be observed experimentally and are often of functional significance. An example is provided by the case of a receptor that becomes phosphorylated only when it is complexed with a second receptor of the same type. Complex graphs are connected at the level of molecular-entity graphs, but because the vertices of a molecular-entity graph need not be connected, a complex graph may be unconnected at the level of component vertices. Note that if we restrict ourselves to consideration of binary interactions (the default assumption), then each vertex of a complex graph is connected by at most one edge. The label of a complex graph may be either assigned or derived from stoichiometry and molecule labels.

2.2   Chemical Species

The material building blocks of a biochemical network, defined above, are its components, molecules, and complexes. Chemical species, one of the two kinds of elements in a chemical reaction network, are particular configurations of these building blocks in specific internal states.

Definition 3. *A Chemical-species Graph C is a molecular-entity or complex graph with any and all variable attributes taking specific values.*

A chemical-species graph is illustrated in Fig. 1(b). Note that, consistent with the layout conventions of [16], molecular-entity graphs comprising the chemical-species graph are enclosed in boxes for clarity and some labels are suppressed to avoid clutter.

2.3   Types of Components and Bonds

The molecular-entity graphs of a system, and all derivative graphs of a system, are typed over a *component-level type graph*, which defines the types of vertices and edges in the system.

Definition 4. *A Component-level Type Graph (CTG) of a biochemical system comprises a pair (CV, CE), where CV is a set of vertex (component) types, and CE is a set of edge (bond) types. Each type is associated with a set of attributes, which may be variable or fixed. Values of fixed attributes are defined, and the allowable values of variable attributes are enumerated or otherwise indicated. Any graph G of a system comprised of or derived from the system's set of molecular-entity graphs is typed over CTG via a mapping $g : G \rightarrow CTG$.*

As indicated in Fig. 1(c), we consider the components of molecules in the FcεRI model to belong to one of two types. Each component is a site of binding and/or a site of phosphorylation. A site of phosphorylation has a variable attribute, which has two possible values, Y (not phosphorylated) or pY (phosphorylated). Components α, β, γ, Fc, unique/SH2, and SH2 are sites of binding. Components β, γ, L, and A are sites of phosphorylation. The type graph of Fig. 1(c) further indicates that two types of bonds are considered. A bond is allowed between two binding sites or between a binding site and a phosphorylation site. A typing mapping is partially illustrated in Fig. 1(d).

2.4   Pattern Graphs and Ensembles of Chemical Species

Pattern graphs are derived from molecular-entity graphs. They appear in *reaction rules* and *function evaluation rules*, defined later, and they can be considered subgraphs of chemical-species graphs. We refer to the set of chemical-species graphs matching a pattern graph as an ensemble, because these graphs represent chemical species that all have a common reactivity or all contribute to a common quantity (the value of an output function).

Definition 5. *A Pattern Graph* $P = (V_P, E_P)$ *is a set of molecular-entity and/or complex graphs. These graphs need not be connected. The components, molecular entities, and complexes of P may each be associated with a set of variable attributes. In addition, connectivity of the graphs of P to external components is specified via an interface. The* Interface *of a Pattern Graph* I_P *is a partition of* V_P *into three sets:* $V_P = V_P^0 \bigsqcup V_P^1 \bigsqcup V_P^{01}$, *where* V_P^0 *is a set of components that* cannot *be bound to components external to the pattern graph,* V_P^1 *is a set of components that* must *be bound to components external to the pattern graph, and* V_P^{01} *is a set of components that are free to be either bound or unbound to components external to the pattern graph.*

A pattern graph is illustrated in Fig. 1(e). According to the conventions of [16], the interface of a pattern graph is specified by the symbol used for a node (open, half-filled, or filled circle). An open circle represents a component $v \in V_P^0$. A half-filled circle represents a component $v \in V_P^{01}$. A filled circle represents a component $v \in V_P^1$. By convention, a half-filled circle is omitted in the diagrammatic representation of a graph if values of variable attributes of this component are unrestricted. As indicated earlier, a pattern graph is used to define an ensemble of chemical-species graphs.

Definition 6. *An* Ensemble *of Chemical-species Graphs* Ω_P *is a set of chemical-species graphs each matched by an identical pattern graph P.*

A chemical species graph $C = (V, E)$ is matched by a pattern graph $P = (V_P, E_P)$ iff

1. there exists a subgraph $C' = (V', E') \subseteq C$ isomorphic to P via an isomorphism $f : P \to C'$;
2. f is consistent with the interface I_P; and
3. f preserves attributes of components, molecular entities, and complexes, e.g., for a vertex $v \in V_P$ attributes of $f(v) \in V'$ fall within the set of attributes defined for $v \in V_P$.

Figure 1(f) shows an ensemble of chemical-species graphs, each of which is matched by the pattern graph of Fig. 1(e). Note that chemical-species graphs containing multiple subgraphs isomorphic to a pattern graph may be matched multiple times. For example, the simple string pattern AB matches BAB twice. In the future, it may be useful to associate 'context' attributes with vertices of a pattern graph to restrict or otherwise control the number of matches, which affects parameterization of reactions (see below).

The observables of an experiment typically correspond to properties of ensembles. Thus, it is important to be able to determine such properties so that model predictions can be tested. This capability is obtained by specifying a function evaluation rule [4,17].

Definition 7. *A* Function Evaluation Rule *is a pattern P and a function of attributes of chemical-species graphs belonging to* Ω_P. *This function is referred to as an* output function.

A function evaluation rule is processed by first finding the chemical-species graphs matched by the pattern graph of the rule and then calculating the value of the rule's output function. An example of an output function is a weighted sum of concentrations. A rule associated with this type of function is useful, for example, for determining the total concentration of a protein X in a particular state of phosphorylation when the protein may be distributed among numerous chemical species, as is usually the case. Concentrations of chemical species are weighted by the number of X proteins in each species.

2.5   Chemical Reactions

We have now introduced definitions needed to consider one of the two kinds of elements in a biochemical reaction network, a chemical species. The second kind of element is a chemical reaction.

Definition 8. *A* Chemical Reaction ρ *comprises a set of reactant chemical species graphs* R_ρ, *a set of product chemical species graphs* P_ρ, *and a rate law* ν_ρ. *Product chemical species graphs are obtained from reactant chemical species graphs via graph rewriting* consistent with chemistry.

Graph rewriting consistent with chemistry in the case of a closed system means that P_ρ is obtained from R_ρ via composition of the following operations:

- addition/removal of intra- or inter-molecular edge(s),
- change of values of variables attribute(s), and
- replacement of a molecular entity or set of molecular entities with another molecular entity or set of molecular entities having the same components.

The first two classes of operations are found in the FcεRI model. The third class of operations is allowed so that one may model assembly and disassembly of a multimeric protein (Fig. 2(d)), covalent reactions between proteins, and proteolytic cleavage of a protein. Examples of the latter reactions occur in activation of the complement system via the classical pathway. (The enzyme C1 assembles on the surface of an antigen, which leads to cleavage of complement component C3 to generate fragments C3a and C3b. C3b may then attach covalently to the antigen.) Two additional operations are allowed for an open system: synthesis and degradation of a set of molecular entities. Degradation of a molecule means that its corresponding molecular-entity graph is removed (to a sink external to the system being modeled) along with any and all bonds to which it is connected. Synthesis of a molecule means that a new molecular entity appears (from a source external to the system being modeled). Finally, we note that the second class of operations includes transport between compartments if compartment location is included as a variable attribute of molecular entities in a multicompartment system.

Figure 2 illustrates chemical reactions involving representative rewriting operations. The composition of the rewriting operations of a reaction implies a mapping f_ρ between vertices of R_ρ and P_ρ. This mapping must preserve, add, and remove molecular-entity graphs as units. In other words, if any vertex of a molecular entity in R_ρ maps to $\emptyset$ then all other vertices of this molecular entity must also map to $\emptyset$ (Fig. 2(e)). Vice versa, if some vertex $v \in M \subseteq P_\rho$ lacks a preimage, then no other vertices of M may have preimages. Importantly, up to synthesis/degradation of molecular entities, f_ρ preserves components, i.e., vertices of chemical species in R_ρ and P_ρ are the same even if molecular entities are replaced with other molecular entities (Fig. 2(d)).

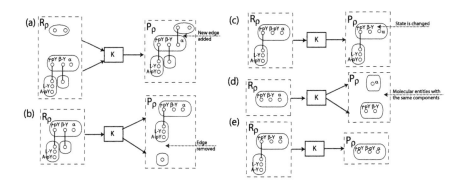

Fig. 2. Different types of reactions. (a) Addition of an intermolecular chemical bond. (b) Breaking of an intermolecular chemical bond. Note that breaking a bond does not necessarily lead to two separate chemical species, because molecular entities may be connected by more than one bond and bonds may be intramolecular as well as intermolecular. (c) Change of a component's attribute value. (d) Replacement of a molecular entity with two molecular entities having the same components. (e) Degradation of a molecular entity. Note that, as suggested by the layout of the diagrams in this figure, if the chemical-species graphs in R_ρ and P_ρ are each replaced with a single node, then a chemical reaction can be represented as a directed bipartite graph.

2.6   Reaction Rules

A reaction rule is a generalization of an individual reaction. It defines a class of chemical transformations of reactants to products; the reactants have common properties, as do the products.

Definition 9. *A* Reaction Rule *is a graph transformation rule* $r : RP \to PP$, *a rate law* ν, *an application condition* α, *and precedence index* N, *where*

1. *A disjoint union of* m *reactant pattern graphs* RP *is used to match and select* m *reactant chemical species* C_r.
2. *The transformation rule* r *includes a component-level mapping function* $f :$ $RP \to PP$ *consistent with chemistry (see above). It maps* RP *to a set of* n *product pattern graphs* PP. *A set of reactant chemical species* C_r *undergoes transformation by replacing the image of* RP *in* C_r *with* PP *via* f. *Dangling edges are removed. This process of graph rewriting corresponds to the well-known single-pushout approach [13]. Note that, to avoid ambiguity*

while embedding PP in C_r, any vertex of RP in V_{RP}^0 of the interface I_{RP} must remain in the same set in PP, i.e., $f(V_{RP}^0) \subseteq V_{PP}^0$.

3. *The rate law ν is a function of rate parameters, such as a single-site rate constant, and properties of chemical species C_r, such as their concentrations.*
4. *The application condition α may include, for example, a pattern selecting species that may not serve as reactants.*
5. *The precedence index N is the priority of reactions generated by the rule. It is sometimes convenient to specify a rule that will generate reactions that replace a subset of reactions generated by another rule [17].*

A reaction rule is illustrated in Fig. 3(a). It should be noted that a negative application condition can be specified by assigning a zero-valued rate law to a rule. All reactions with lower precedence generated by other rules are overridden. A practical application of this idea is the case in which an inhibitor of an enzyme is introduced to a model. An old rule that generates reactions catalyzed by the enzyme can be overridden by a new rule that additionally contains the inhibitor in RP and generates with higher precedence a reaction with a zero-valued or reduced rate.

3   Model Generation

3.1   Application of Reaction Rules

A biochemical reaction network can be generated through iterative application of a set of reaction rules to a seed set of chemical species until no further change is possible (exhaustive generation) or a specified termination condition is reached (such as iteration until a given number of product species or reactions has been generated).

The process of applying reaction rules to a set of distinct chemical species graphs $\mathcal{C}^0$ consists of the following steps, generalizing the algorithm of [17]. For each chemical species C matched by RP, a transformation replaces RP in C with PP according to a procedure of *graph rewriting*, which as mentioned earlier corresponds to the standard single-pushout approach [13].

1. For each reaction rule $r_{m,n}, RP_1 + \ldots RP_m \rightarrow PP_1 + \ldots PP_n$, identify all sets of species graphs in $\mathcal{C}^0$ that qualify as reactants. Then, for each RP_i, find all matching species graphs $C_i \in \mathcal{C}^0$. If an application condition is specified, exclude all sets of species graphs that do not satisfy the condition.
2. For each set of reactant species $\bigsqcup C_i$, define a chemical reaction (graph transformation) by replacing the image of $\bigsqcup RP_i$ in $\bigsqcup C_i$ with $\bigsqcup PP_j$. In this operation, attributes of vertices in $\bigsqcup C_i$ that do not differ between the corresponding vertices of $\bigsqcup RP_i$ and $\bigsqcup PP_j$ are preserved. Incident edges of $\bigsqcup C_i$ not indicated in $\bigsqcup RP_i$ or $\bigsqcup PP_j$ are also preserved. Any edge (l, c) between a vertex $l \in \bigsqcup RP_j$ and $c \in C \setminus \bigsqcup RP_i$ is either replaced with an edge $(f(l), c)$, if $f(l) \in \bigsqcup PP_j$, or removed, if $f(l) = \emptyset$. Assign the precedence index N of the reaction rule to each reaction.

3. Applying all reaction rules to the set of seed species, generate a list of distinct reactions $\mathcal{R}^0$. If the list $\mathcal{R}^0$ contains identical reactions with different precedence indices, delete reactions with indices less than the maximum index. All identical reactions of the same precedence remain in $\mathcal{R}^0$.
4. Identify chemical species that are products in the list $\mathcal{R}^0$ but that are not isomorphic to any in the list $\mathcal{C}^0$ to obtain a list of new species graphs $\mathcal{C}^1$.

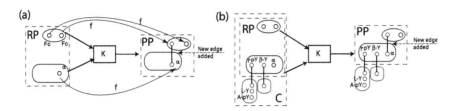

Fig. 3. Reaction rule for ligand-receptor binding in the model of [19]. (a) The rule consists of a reactant pattern graph RP, a product pattern graph PP, and a mapping f. The interface of RP specifies that two Fc components and an α component of RP should be unbound. The rule generates a reaction in which one Fc component is bound to the α component; the other Fc component is unaffected. The remaining components of species matched by the rule are also unchanged. (b) An example of a reaction that may be generated by the rule.

After the initial steps listed above, we continue the network generation procedure by iteratively applying each of the reaction rules to the set of species in $\bigcup_{i=0}^{k} \mathcal{C}^i$, where k is a counter that is updated after each round of rule application. Note that reactions need only be generated when reactant species include at least one reactant in the list $\mathcal{C}^k$. After each round of exhaustive application of the rules, we obtain a list of new reactions $\mathcal{R}^k$ and a list of new product species $\mathcal{C}^{k+1}$. Termination occurs when either no new species are found or a specified termination condition is satisfied. Application of the reaction rule of Fig. 3(a) is illustrated in Fig. 3(b). In general, finding subgraph and graph isomorphisms can be computationally expensive (the subgraph isomorphism problem is NP-complete [27]), but efficient methods are available for many problems of practical concern [50,39]. Also, for two labeled attributed graphs, (sub)graph isomorphism can be ruled out in many cases by a simple comparison of labels and attributes. Issues of termination and computational complexity are discussed further below.

Termination. Figure 4 illustrates a set of rules for which the rule-evaluation procedure described above is non-terminating [11,16]. The rules of Fig. 4 describe interaction of a symmetric bivalent ligand with a symmetric bivalent cell-surface receptor. Rules (a) and (b) and their reverse forms describe the formation and break up of polymer chains of alternating ligands and receptors. Rule (c) and its reverse form describe ring closure and opening. The potential size of the network is limited physically by the numbers of ligands and receptors and binding parameters, but without regard to these quantities, the network is of infinite size.

Rule evaluation can be terminated by specifying an arbitrary cutoff for chain size, number of species, etc. or a maximum number of iterations of rule evaluation. With such an approach, one must be careful to ensure that a generated network is of sufficient size to encompass the species populated in a simulation. Alternatively, as described below, rule evaluation can be embedded in network simulation. With this approach, network elements (species and reactions) are generated as needed and arbitrary termination of network generation is avoided. The fact that a set of reaction rules can generate sets of species and reactions of unbounded size demonstrates that membership of a given species in a reaction network is semi-decidable, meaning that membership cannot generally be ruled out in a finite number of steps. Also, in general, it cannot be determined if evaluation of a set of rules will eventually terminate in the absence of a specified termination condition, such as a maximum number of iterations. For biochemical systems, it is difficult to imagine a situation in which non-terminating rule evaluation could pose a major problem. The effective size of a network is always limited for physical reasons (e.g., as when only a finite number of molecules is available to populate the species of a network). An example of network size being limited by protein copy number is discussed in [15].

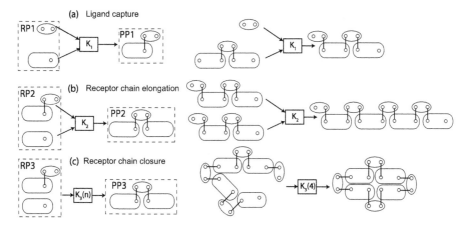

Fig. 4. Reaction rules for interaction of a bivalent ligand with a bivalent cell-surface receptor. Evaluation of these rules is non-terminating. (a) Rule for ligand capture rule and an example of rule application. (b) Rule for receptor chain elongation and an example of rule application. (c) Rule for receptor chain closure and an example of rule application. Note that the rate law in this rule depends on ring size [11]. Also note that pattern RP3 selects a single species, whereas the pattern RP2 above selects two species.

Computational Complexity. The procedure of rule evaluation may be computationally expensive for several reasons. Two important issues are as follows.

1. *A problem of subgraph isomorphism must be solved to map a pattern graph onto a species graph.* Each reactant pattern in a rule set must be tested for isomorphism against all of the species arising in a network.

2. *A problem of graph isomorphism must be solved to determine the uniqueness of a species graph appearing in a new reaction.* Each product of a new reaction must be checked for uniqueness against the other species arising in a network, which can be accomplished by generating a canonical label (a string) for each product of each reaction.

The need to solve these problems in the procedure of rule evaluation could limit the applicability of our modeling approach to 'small' systems in some circumstances. However, we expect the procedure to be practical more often than not. Two factors serve to mitigate the computational costs. First, the vertices of graphs are labeled and attributed, and as a result, the computational cost of isomorphism scales as the number of *identical* vertices (those sharing the same label and attributes). This number is small in most cases we have considered, for example, as in two models we have reported for signal-transduction systems [19,5]. It should be noted that these models are among the largest ever considered for such systems, comparable in size to models developed for other systems using distinct rule-based methods [36,37]. Second, even in cases where the first property does not hold, as in the model of Fig. 4, the maximum degree of vertices is generally small, one to three, and thus low-complexity algorithms are applicable [38,21]. An unoptimized prototype implementation of our algorithm in Perl (available upon request) demonstrates the practicality of the algorithm, which we have used to generate an array of biological networks ranging in size from scores of species to more than 10^4 species (unpublished material). Compared with the method of BioNetGen 1.1 [4,17], which is based on string matching and substitution, we find that graph-based network generation is currently about an order of magnitude slower. However, the method is still feasible. For example, with a laptop computer, the model of [19], which includes 354 species, is generated in about 2 s using BioNetGen 1.1 [4,17], and it is generated using the prototype software in about 45 s. An extension of this model that includes 2954 species (available at http://cellsignaling.lanl.gov) is generated in about 40 s and 1400 s using the two software tools. Again, the prototype software has not been optimized: the algorithm for (sub)graph isomorphism implemented at this time is simply that of Ullmann [50]. Substantial improvements in performance should be possible.

3.2 Assigning Reaction Parameters

Although the rate law is the same for all reactions generated by a rule, rate constants assigned to individual reactions may be different [17,37]. For purposes of discussion, we will now assume that rate laws in reaction rules are rate laws for elementary reactions (i.e., they have the form $\nu_r = \kappa_r \Pi_{i=1}^{m}[C_i]$, where $[C_i]$ denotes the concentration of chemical species C_i) and that the rate constant of the rate law, κ_r, is a single-site rate constant. For a given individual reaction, the rate constant κ_r may need to be multiplied by any of a variety of factors to ensure consistency with other reactions generated by the same rule r. A factor may arise for reasons related to collision frequency. For example, the collision frequency of $A + B$ reactions, in the limit of large numbers, is twice that of $A + A$ reactions, all other factors being equal. A statistical factor may arise if there is reaction path degeneracy (multiple chemically indistinguishable reaction paths from reactants to products). A factor may arise for reasons related to turnover frequency in the case of a catalytic reaction. For example, if formation of a complex facilitates an enzymatic reaction by co-localizing enzyme and substrate, then we must consider the number of enzymes in the complex. A factor, which equals a volume ratio, may arise if reactions take place in separate compartments of different volumes. Rate constants may also be modified by the properties of the reactant chemical species (Fig. 4(c)).

Statistical factors are related to symmetries [17]. Factors greater than 1 arise when a pattern RP is symmetric, meaning there exist non-trivial automorphisms $\psi : RP \to RP$, and the reaction rule breaks the symmetry of the pattern. A transformation that completely breaks pattern symmetry is associated with a statistical factor of $|\mathtt{Aut}(RP)|$, where $\mathtt{Aut}(RP)$ is the automorphism group of RP. Consider, for example, the reaction rule $A.A \to A + A'$ in which A is a molecular entity graph, A' is a form of A that differs with respect to attribute values, $RP \equiv A.A$, '.' represents an edge connecting molecular entities, and '$+$' serves to indicate that $PP \equiv A + A'$ is disjoint union of the graphs A and A' and that the molecularity of each reaction defined by the rule is 2. The reactant pattern is symmetric, with $|\mathtt{Aut}(RP)| = 2$, but the nontrivial automorphism is not preserved under the mapping onto the product patterns. This reaction rule, applied to the chemical species $B.A.A.B$, has a statistical factor of 2, because either of the two A molecules can be transformed into A' and the reactions $B.A.A.B \to B.A + A'.B$ and $B.A.A.B \to B.A' + A.B$ are chemically indistinguishable. When an automorphism is preserved under the mapping onto product patterns, it does not contribute to the statistical factor of a reaction. For example, the rule $A.A \to A + A$ applied to the chemical species $B.A.A.B$ generates the reaction $B.A.A.B \to B.A + A.B$ with a statistical factor of one. In general, the statistical factor arising from pattern symmetry is given by the ratio $\frac{|\mathtt{Aut}(RP)|}{|\mathtt{Aut}(RP \to PP)|}$, where the denominator indicates the size of the group of automorphisms of RP that are preserved under the mapping of RP onto PP. Statistical factors also arise when the reactant chemical species C_r contain symmetric instances of RP. For example, the rule $A \to A'$ applied to $A.A$ would generate the reaction $A.A \to A.A'$ with a statistical factor of 2.

3.3   Embedding Rule Evaluation in Simulation

The method of network generation described above does not rely on the populations of species in the seed set or rate laws. Once a biochemical reaction network has been generated, it can be used to formulate different types of models. For example, one can generate a system of coupled ordinary differential equations (ODEs) or a stochastic simulation algorithm (SSA) [23,24], which is a Monte Carlo procedure for simulating discrete-event reaction kinetics. However, there are cases when all potential species of a reaction network cannot be exhaustively enumerated, as for interaction of a bivalent ligand with a bivalent receptor (Fig. 4). For such a system, rule evaluation would proceed indefinitely unless an arbitrary termination condition is specified. A solution to this problem is to embed rule evaluation in the simulation procedure, such that chemical species are generated only as needed. Two methods for embedding rule evaluation in SSA-based simulation of biochemical reaction kinetics have been proposed [37,17], and both are now implemented in BioNetGen. With lazy rule evaluation [37], only reactions and species connected to newly populated species are generated. With layered rule evaluation [17], the network is extended when a species is populated for the first time by applying the reaction rules for a specified number of iterations (the default is one round), as in the procedure described earlier, to all current species. The relative efficiencies of the various simulation procedures have yet to be fully evaluated, but preliminary (unpublished) results indicate that pregeneration of a network followed by simulation and on-the-fly generation of a network during simulation are complementary. Lazy and layered simulation-embedded evaluation of rules are comparable for problems we have considered (unpublished material). Embedding rule evaluation in ODE-based simulations is straightforward and may provide better performance than analogous SSA-based simulations.

4   Discussion

The sheer size of some biochemical systems makes it difficult to formulate models for them and represent these models in comprehensible ways. Reaction rules for biomolecular interactions help to solve these problems [29,26]. Rules serve as generators of reactions, which can then be translated into mathematical or computational models, in the way SBML [30] is translated into, say, a system of coupled ordinary differential equations (ODEs). In our experience, the equations of a rule-based model typically far outnumber the rules from which they are derived [19,5]. The ability to generate models through automatic interpretation of rules overcomes limitations of writing models manually, which may be impossible. In mathematics, many combinatorial problems that are intractable become tractable when reformulated in terms of generating functions (rules). Here, we have extended methods for rule-based modeling of biochemical systems by introducing a formalism for *graphical* reaction rules, which can expressively represent biomolecular interactions and the consequences of these interactions.

Our main motivation for introducing graphical reaction rules is that such rules allow the connectivity of proteins in a complex to be explicitly and systematically represented. This ability is needed when connectivity affects the reactivity of a complex. A simple example is provided by the case of a bivalent ligand interacting with a bivalent cell-surface receptor. As illustrated in Fig. 4, such a ligand induces the formation of rings and chains of receptors. However, only a chain, such as the protein complex illustrated on the right side of panel (b), can associate with additional ligand or receptor. A ring, such as the protein complex illustrated on the right side of panel (c), can only break apart. Clearly, chains and rings, which may have identical composition and differ only with respect to connectivity, must be distinguished. The most straightforward way of solving this type of problem, we believe, is through the introduction of graphs. The cost of introducing graphs is computational complexity. This cost seems difficult to avoid if one wishes to track connectivity of complexes, which is important for mechanistic modeling of many biological systems.

Graphical reaction rules have further representational advantages over other means of summarizing and analyzing biological systems. They can be visualized as cartoon-like diagrams and therefore used for the same purpose as diagrammatic interaction maps [34,1], which are in common use. However, unlike most interaction maps, rules have precise interpretations [16]. A set of well-posed rules unambiguously specifies a reaction network, and a model for this network can be generated through a computational procedure that interprets the rules. Because the procedure is automatic, once rules are specified, very little mathematical or computational expertise is required in principle to obtain a mathematical model. Graphical reaction rules are also close in form to the type of biological knowledge usually available about a system, which may consist mainly of a list of proteins, their functional components, and their binding and catalytic activities, even for a well-studied system. Thus, because graphical rules can be specified essentially by drawing cartoon-like diagrams (an interface that provides this capability is in development) and they provide a natural way to formalize biological knowledge, graphical rules may, with maturation of software, allow more biologists to contribute to the development of mathematical models, which are needed for predictive understanding of biological systems, which are exceedingly complex.

Finally, rules for biomolecular interactions may be useful for high-throughput modeling of large numbers of systems and for development of models that include a large number of distinct interacting biomolecules. Rules are independent units of a model specification and sets of rules are compositional, which allows models to be built incrementally. In principle, crude models of a large size could be built at present from information of pairwise protein-protein interactions currently catalogued in electronic databases, such as the Human Protein Reference Database [42]. However, large-scale modeling of higher quality will require cataloging the functional domains involved in interactions and the conditions under which interactions take place. Rules must be expressive enough to encode this information, and graphical rules are a step forward. The independence of rules facilitates not only incremental model building but also the consideration of alternative models and mechanistic hypotheses. For example, to introduce a protein-protein interaction in a system to investigate its effect, one can simply add an appropriate rule instead of adding and modifying possibly large numbers of interrelated equations or lines of code. If rules are stored in a machine-readable format in an electronic database, they can be reused. Rules can be assembled in different ways to define models for different systems, which may share some components, and models for different parts of a larger system can be integrated by combining the corresponding sets of rules. Community standards for storing and exchanging rule-based models of biological systems are currently being discussed [31,22].

4.1   Related Work

We contribute a new application of ideas from formal systems, graph rewriting, and (sub)graph isomorphism. Our formalism is expressive enough to represent protein-protein interactions. There is probably much room for algorithmic improvement. A general framework for graph rewriting closely related to the present work is that of AGG [49]. Graph rewriting has been used to model diverse biological systems [45] and other systems, such as chemical systems [3] and self-assembling robotic systems [33]. This body of work provided inspiration. A number of research groups have developed various methods for rule-based modeling of signal-transduction systems. A few key references not already cited are [40,44,14]. Software tools related to BioNetGen include STOCHSIM [35], Cellerator [46], Maude [14,48], BIOCHAM [20], and Moleculizer [37]. Others have also suggested, like us, the use of graphs to represent proteins and protein-protein interactions [9,10,48].

Acknowledgements

This work was supported by grant RR18754 from the National Institutes of Health and by the Department of Energy through contract W-7405-ENG-36. We thank Joshua Colvin, Andrew Finney, Walter Fontana, Matthew Fricke, Nathan Lemons, Paul Loriaux, Fangping Mu, Richard G. Posner, David C. Torney, and Amitabh Trehan for helpful discussions.

References

1. Aladjem, M.I., Pasa, S., Parodi, S., Weinstein, J.N., Pommier, Y., Kohn, K.W.: Molecular interaction maps—a diagrammatic graphical language for bioregulatory networks. Sci. STKE 2004, pe8.
2. Andries, M., Engels, G., Habel, A., Hoffmann, B., Kreowski, H.J., Kuske, S., Plump, D., Schurr, A., Taentzer, A.: Graph transformation for specification and programming. Sci. Comput. Program. **34** (1999) 1–54
3. Benkö, G., Flamm, C., Stadler, P.F.: A graph-based toy model of chemistry. J. Chem. Inf. Comput. Sci. **43** (2003) 1085–1093
4. Blinov, M.L., Faeder, J.R., Goldstein, B., Hlavacek, W.S.: BioNetGen: software for rule-based modeling of signal transduction based on the interactions of molecular domains. Bioinformatics **20** (2004) 3289–3291
5. Blinov, M.L., Faeder, J.R., Goldstein, B., Hlavacek, W.S.: A network model of early events in epidermal growth factor receptor signaling that accounts for combinatorial complexity. BioSystems (in press).
6. Borisov, N.M., Markevich, N.I., Hoek, J.B., Kholodenko, B.N.: Signaling through receptors and scaffolds: independent interactions reduce combinatorial complexity. Biophys. J. **89** (2005) 951–966
7. Bray, D.: Molecular prodigality. Science **299** (2003) 1189–1190
8. Conzelmann, H., Saez-Rodriguez, J., Sauter, T., Bullinger, E., Allgower, F., Gilles, E.D.: Reduction of mathematical models of signal transduction networks: simulation-based approach applied to EGF receptor signalling. Syst. Biol. **1** (2004) 159–169
9. Danos, V., Laneve, C.: Graphs for core molecular biology. Lect. Note Comput. Sci. **2602** (2003) 34–46
10. Danos, V., Laneve, C.: Formal molecular biology. Theor. Comput. Sci. **325** (2004) 69–110

11. Dembo, M., Goldstein, B.: Theory of equilibrium binding of symmetric bivalent haptens to cell surface antibody: application to histamine release from basophils. J. Immunol. **121** (1978) 345–353
12. Efroni, S., Harel, D., Cohen, I.R.: Towards rigorous comprehension of biological complexity: modeling, execution and visualization of thymic T cell maturation. Genome Res. **13** (2003) 2485–2497
13. Ehrig, H., Heckel, R., Korff, M., Löwe, M. Ribeiro, L., Wagner, A., Corradini, A.: Algebraic approaches to graph transformation. Part II: single pushout approach and comparison with double pushout approach. In *Handbook of Graph Grammars and Computing by Graph Transformation*, vol. 1, ch. 4, pp. 247–312 (Eds: Ehrig, H. Kreowski, H.-J, Montanari, U., Rozemberg, G.), World Scientific, Singapore, 1996.
14. Eker, S., Knapp, M., Laderoute, K., Lincoln, P., Meseguer, J., Sonmez, K.: Pathway logic: symbolic analysis of biological signaling. Pac. Symp. Biocomput. (2002) 400–412
15. Endy, D., Brent, R.: Modelling cellular behaviour. Nature **409** (2001) 391–395bray
16. Faeder, J.R., Blinov, M.L., Hlavacek, W.S.: Graphical rule-based representation of signal-transduction networks. Proc. ACM Symp. Appl. Computing (2005) 133–140
17. Faeder, J.R., Blinov, M.L., Hlavacek, W.S.: Rule-based modeling of biochemical networks. Complexity **10** (2004) 22–41
18. Faeder, J.R., Blinov, M.L., Goldstein, B., Hlavacek, W.S.: Combinatorial complexity and dynamical restriction of network flows in signal transduction. Syst. Biol. **2** (2005) 5–15
19. Faeder, J.R., Hlavacek, W.S., Reischl, I., Blinov, M.L., Metzger, H., Redondo, A., Wofsy, C., Goldstein, B.: Investigation of early events in FcεRI-mediated signaling using a detailed mathematical model. J. Immunol. **170** (2003) 3769–3781
20. Fages, F., Soliman, S., Chabrier-Rivier, N.: Modelling and querying interaction networks in the biochemical abstract machine BIOCHAM. J. Biol. Phys. Chem. **4** (2004) 64–73
21. Faulon, J.-L.: Isomorphism, automorphism partitioning, and canonical labeling can be solved in polynomial-time for molecular graphs. J. Chem. Inf. Comput. Sci. **38** (1998) 432–444.
22. Finney, A.: Developing SBML beyond level 2: proposals for development. Lect. Note Comput. Sci. **3082** (2005) 242–247
23. Gillespie, D.T.: A general method for numerically simulating the stochastic time evolution of coupled chemical reactions. J. Comput. Phys. **22** (1976) 403–434
24. Gillespie, D.T.: Exact stochastic simulation of coupled chemical reactions. J. Phys. Chem. **81** (1977) 2340–2361
25. Goldstein, B., Faeder, J.R., Hlavacek, W.S., Blinov, M.L., Redondo, A., Wofsy, C.: Modeling the early signaling events mediated by FcεRI. Mol. Immunol. **38** (2002) 1213–1219
26. Goldstein, B., Faeder, J.R., Hlavacek, W.S.: Mathematical and computational models of immune-receptor signalling. Nat. Rev. Immunol. **4** (2004) 445–456
27. Garey, M.R., Johnson, D.S.: *Computers and Intractability: A Guide to the Theory of NP-Completeness*, W.H. Freeman and Company, San Francisco, 1979
28. Haugh, J.M., Schneider, I.C., Lewis, J.M.: On the cross-regulation of protein tyrosine phosphatases and receptor tyrosine kinases in intracellular signaling. J. Theor. Biol. **230** (2004) 119–132
29. Hlavacek, W.S., Faeder, J.R., Blinov, M.L., Perelson, A.S., Goldstein, B.: The complexity of complexes in signal transduction. Biotechnol. Bioeng. **84** (2003) 783–794

30. Hucka, M., Finney, A., et al.: The systems biology markup language (SBML): a medium for representation and exchange of biochemical network models. Bioinformatics **19** (2003) 524–531.

31. Hucka, M., Finney, A., et al.: Evolving a lingua franca and associated software infrastructure for computational systems biology: the Systems Biology Markup Language (SBML) project. Syst. Biol. **1** (2004) 41–53

32. Kitano, H.: A graphical notation for biochemical networks. BioSilico **1** (2003) 169–176

33. Klavins, E., Christ, R., Lipsky, D.: Graph grammars for self assembling robotic systems. Proc. IEEE Int. Conf. Rob. Autom. (2004) 5293–5300

34. Kohn, K.W.: Molecular interaction maps as information organizers and simulation guides. Chaos **11** (2001) 84–97

35. Le Novère, N., Shimizu, T.S.: STOCHSIM: modelling of stochastic biomolecular processes. Bioinformatics **17** (2001) 575–576

36. Li, Q., Dinner, A.R., Qi, S., Irvine, D.J., Huppa, J.B., Davis, M.M., Chakraborty, A.K.: CD4 enhances T cell sensitivity to antigen by coordinating Lck accumulation at the immunological synapse. Nat. Immunol. **5** (2004) 791–799

37. Lok, L., Brent, R.: Automatic generation of cellular reaction networks with Moleculizer 1.0. Nat. Biotechnol. **23** (2005) 131–136

38. Luks, E.M.: Isomorphism of graphs of bounded valence can be tested in polynomial time. J. Comput. Syst. Sci. **25** (1982) 42–65

39. McKay, B.D.: Practical graph isomorphism. Congressus Numerantium **30** (1981) 45–87.

40. Morton-Firth, C.J., Bray, D.: Predicting temporal fluctuations in an intracellular signalling pathway. J. Theor. Biol. **192** (1998) 117–128

41. Pawson, T., Nash, P.: Assembly of cell regulatory systems through protein interaction domains. Science **300** (2003) 445–452

42. Peri, S., et al.: Development of human protein reference database as an initial platform for approaching systems biology in humans. Genome Res. **13** (2003) 2363–2371

43. Priami, C., Regev, A., Shapiro, E., Silverman, W.: Application of a stochastic name-passing calculus to representation and simulation of molecular processes. Inf. Process Lett. **80** (2001) 25–31

44. Regev, A., Silverman, W., Shapiro, E.: Representation and simulation of biochemical processes using the π-calculus process algebra. Pac. Symp. Biocomput. (2001) 459–470

45. Rosello, R., Valiente, G.: Graph transformation in molecular biology. Lect. Note Comput. Sci. **3393** (2005) 116–133

46. Shapiro, B.E., Levchenko, A., Meyerowitz, E.M., Wold, B.J., Mjolsness, E.D.: Cellerator: extending a computer algebra system to include biochemical arrows for signal transduction simulations. Bioinformatics **19** (2003) 677–678

47. Shimizu, T.S., Aksenov, S.V., Bray, D.: A spatially extended stochastic model of the bacterial chemotaxis signalling pathway. J. Mol. Biol. **329** (2003) 291–309

48. Talcott, C., Eker, S., Knapp, M., Lincoln, P., Laderoute, K.: Pathway logic modeling of protein functional domains in signal transduction. Pac. Symp. Biocomput. (2004) 568–580

49. Taentzer, G.: AGG: a graph transformation environment for modeling and validation of software. Lect. Note Comput. Sci. **3062** (2003) 446–453

50. Ullmann, J.R.: An algorithm for subgraph isomorphism. J. ACM **23** (1976) 31–42

Adapting Biochemical Kripke Structures for Distributed Model Checking

Susmit Jha[1] and R.K. Shyamasundar[2,*]

[1] Department of Computer Science, Indian Institute of Technology, Kharagpur, India
susmit.kumar.jha@ieee.org
[2] School of Technology and Computer Science, Tata Institute of Fundamental Research,
Bombay, India
shyam@tcs.tifr.res.in

Abstract. In this paper, we use some observations on the nature of biochemical reactions to derive interesting properties of qualitative biochemical Kripke structures. We show that these characteristics make Kripke structures of biochemical pathways suitable for assumption based distributed model checking. The number of chemical species participating in a biochemical reaction is usually bounded by a small constant. This observation is used to show that the Hamming distance between adjacent states of a qualitative biochemical Kripke structures is bounded. We call such structures as Bounded Hamming Distance Kripke structures (BHDKS). We, then, argue the suitability of assumption based distributed model checking for BHDKS by constructively deriving worst case upper bounds on the size of the fragments of the state space that need to be stored at each distributed node. We also show that the distributed state space can be mapped naturally to a hypercube based distributed architecture. We support our results by experimental evaluation over benchmarks and biochemical pathways from public databases.

1   Introduction

Recently, there has been a lot of work in the application of formal methods for the modeling and reasoning of biochemical pathways. A popular approach uses the formal model of Kripke structure derived from boolean abstractions of biochemical reactions [6,4]. Model checking of these Kripke structures is capable of deriving valuable information about the underlying biochemical pathways that cannot be understood from classical simulation techniques. However, model checking techniques suffer from state space explosion and there have been several investigations into the scalability of model checking techniques [1,3,7].One such method is the technique of assumption based distributed model checking as envisaged in [2].

However, little effort has been made in the direction of exploiting properties specific to biochemical Kripke structures for the design of scalable model checking approaches. We take the assumption based distributed model checking paradigm [2], where the state space of a system is partitioned into several distributed nodes, as the basis of our work.

---

* Current address. IBM India Research Lab Block1, IIT Delhi, Hauz Khas, New Delhi 110016, India, rshyamas@in.ibm.com

C. Priami et al. (Eds.): Trans. on Comput. Syst. Biol. VII, LNBI 4230, pp. 107–122, 2006.
© Springer-Verlag Berlin Heidelberg 2006

Biochemical Kripke structures have been well studied in BIOCHAM [6,4]. We develop a framework for distributing the state space of a biochemical Kripke structure among several distributed nodes for model checking, by using structural properties of Kripke structures derived from biochemical systems. In this paper, we present the following results:

- Two states in a Kripke structure derived from biochemical pathways are connected by a transition only if the Hamming distance between their propositional labels is bounded by a small constant derived from the stoichiometry of the underlying biochemical reactions. We call such structures as k - Bounded Hamming Distance Kripke structures (BHDKS) where k is a small constant obtained from the stoichiometry of the reactions .
- Bounded Hamming Distance Kripke structures can be well partitioned into fragments each having a size that can be made small enough to be only polynomial in the number of propositions of the Kripke structure (N), and hence amenable to extensive fragmentation [1] for assumption based distributed model checking. The result shows that it is possible to split the exponential state space of the BHDKS $(O(2^N))$ into fragments each of which is only polynomial in the number of the propositions involved $(O(N^p)$, where p is a small constant).
- When the number of distributed nodes across which the state space is to be distributed is not too large (smaller than $2^{N/k}$ for a k - Bounded Hamming Distance Kripke structure with N atomic propositions), we present a hypercube based fragmentation approach which forms smaller fragments and ensures that the neighbours of all the states on a distributed node lie only on the adjacent distributed nodes in the hypercube.

We also note that a k - BHDKS with n states can be partitioned into $n^{1-1/k}$ size fragments along the nodes of a hypercube despite the fact that, in general, the corresponding class of graphs do not have "good" vertex separators i.e., $n^{1-\epsilon}$ separators for any $\epsilon > 0$.

We organize the rest of the paper as follows: Section 2 presents new insights into Kripke structures formed from biological systems by showing that the Hamming distance between any two successive states in the Kripke structure is bounded by a small constant. Such Kripke structure are referred to as bounded Hamming distance Kripke structures (BHDKS). We use these structures to derive a bound on the edge density in Section 3. Section 4 presents relevant background results and definitions related to distributed model checking. In section 5, we use the existence of a small bound on the Hamming distance between successive states in BHDKS to argue that biochemical pathways are more amenable to distributed model checking techniques by presenting the worst case bounds on the size of the fragments of the distributed Kripke structure. The proof presented is constructive and suggests methods of partitioning BHDKS. We discuss the results of our experimental evaluation on benchmarks and public databases in Section 6. The paper concludes with section 7 identifying scopes for further work.

---

[1] We will also illustrate that general Kripke structures need not have any reduction in size during fragmentation.

2   Bounded Hamming Distance of Biochemical Kripke Structures

In this section, we shall describe the modeling of biochemical pathways and demonstrate as to how the characteristics of biochemical pathways lead to their representation as BHDKS.

2.1   Background

In the abstract boolean Kripke structure model [4,5,6], a biochemical reaction takes the system from a state with biochemical entities matching the lefthand side of the reaction rule, into one of the other states in which the biochemical entities of the righthand side have been added. The biochemical entities which appear only in the lefthand side of the rule and not in the righthand side may be nondeterministically present or absent in the target state. By using this boolean abstraction, such models are capable of reasoning about all possible behaviors of the system with unknown concentration values and unknown kinetic parameters[4]. This modeling is particularly useful for complex chemical systems like biochemical pathways where even a boolean abstraction can generate valuable results. It is also now well appreciated that biological models, despite their hybrid nature, indeed have many digital (boolean) controls. In the model checking algorithm, each biochemical entity is associated with a proposition. If the biochemical entity is present in a state, the associated boolean proposition is *true*; other wise, it is *false*. Thus, the biochemical Kripke structure makes a transition from one state to another by "executing" a biochemical reaction and the truth values of the boolean propositions change to reflect the biochemical entities added or removed from the system.

The detailed methodology which takes a biochemical pathway as input and forms a Kripke structure is presented in [5]. In the following, we shall illustrate the derivation of Kripke structures for biochemical pathways through some examples.

Example 1. Simple modeling of a chemical reaction.
Here, the presence and absence of reactants is encoded in the state tuple of the Kripke structure. This is an implicitly assumed reasonable assumption in biochemical pathway representations. Let us try to capture a transition wherein A and B react to form C and D. A typical one is denoted:

$$A + B + \neg C + \neg D \rightarrow A + B + C + D$$

which is interpreted as follows: The transition is defined from all states where the propositions associated with A and B are true, and C and D are false to those states where propositions associated with C and D are true as well as A and B are true. The reasonable assumption is that the reaction does not consume all its reactants and hence, some quantity of reactants A and B are still present after the reaction.

Example 2. Abstract Modeling.
Consider the scenario of A and B reacting to form C and D,

$$A + B \rightarrow C + D$$

and we want to nondeterministically capture all possible scenarios. This is captured by

$$
\begin{aligned}
A + B + \neg C + \neg D &\rightarrow \neg A + B + C + D \\
A + B + \neg C + \neg D &\rightarrow A + \neg B + C + D \\
A + B + \neg C + \neg D &\rightarrow \neg A + \neg B + C + D \\
A + B + \neg C + \neg D &\rightarrow A + B + C + D \\
A + B + C + \neg D &\rightarrow \neg A + B + C + D \\
A + B + C + \neg D &\rightarrow A + \neg B + C + D \\
A + B + C + \neg D &\rightarrow \neg A + \neg B + C + D \\
A + B + C + \neg D &\rightarrow A + B + C + D \\
A + B + \neg C + D &\rightarrow \neg A + B + C + D \\
A + B + \neg C + D &\rightarrow A + \neg B + C + D \\
A + B + \neg C + D &\rightarrow \neg A + \neg B + C + D \\
A + B + \neg C + D &\rightarrow A + B + C + D \\
A + B + C + D &\rightarrow \neg A + B + C + D \\
A + B + C + D &\rightarrow A + \neg B + C + D \\
A + B + C + D &\rightarrow \neg A + \neg B + C + D \\
A + B + C + D &\rightarrow A + B + C + D
\end{aligned}
$$

In an abstract model, each chemical reaction is interpreted as a set of chemical reactions where some of the reactants may be present even after the execution of the reaction and the products may be present even before the execution.

Example 3. The E. Coli K-12 Pathway: leucine biosynthesis [9].
Using the following abbreviations: K — 2-keto-isovalerate, AC — Acetyl-CoA, C— Coenzyme A, H— 3-carboxy-3-hydroxy-isocaproate, T — 2-D-threo-hydroxy-3-carboxy-isocaproate, CN — CO_2 NADH, N — NADH, M — 2-keto-4-methyl-pentanoate, L — L-leucine, AG — α-ketoglutarate, G — L-glutamate, the biochemical pathway is given by the following reactions:

$$K + AC \rightarrow C + H$$
$$H \rightarrow T$$
$$T + N \rightarrow M + CN$$
$$M + G \rightarrow L + AG$$
$$AG \rightarrow K$$

The reactions can be easily extrapolated to their abstract interpretation.

It may be noted that a Kripke structure is an asynchronous formalism. In particular, two reactions occurring "simultaneously" can be modeled as one occurring after another because of the nondeterministic modeling with respect to the reactants and the asynchronous interleaving semantics of Kripke structures.

2.2 Bound on the Number of Chemical Entities Involved in a Reaction

A study of pathways [9,11] shows that for biochemical pathways, the number of biochemical entities reacting in a chemical reaction is fairly small. As illustrated in Fig. 1, almost 60% of the reactions in each of these databases have no more than two reactants or two products. Also, no reaction was found with more than six reactants or products in these databases. The statistics gathered from the databases of these widely differing organisms shows that there is a very low probability of the interaction of more than a few entities at the atomic level. Hence, all biochemical reactions indeed involve interaction of a fairly small number of chemical entities, and the number of chemical entities produced as a result of biochemical reactions are also small. We may contrast this with an arithmetic operation $a := a \times b$, a system wide reset in a VLSI chip or the setting of bits in a long flag register. Each of these can take the Kripke structure of these hardware or software systems from one state to another such that the Hamming distance between them is arbitrarily large.

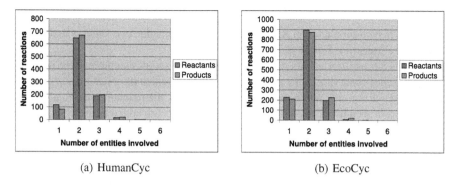

(a) HumanCyc   (b) EcoCyc

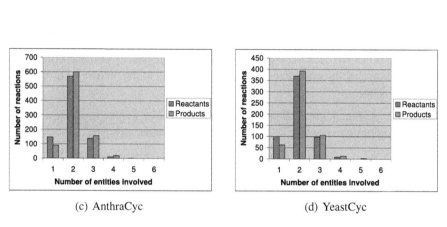

(c) AnthraCyc   (d) YeastCyc

Fig. 1. The HumanCyc, EcoCyc, AnthraCyc and YeastCyc Databases Reactions Summary: The bar charts clearly show that most reactions have small number of reactants and products. There is no reaction having more than 6 reactants or products among some 3000 biochemical reactions in these databases.

2.3   Bounded Hamming Distance Kripke Structures

In order to separate the development of the partitioning algorithm from the details of the biochemical Kripke structure [6], we consider the earlier introduced BHDKS model. This abstract model is sufficient for the construction of our partitioning algorithm.

Definition 1. *Let $K = (S,R,\mathcal{AP},\mathcal{L},F)$ be a Kripke structure, where S is the set of states, R is the transition relation, $\mathcal{AP}$ is the set of atomic propositions, $\mathcal{L}$ is the labeling of states with atomic propositions, F is the set of final states, and H(x,y) denotes the Hamming distance between x and y. Then, K is called a k - Bounded Hamming Distance Kripke structure iff*

$$\forall s, s' \in S, \quad R(s,s') \implies (H(\mathcal{L}(s), \mathcal{L}(s')) \le k)$$

Intuitively, a k-BHDKS has a transition between two states in the Kripke structure only if the Hamming distance between the propositional labels of these states is at most k.

Theorem 1. *A biochemical Kripke structure is a k-BHDKS for some small k.*

Proof. Let K be a biochemical Kripke structure[6]. Consider two states s and s' in K. If there is no transition from s to s', we are done.

If there is a transition from s to s', then the system executes some reaction at state s. From our earlier observation, the reaction has at most r reactants and at most p products, where r and p are small. When the reaction is executed, the reactants can nondeterministically be removed from the system, while the products are added to the system. Thus, s' can differ from s in at most $k = r + p$ chemical entities, that is $H(s, s')^2 \le k$. Hence, the biochemical Kripke structure is a k-BHDKS for some small k.

3 Density of Bounded Hamming Distance Kripke Structures

In this section, we shall establish certain properties of BHDKS and show that they are "reasonably sparse" in nature. We use the bound on the Hamming distance of neighbouring states in a BHDKS to derive a bound on the edge density of these Kripke structures. We show that the edge density is only polynomial in the number of propositions of the state space.

Theorem 2. *A state in the k - Bounded Hamming Distance Kripke structure with $\log n$ number of propositions (where $n > 1$) has a degree of at most $(\log n)^k$.*

Proof. Let s be any state such that $s \in S$, where S is the state space of the k - Bounded Hamming Distance Kripke structure. Now, consider all possible neighbours $N(s)$ of s. From the definition of BHDKS, we know that $s' \in N(s)$ only if $H(s, s') \le k$. Now, we define a set of states P_i such that $p \in P_i$ if and only if $H(s, p) = i$. Further, let us define $P = \bigcup_{i=0\ldots k} P_i$. Clearly,

- $|P_i| = \binom{log(n)}{i}$
- $P_i \cap P_j = \phi$

So, $|P| = |\bigcup_{i=0\ldots k} P_i|$
$= \sum |P_i| \quad (\because P_i \cap P_j = \phi)$
$= \sum_{i=0}^{k} \binom{log(n)}{i}$
$\le (log(n))^k$

Also, $N(s) \subset P$. Hence, $|N(s)| \le |P| \le (log(n))^k$
Thus, each state has no more than $(log(n))^k$ neighbours.

Thus, the number of transitions in a Bounded Hamming Distance Kripke structure are no more than polynomially (in the number of propositions in the Kripke structure) larger than the number of states.

4 Background on Assumption Based Distributed Model Checking

Distributed model checking as presented in [1,2] decomposes the Kripke structure into fragments. Each distributed node in the distributed computing cluster stores only one of

---

[2] Eventually, we will use the notation H(s,s') to mean $H(\mathcal{L}(s), \mathcal{L}(s'))$.

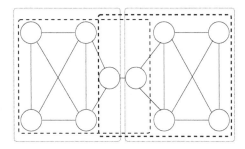

Fig. 2. An example of a Kripke structure and the fragments formed by dividing into two parts. The dotted boxes surround the subsets used for constructing the partition. The dashed lines show the actual partitions themselves. Observe that the partition was able to reduce the size of the Kripke structure rather well. Also, the undirected edges indicate transitions possible in both directions.

these fragments; hence, the size of the model checking problem which can be processed by the distributed model checking algorithm is bounded by the size of the smallest fragments we can construct.

Definition 2. *A Kripke structure* $M' = (S', R')$ *is a fragment of a Kripke structure* $M = (S, R)$ *iff*

- $S' \subseteq S$,
- $R' \subseteq R$ *and*
- $\forall (s, s') \in R$ *if* $s \in S'$, *then either* $(s, s') \in R'$ *or* $\nexists t \in S'$ *such that* $(s, t) \in R'$.

Given a Kripke structure M, it is now pertinent to generate these fragments. Any subset of the state space can be naturally extended to form a fragment by including those states which are immediate neighbours of the states in this subset and the rest of the Kripke structure, as shown in Fig 2. Formally,

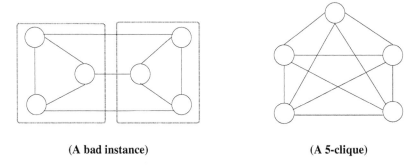

(A bad instance)   (A 5-clique)

Fig. 3. Bad instances for distributed model checking:In the left figure, the subsets are shown by dotted boxes. For these subsets, each of the fragment will be as large as the original Kripke structure and the purpose of the distributed algorithm will fail. In the right figure, a 5-clique is shown. Irrespective of the choice of our subsets, each fragment will be as large as the whole Kripke structure once again.

Definition 3. *Let $M = (S, R)$ be a Kripke structure and $T \subseteq S$. The distributed fragment of the Kripke structure $Fragment_M(T) = (S_T, R_T)$ is defined as*

- $S_T = \{s \in S | s \in T \vee \exists s' \in T \text{ such that } (s', s) \in R\}$
- $R_T = \{(s_1, s_2) \in R | s_1 \in T, s_2 \in S_T\}$

Thus, a distributed computation node i in the distributed model checking paradigm contains all states from T (called *core* states) and their immediate predecessors $S_T \setminus T$(called *border* states).

The central idea of the distributed algorithm in [2] is presented in the following algorithm:

---

proc Distributed Algorithm(input: total Kripke Structure M, ψ, f; output:$A_{f(s_0)}(s_0, \psi))$

Split M into K_i;
for all $i \in \{1, \ldots, n\}$ do in parallel $\{$ for all K_i $\}$
Take the initial assumption function;

repeat

repeat
Compute all you can;

Send relevant information to other nodes;
Receive relevant information from other nodes;
until all processes reach fixpoint;
Extrapolate additional information;

until all is computed;

Return result for the initial state s_0;
od

end

In order to abstract the concerns of the assumption based distributed model checking problem and allow a mathematical formulation of the fragmentation problem, we define the notion of a separator of a set of states in a Kripke structure.

Definition 4. *Given a set of states $T \subset S$ of the Kripke structure K, the set V is said to be a separator of T w.r.t S iff*

- $V \subset S$
- *There is no path from a state in $S \setminus (T \cup V)$ to a state in T which does not pass through some state in V.*
  That is, in the graph formed by removing V from S, $K_V = (S \setminus V, R \setminus R_V)$, $\forall t \in T, \forall s \in S \setminus (V \cup T)$, there is no path from s to t in K_V.
  Clearly, $R_V = \{(x, y) \in R | x \in V \text{ or } y \in V\}$.

Intuitively, T is the *core* of the fragment and V is the set of *border* states. Thus, any set of states along with its separator with respect to the rest of the Kripke structure contains a fragment for assumption based distributed model checking.

5 Fragmentation of BHDKS

Several efforts have been made to solve the problem of state space explosion in model checking. The art and science of symbolic model checking [3] has made considerable progress in increasing the size of the state space that can be model checked. Distributed Model Checking is a technique which aims at exploiting the memory of a large number of systems in a distributed environment. In the past, there has been work on developing good distributed model checking algorithms for software by making use of the information in control flow graphs [8]. However, to the best of our knowledge, there has been no work on developing distributed algorithms for biochemical systems that establishes worst case bounds on the size of each fragment by the use of structural properties of biochemical Kripke structures. The background definitions related to assumption based distributed model checking are presented in Sec. 4. We just recall the definition of a fragment here.

Definition 5. *Let* $M = (S, R)$ *be a Kripke structure and* $T \subseteq S$. *The distributed fragment of the Kripke structure* $Fragment_M(T) = (S_T, R_T)$ *is defined as*

- $S_T = \{s \in S | s \in T \vee \exists s' \in T \text{ such that } (s, s') \in R\}$
- $R_T = \{(s_1, s_2) \in R | s_1 \in T, s_2 \in S_T\}$

Thus, a distributed computation node i in the distributed model checking paradigm contains all states from some subset T of S(called *core* states) and their immediate predecessors $S_T \setminus T$(called *border* states). Thus, any set of states, along with its vertex separator with respect to the rest of the Kripke structure, contains a fragment for assumption based distributed model checking. A set of vertices V is said to be a vertex separator of T with respect to S if all paths from $S \setminus T$ to T pass through some vertex in V. Now, we will present results on the size of separators for BHDKS.

5.1 Polynomial Separators for BHDKS

We will first show that the size of the separator of an arbitrary subset of the state space of a BHDKS is at most polynomially (in the number of propositions in the Kripke structure) larger than the subset itself.

Theorem 3. *Given any set* $T \subset S$ *of the state space of a k - Bounded Hamming Distance Kripke structure* $K = (S, R)$ *with log(n) propositions, the size of the smallest separator V of T with respect to S is no more than* $|T|.(log(n))^k$.

Proof. For each state $t \in T$, consider the neighbours of t. As shown earlier, $N(t) \leq (log(n))^k$. Clearly, $\bigcup_{t \in T} N(t)$ is a separator of T with respect to S. Hence, the size of the smallest separator of $T = |V|$

$$\leq |\bigcup_{t \in T} N(t)|$$
$$\leq \sum_{t \in T} |N(t)|$$
$$\leq |T|.(log(n))^k.$$

Corollary 1. *Given any set* $T \subset S$ *of the state space of a k - Bounded Hamming Distance Kripke structure* $K = (S, R)$ *with log(n) propositions, the size of the fragment associated with T is no more than* $|T|.(1 + (log(n))^k)$.

Proof. Any set of states with its separator with respect to the rest of the Kripke structure contains a fragment.

This shows that the size of the state space which needs to be put at one node of the distributed computation grows only polynomially in the number of propositions in the Bounded Hamming Distance Kripke structure. It is noted that this distribution can compute the separators for only the reachable set of states in T, which can be useful if the reachable set is significantly small.

5.2 Hypercube Based Fragmentation

Now, we present another approach to distribute the state space which shows that BHDKS are very suitable for distributed computation in a hypercube grid. We prove the following results on the hypercube based partition in this section:

- A k - BHDKS with $\log n$ atomic propositions can be embedded in a l -hypercube as long as $l < \log(n)/k$.
- When embedded in a l-dimensional hypercube of distributed nodes, the size of the separator for the *core* set of states, mapped to each node in the distributed system, is no more than $\frac{l}{2^l}.n$.
- The separator for the set of *core* states associated with any node then lie only on the adjacent nodes of the hypercube. Also, there exist several states in the *core* which do not have any transitions connecting them to states outside this node.
- Thus, the size of the state space of the fragment (*core* and *border*) associated with each distributed node is given by $\frac{l+1}{2^l}.n$. Thus, the ratio of the *border* states to the *core* states is only $l < \log n$ as opposed to a ratio of $(\log n)^k$ in the polynomial fragmentation case.
- The partition ensures that only neighboring nodes in the hypercube grid need to interchange any information during the operation of the distributed model checking algorithm.

Construction of the Partitioning. We select $d = 2^l$ centers which are symmetrically placed d points, $P_1, P_2 \ldots P_d$, using the Hamming distance as a metric. It is easy to verify that these d points exist whenever $d = 2^l$ for any $l < log(n)$, where log(n) is the number of propositions.

- $000 \ldots 000 : 0$
- $000 \ldots 001 : 1$
- $000 \ldots 010 : 2$
- $000 \ldots 011 : 3$
- $\ldots \ldots \ldots$
- $\ldots \ldots \ldots$
- $111 \ldots 111 : 2^l - 1$

Using this list of binary numbers of length l, we generate the points P_i by replacing each 0 by the string made of $(log(n)/l)$ zeroes and similarly each 1 is replaced by the string made of $(log(n)/l)$ ones. The case of $l = 2$ is shown in Fig. 4.

P0 Partition around 00	P1 Partition around 01
P2 Partition around 10	P3 Partition around 11

Fig. 4. The figure shows the distribution of states among 4 subsets - a 2-hypercube. The center of each subset is a P_i with the binary representation corresponding to 00,01,10 or 11 respectively in our list. For $log(n) = 6$, these may be 000000, 000111, 111000 and 111111.

It can be observed that these 2^l centers satisfy the following:

- $\forall i \exists j$ such that $H(P_i, P_j) = log(n)/l$
- $\forall i \; \not\exists j \neq i$ such that $H(P_i, P_j) < log(n)/l$.

Given a state s in the Kripke structure, $L(s)$ associates a binary label with s. We define the partition $P^{Hamming} = \{S_0^h, S_1^h, \ldots S_d^h\}$ such that $s \in S_i^h$ iff $\forall j \neq i, H(s, P_i) < H(s, P_j)$, or $\exists j \neq i H(s, P_i) = H(s, P_j)$ and *generate_fair_partition(i, j) = i*. *generate_fair_partition* returns i or j with equal probability. These conditions ensure that the sets in the partition are disjoint as well as balanced. The *generate_fair_partition* ensures the points equidistant from more than one P_i to be distributed in a balanced manner among the nodes. Each S_i^h is associated with the ith node of the distributed system as its *core* set of states. We will later add the separator of this *core* set of states with respect to the rest of the Kripke structure as the set of *border* states. We illustrate such a partition by a small example.

An Example of Hypercube Fragmentation. Consider Fig. 5 which corresponds to the case with $l = 2$. The sets $S1, S2, S3$ and $S4$ are formed as before by dividing the state space into 4 parts around 4 equidistant centers $0^{2p}, 0^p 1^p, 1^{2p}$ and $1^p 0^p$ respectively as

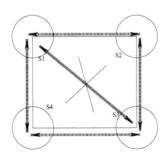

Fig. 5. For each subset around a point, it is connected only to two other sets and not to the diagonally opposite points

before. These form the core states of the fragment. We now motivate our next result by showing that for sufficiently large Kripke structures, if we take these P_is as the corners of a 2-D hypercube (square), then there can be no transitions between the distributed nodes along the diagonals.

Theorem 4. *For a BHDKS Kripke structure split uniformly around four centers $0^{2p}, 0^p 1^p, 1^{2p}$ and $1^p 0^p$, there can be no transition along the diagonal as long as $p > k$.*

Proof. Suppose the contrary; without loss of generality, assume that there is a transition from the set around 0^{2p} to the set around 1^{2p} say from x to y. Then, $H(x, y) \leq k$. Also, by construction, $H(x, 0^{2p}) \leq p/2$ and $H(y, 1^{2p}) \leq p/2$. By triangle inequality, $H(y, 0^{2p}) + H(y, 1^{2p} \geq H(0^{2p}, 1^{2p}$ i.e., $H(y, 0^{2p}) \geq 2p - p/2$.

Again, by triangle inequality, $H(x, y) + H(x, 0^{2p}) \geq H(y, 0^{2p})$
i.e., $H(x, y) \geq H(y, 0^{2p}) - H(x, 0^{2p})$
i.e., $H(x, y) \geq 2p - p/2 - p/2$
i.e., $H(x, y) \geq p$

Thus, as long as $p > k$, there can be no transition along the diagonal. So the size of each fragment is at most 3 times the size of the core set at each node i.e., $(2 + 1)/2^2$ of the whole Kripke structure.

Bound on the Size of Fragment Associated with Each Distributed Node. Now consider a state space split into 2^l parts in a l-dimensional hypercube. Recall that we map each S_i^h to the node i of the hypercube, formed naturally by the binary encoding of i. We show that there can be no transition along any of the diagonals of this hypercube. The case of a 3-D cube is illustrated in Fig. 6

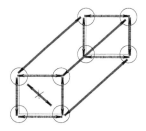

Fig. 6. A 3-D cube. There can be no transitions along any of the diagonals.

Theorem 5. *For a k-BHDKS Kripke structure with $(log(n))$ propositions split uniformly around 2^l centers $0^{lp}, 0^{(l-1)p} 1^p, \ldots \ldots 0^p 1^{(l-1)p}, 1^{lp}$ (where $p = (log(n)/l)$) and $p > k$, there can be no transition along any of the diagonals of this l-dimensional hypercube.*

Proof. Suppose the contrary; without loss of generality, assume that there is a transition from the set around θ to the set around δ say from x to y. Then, $H(x, y) \leq k$ Also, δ, θ are along some diagonal and not adjacent. So, $H(\theta, \delta) \geq 2p$. By construction, $H(x, \theta) \leq p/2$. and $H(y, \delta) \leq p/2$. By triangle inequality $H(y, \theta) + H(y, \delta) \geq$

$H(\theta, \delta)$ i.e., $H(y, \theta) \geq 2p - p/2$ (assuming the worst case that δ and θ are as close as possible without being neighbors in the l-dimensional hypercube) .

By triangle inequality, $H(x, y) + H(x, \theta) \geq H(y, \theta)$ i.e., $H(x, y) \geq H(y, \theta) - H(x, \theta)$

  i.e., $H(x, y) \geq 2p - p/2 - p/2$

  i.e., $H(x, y) \geq p$

Thus, as long as $p > k$, there can be no transition along the diagonal. Hence, there cannot be a transition along any diagonal of the l-dimensional cube.

Corollary 2. *The size of the separator of the set associated with each distributed node in the l-Dimensional hypercube is at most l times the size of the largest possible core set at each node i.e., $\frac{l}{2^l}.n$.*

Proof. Each node in the l-dimensional hypercube has transitions only to the neighbouring nodes in the hypercube. In an l-dimensional hypercube, there are l neighbours. By construction, each neighbour has no more than $\frac{1}{2^l}.n$ *core* states. Hence, the size of the separator of a node $\leq$ sum of the size of the *core* sets associated with all the neighbouring nodes in the hypercube (since the *border* states of a node do not have any transitions to any other node)$\leq \frac{l}{2^l}.n$

Corollary 3. *The size of the fragment associated with each node in the l-Dimensional hypercube is at most $(l + 1)$ times the size of the largest possible core set at each node i.e., $\frac{(l+1)}{2^l}.n$.*

Proof. A set and its separator form a fragment corresponding to that set.

Corollary 4. *The fragment associated with each node in the distributed system can be made as small as $(\frac{2.log(n)}{k}).n^{1-1/k}$ in the size of the k-BHDKS*

Proof. We know that the size of a fragment is bounded by $\frac{(l+1)}{2^l}.n$, as long as $l < log(n)/k$. Let us choose: $l = (log(n)/k) - 1$. Then the size of the fragment is bounded by $\frac{(l+1)}{2^l}.n = (\frac{2.log(n)}{k}).n^{l-1/k}$.

At first sight one might feel that the hypercube based approach produces fragments larger the simple subset construction presented earlier. However, the hypercube based approach trades off the size of the fragment for both a structure in the resulting partition and the greater ratio of core to fragment states in each node, which implies that less of the state space has to be copied across multiple nodes. Also, because of the small value of k and the large values of n the result is practically significant for model checking; e.g., for a 2^{20} state Kripke structure, one could partition it into 2^4 nodes each of size 2^{16} for k = 4. We remark here that the hypercube based partitioning not only provides a bound on the size of the fragment but also ensures that the communication among the nodes of the distributed computation having these fragments occurs only along the edges of the hypercube and not along its diagonals. As such, it also suggests the architecture of the distributed system and bounds the cost of the links required to connect these distributed nodes.

An important point to note is that the traditional way of recursively finding vertex separators [10] of the underlying graph to break it into smaller graphs is not feasible for the case of BHDKS. It is a well known result that the existence of $O(n^{1-\epsilon})$ vertex separator for a class of graphs implies that the class of graphs has no more than constant degree for each vertex. However, we know that the BHDKS vertex degree polylogarithmic in the number of vertices $((\log n)^k)$. As such, BHDKS do not have good vertex separators. Our hypercube based fragmentation approach avoids the construction of vertex separators and actually creates fragments $O(n^{1-\epsilon})$ in size, where $\epsilon = 1/k$, by exploiting the difference between "good" fragments and "good" vertex separators.

6 Experimental Results

We used the Cyc public database [9,11] and the CMBSLib benchmark [12] to study the performance of the hypercube based partitioning method. We took all of the thousand biochemical reactions for the Humancyc and the Ecocyc reaction pathway databases and computed an upper bound on the size of the fragment in the hypercube based fragmentation of the Kripke structure for these reaction pathways. We counted the number of edges into the core state (around the center 1111...11) using on-the-fly traversal of the state space and then used the number of edges as an upper bound on the number of *border* states. The upper bound on the size of the fragment clearly shows that the size of the fragment obtained using our worst case analysis is slightly larger than that obtained in experimental results (though of the same order).

We also took the boolean biochemical benchmark systems in CMBSLib benchmark [12] and calculated the exact size of the fragment using hypercube based partitioning method. These results indicate that the size of the fragment built using hypercube based partitioning method is of the same order as the size of the core around which it is built.

Table 1. HumanCyc 1120 atoms and EcoCyc 1313 atoms: the ratios are approximate

Sl No	Database	Radius of the Fragment	Number of States in the core	Maximum number of states in the fragment	Ratio of fragment to the core
1	HumanCyc	8	60321482688944611644	58218118459069712450424	965
2	HumanCyc	9	7459853563127158123804	7198818881724135645151 56	965
3	HumanCyc	10	8295478676998126793247 80	80043157043255991509859 6984	964
4	HumanCyc	11	8378570202149262436415 0540	80835123199556021465682 097364	964
5	HumanCyc	12	7750316948401178304236 797860	74764684646408464350771 37076096	964
6	EcoCyc	8	215766787047246662253	286658426283477266973032	1328
7	Ecocyc	9	313104532701149256451 93	41591878653908316107275 044	1328
8	Ecocyc	10	408605757066214026502 0569	54270306998590744772102 84960	1328
9	Ecocyc	11	484389284294462960011 031017	64326583496672658366811 0535208	1327
10	Ecocyc	12	525972893838268519024 53164625	69838841881773224220828 914800104	1327

Table 2. Fragmentation results for the CMBSLib Benchmark: http://contraintes.inria.fr/CMBSlib/

Sl No	Benchmark	Hamming Diameter	Size of core	Size of border	Fraction of core to fragment size
1	Circadian oscillations	2	10	59	0.1449
2	Circadian oscillations	3	51	127	0.2865
3	Circadian Oscillations	4	140	149	0.48445
4	Circadian Oscillations	5	251	102	0.7110
5	Circadian Oscillations	6	333	41	0.8904
6	Cell Division Cycle	2	7	25	0.2187
7	Cell Division Cycle	3	29	48	0.3766
8	Cell Division Cycle	4	71	63	0.5299
9	Cell Division Cycle	5	126	59	0.6811
10	Cell Division Cycle	6	179	41	0.8136

It shows that the hypercube based approach performs better than our worst case bounds on real benchmarks. [3]

7   Conclusion and Future Work

In this paper, the focus has been on showing that the biochemical Kripke structures are BHDKS and are very amenable to fragmentation. In particular, it is shown that such Kripke structures can be divided into fragments as small as polynomial in the number of atomic propositions present in the Kripke structure. The hypercube algorithm tends to distribute the exponential state space in a uniform manner, and one may raise the question as to the benefit of this exercise when the reachable state space is small. A simple heuristic of merging those nodes, which can be merged into one without violating the bound on the size of the core set $(n/2^l)$, helps to handle this scenario when the distribution of the reachable state space in the hypercube is not uniform.

In particular, our explicit distributed construction of the state space partitioning assumes that there is a number close to $\log n$ which has factors that can be used as l – the dimension of the embedding hypercube. A naive recursive bi-partitioning approach which splits the entire state space around two maximally separated points in the Hamming distance space can overcome this difficulty. However, an explicit centralized construction of the state space for partitioning would defeat the purpose of the distributed model checker. Future directions of research include the development of distributed algorithms to distribute the reachable state space onto a hypercube. Also, the choice of the hypercube in which the system is embedded and the assignment of different embeddings onto the same hypercube (by changing the order of propositions in the state space) needs to studied. In short, BHDKS are very suitable for bounded model checking. Hamming Distance Kripke structures are also very suitable for Bounded Model Checking.

---

[3] The result of the benchmark differs from that of the public databases because we abstract all the reactions in the public databases for nondeterministic vanishing of reactants after the reactions to illustrate a worst case scenario.

Acknowledgement

The author acknowledges the support of the Indian Academy of Sciences Summer Fellowship 2004 and grateful to Prof. D. Sarkar for the encouragement and support for the work. The second author thanks ITPAR (Indo-Italian Promotion of Advanced Research) for his visit to University of Trento during which some initial exploration of such applications was done.

References

1. Luboš Brim, Karen Yorav, and Jitka Žídková. Assumption-based distribution of CTL model checking. *International Journal on Software Tools for Technology Transfer (STTT)*, 7(1):61–73, February 2005.
2. Luboš Brim, Jitka Žídková, and Karen Yorav. Using assumptions to distribute CTL model checking. *Electr. Notes Theor. Comput. Sci.*, 68(4), 2002.
3. J. R. Burch, E. M. Clark, K. L. McMillan, D. L. Dill, and L. J. Hwang. Symbolic model checking: 10^{20} states and beyond. In John C. Mitchell, editor, *Proceedings of the 5th Annual IEEE Symposium on Logic in Computer Science*, pages 428–439, Philadelphia, PA, June 1990. IEEE Computer Society Press.
4. Nathalie Chabrier and François Fages. Symbolic model checking of biochemical networks. In Corrado Priami, editor, *CMSB*, volume 2602 of *Lecture Notes in Computer Science*, pages 149–162. Springer, 2003.
5. Nathalie Chabrier-Rivier, Marc Chiaverini, Vincent Danos, François Fages, and Vincent Schächter. Modeling and querying biomolecular interaction networks. *Theoretical Computer Science*, 325(1):25–44, September 2004.
6. Nathalie Chabrier-Rivier, François Fages, and Sylvain Soliman. The biochemical abstract machine biocham. In Vincent Danos and Vincent Schachter, editors, *CMSB*, volume 3082 of *Lecture Notes in Computer Science*, pages 172–191. Springer, 2004.
7. Edmund M. Clarke, Orna Grumberg, and Doron A. Peled. *Model Checking*. The MIT Press, Cambridge, Massachusetts, 1999.
8. Matthew B. Dwyer, editor. *Model Checking Software, 8th International SPIN Workshop, Toronto, Canada, May 19-20, 2001, Proceedings*, volume 2057 of *Lecture Notes in Computer Science*. Springer, 2001.
9. Peter D. Karp, Monica Riley, Suzanne M. Paley, and Alida Pellegrini-Toole. Ecocyc: an encyclopedia of escherichia coli genes and metabolism. *Nucleic Acids Research*, 24(1):32–39, 1996.
10. George Karypis and Navaratnasothie Selvakkumaran. Multi-objective hypergraph partitioning algorithms for cut and maximum subdomain degree minimization. In *ICCAD '03: Proceedings of the 2003 IEEE/ACM international conference on Computer-aided design*, page 726, Washington, DC, USA, August 18 2003. IEEE Computer Society.
11. Cynthia J. Krieger, Peifen Zhang, Lukas A. Mueller, Alfred Wang, Suzanne M. Paley, Martha Arnaud, John Pick, Seung Yon Rhee, and Peter D. Karp. Metacyc: a multiorganism database of metabolic pathways and enzymes. *Nucleic Acids Research*, 32(Database-Issue):438–442, 2004.
12. Sylvain Soliman and François Fages. Cmbslib: A library for comparing formalisms and models of biological systems. In Vincent Danos and Vincent Schachter, editors, *CMSB*, volume 3082 of *Lecture Notes in Computer Science*, pages 231–235. Springer, 2004.

A Graphical Representation for Biological Processes in the Stochastic pi-Calculus

Andrew Phillips[1], Luca Cardelli[1], and Giuseppe Castagna[2]

[1] Microsoft Research, 7 JJ Thomson Avenue, CB3 0FB Cambridge UK
{andrew.phillips, luca}@microsoft.com
[2] École Normale Supérieure, 45 rue d'Ulm, 75005 Paris France
giuseppe.castagna@ens.fr

Abstract. This paper presents a graphical representation for the stochastic π-calculus, which is formalised by defining a corresponding graphical calculus. The graphical calculus is shown to be reduction equivalent to stochastic π, ensuring that the two calculi have the same expressive power. The graphical representation is used to model a couple of example biological systems, namely a bistable gene network and a mapk signalling cascade. One of the benefits of the representation is its ability to highlight the existence of cycles, which are a key feature of biological systems. Another benefit is its ability to animate interactions between system components, in order to visualise system dynamics. The graphical representation can also be used as a front end to a simulator for the stochastic π-calculus, to help make modelling and simulation of biological systems more accessible to non computer scientists.

1 Introduction

The stochastic π-calculus has been used to model and simulate a range of biological systems [9,18,20]. One of the main benefits of the calculus is its ability to model large systems incrementally, by composing simpler models of subsystems in an intuitive way [2]. Various stochastic simulators have been developed for the calculus [20,15], in order to perform virtual experiments on biological system models. Such *in silico* experiments can be used to formulate testable hypotheses on the behaviour of biological systems, as a guide to future experimentation *in vivo*. The calculus also facilitates mathematical analysis of systems using a range of techniques, including types, behavioural equivalences and model checking. In future, such analysis could help provide insight into some of the fundamental properties of biological systems. In spite of these benefits, the mathematical nature of the stochastic π-calculus can sometimes limit its accessibility to a wider audience. In such cases, it can be useful to present an alternative graphical representation for the calculus, to complement its textual notation. From our experience, such a representation would be particularly welcomed by experimental systems biologists.

This paper presents a graphical representation for the stochastic π-calculus, which is formalised by defining a corresponding graphical calculus. The paper

C. Priami et al. (Eds.): Trans. on Comput. Syst. Biol. VII, LNBI 4230, pp. 123–152, 2006.
© Springer-Verlag Berlin Heidelberg 2006

is structured as follows. Section 2 presents a variant of the stochastic π-calculus that supports internal transitions and recursive definitions, based on [19]. Section 3 presents a graphical representation for the stochastic π-calculus, and explains why additional syntax constraints are needed to define a corresponding graphical execution model. Section 4 presents the graphical stochastic π-calculus, which formalises the syntax constraints identified in Sec. 3. The graphical calculus is shown to be reduction equivalent to the stochastic π-calculus of Sec. 2, ensuring that the two calculi have the same expressive power. Section 5 uses the graphical stochastic π-calculus to model a couple of example biological systems, namely a bistable gene network [4] and a mapk signalling cascade [8]. Finally, Section 6 shows how the graphical representation can be used as a front end to a simulator for the stochastic π-calculus.

2   The Stochastic π-Calculus

This section presents a variant of the stochastic π-calculus that supports internal transitions and recursive definitions, based on [19]. Recursive definitions have been argued in [20] to be a more practical programming abstraction for biological systems than the basic replication semantics of the π-calculus. This paper also shows how internal transitions labelled with a stochastic delay can provide a useful programming abstraction.

The syntax of the stochastic π-calculus ($S\pi$) used in this paper is summarised in Definition 1. A system $E \vdash P$ of the calculus consists of a process P together with a constant environment E. Each definition $X(m) = P$ in the environment maps a given identifier X to a corresponding process P, parameterised by m. Since the definitions themselves do not change over time, the environment E remains constant during execution. Stochastic behaviour is incorporated into the calculus by associating each channel x with a corresponding interaction rate given by $rate(x)$, and by associating each internal transition τ with a rate r. Each rate characterises an exponential distribution, such that the probability of an interaction with rate r occurring within time t is given by $F(t) = 1 - e^{-rt}$. The average duration of the interaction is given by the mean of this distribution, which is $1/r$. In this paper, it is assumed that all recursive calls to definitions are *guarded* inside an action prefix π. This prevents undesirable definitions such as $X = X$, or $X = Y, Y = (X \mid X)$. More precisely, it is assumed that for every infinite unfolding of definitions there are infinitely many occurrences of actions.

The execution rules for the calculus are summarised in Definition 3. In the general case, each rule is of the form $E \vdash P \xrightarrow{\alpha} E \vdash P'$, which states that a system $E \vdash P$ can reduce to a system $E \vdash P'$ by doing an interaction α. The definition of interaction labels is summarised in Definition 2. Since the environment E remains constant over time, the rules can be abbreviated to the form $P \xrightarrow{\alpha} P'$. Where necessary, additional predicates are used to denote the presence of specific definitions in the environment.

$P, Q ::=$	$\nu x\, P$	Restriction	$E ::=$	$X(m) = P$	Definition, $\mathrm{fn}(P) \subseteq m$
	$\mid \quad P \mid Q$	Parallel		$\mid \quad E_1, E_2$	Union
	$\mid \quad M$	Choice		$\mid \quad \emptyset$	Empty
	$\mid \quad X(n)$	Instance			
			$\pi ::=$	$?x(m)$	Input
$M ::=$	$\pi.P + M$	Action		$\mid \quad !x(n)$	Output
	$\mid \quad \mathbf{0}$	Null		$\mid \quad \tau_r$	Delay

Definition 1. *Syntax of* $S\pi$*, with processes* P, Q*, actions* π*, channels* x, y *and tuples* m, n. In a biological setting, each process typically describes the behaviour of a molecule, such as a gene or protein, and each action describes what a given molecule can do. A delay action τ_r describes a change in the internal structure of a molecule, such as a radioactive decay or a change in shape. Each delay is associated with a rate r that characterises an exponential distribution. In the case of radioactive decay, the rate determines the half-life of the reaction. Two molecules can interact by performing a complementary input $?x(m)$ and output $!x(n)$ on a common channel x. This can represent two proteins with complementary shapes, or two chemicals with complementary electronic configurations. In practice, reactions between more than two molecules are extremely rare, since the probability of three or more molecules interacting simultaneously is very low. Thus, the binary interaction model of the stochastic π-calculus fits well with the biological reality. Values m, n can also be sent and received during a reaction, e.g. to represent the transfer of an electron or a phosphate from one molecule to another. A choice of actions $\pi_1.P_1 + \ldots + \pi_N.P_N$ represents the ability of a molecule to react in N different ways, while a parallel composition $P_1 \mid \ldots \mid P_M$ represents the existence of M molecules in parallel. A definition of the form $X(m) = P$ represents a particular type of molecule X, parameterised by m. The parameters are assumed to contain all of the free names of P, written $\mathrm{fn}(P) \subseteq m$. The definitions are recorded in a constant environment E, which is assumed to contain a single definition for each instance $X(n)$. A process P together with its constant environment E denotes a *system* in the calculus, written $E \vdash P$. Finally, a restriction $\nu x\, P$ is used to represent the formation of complexes between molecules, where a complex of two processes P and Q is modelled as $\nu x\, (P \mid Q)$. The restriction denotes a private channel x on which the two molecules can synchronise to split the complex.

The probability of performing an interaction is determined by basic principles of chemical kinetics, and is proportional to the apparent rate of the interaction [6]. The apparent rate of a delay τ_r is simply the rate r of the delay, while the apparent rate of an interaction on a given channel x is equal to the number of possible combinations of inputs and outputs on x, multiplied by the rate of x [16]. The function $R(x, P)$ calculates the apparent rate of channel x in process P and is defined by:

α	Description	$\text{fn}(\alpha)$	$\text{bn}(\alpha)$
$?x(n)$	Receive a value n on channel x	$\{x,n\}$	$\emptyset$
$!x(n)$	Send a value n on channel x	$\{x,n\}$	$\emptyset$
$!x(\nu y)$	Send a private channel y on channel x	$\{x\}$	$\{y\}$
x	Interact on channel x	$\{x\}$	$\emptyset$
r	Perform an action with apparent rate r	$\emptyset$	$\emptyset$

Definition 2. *Interaction labels in* Sπ, *where* $\text{fn}(\alpha)$ *and* $\text{bn}(\alpha)$ *denote the set of free and bound names in* α, *respectively.* Each label α denotes an interaction that a given process can perform. The labels for receive $?x(n)$, send $!x(n)$ and private send $!x(\nu y)$ are defined as in [19]. The label x denotes an interaction on channel x, where the rate of interaction depends on the number of inputs and outputs on the channel. The label keeps track of the channel name so that the rate can be re-calculated whenever new inputs or outputs are added in parallel. Finally, the label r denotes an interaction with constant apparent rate r, such as a stochastic delay or an interaction on a private channel.

$$!x(n).P + M \xrightarrow{!x(n)} P \tag{1}$$

$$?x(m).P + M \xrightarrow{?x(n)} P_{\{n/m\}} \tag{2}$$

$$\tau_r.P + M \xrightarrow{r} P \tag{3}$$

$$P \xrightarrow{!x(n)} P' \quad Q \xrightarrow{?x(n)} Q' \quad \Rightarrow \quad P \mid Q \xrightarrow{x} P' \mid Q' \tag{4}$$

$$n \notin \text{fn}(Q) \quad P \xrightarrow{!x(\nu n)} P' \quad Q \xrightarrow{?x(n)} Q' \quad \Rightarrow \quad P \mid Q \xrightarrow{x} \nu n\,(P' \mid Q') \tag{5}$$

$$P \xrightarrow{x} P' \quad \Rightarrow \quad \nu x\, P \xrightarrow{R(x,P)} \nu x\, P' \tag{6}$$

$$x \neq y \quad P \xrightarrow{!x(y)} P' \quad \Rightarrow \quad \nu y\, P \xrightarrow{!x(\nu y)} P' \tag{7}$$

$$x \notin \text{fn}(\alpha) \cup \text{bn}(\alpha) \quad P \xrightarrow{\alpha} P' \quad \Rightarrow \quad \nu x\, P \xrightarrow{\alpha} \nu x\, P' \tag{8}$$

$$M \xrightarrow{\alpha} P' \quad \Rightarrow \quad \pi.P + M \xrightarrow{\alpha} P' \tag{9}$$

$$\text{bn}(\alpha) \cap \text{fn}(Q) = \emptyset \quad P \xrightarrow{\alpha} P' \quad \Rightarrow \quad P \mid Q \xrightarrow{\alpha} P' \mid Q \tag{10}$$

$$X(m) = P \quad P_{\{n/m\}} \xrightarrow{\alpha} P' \quad \Rightarrow \quad X(n) \xrightarrow{\alpha} P' \tag{11}$$

Definition 3. *Reduction in* Sπ. An output $!x(n).P$ can send the value n on channel x and then execute process P (1). An input $?x(m).P$ can receive a value n on channel x and then execute process P, in which the received value is assigned to m (2). A delay $\tau_r.P$ can perform an internal action with apparent rate r and then execute the process P (3). If a process P can send a value n on channel x and a process Q can receive a value n on channel x then P and Q can interact on x (4). If n is private then the scope of n is extended over the resulting processes, where $\nu n\,(P' \mid Q')$ denotes the formation of a complex between P' and Q' (5). If two processes interact on a private channel x then the apparent rate of the interaction is constant, and is given by $R(x,P)$ (6). Rule (7) allows a private channel to be sent. Finally, rules (8), (9), (10) and (11) allow an action to be performed inside a restriction, a choice, a parallel composition and a definition, respectively. For each of the rules (4), (5) and (10) there exists a symmetric rule (not shown) in which $P \mid Q$ and $P' \mid Q'$ are commuted.

$$R(x, P) = rate(x) \times (\text{In}_x(P) \times \text{Out}_x(P) - \text{Mix}_x(P)) \qquad (12)$$

where $\text{In}_x(P)$ and $\text{Out}_x(P)$ are the number of unguarded inputs and outputs on channel x in P, respectively, and $\text{Mix}_x(P)$ is the sum of $\text{In}_x(M_i) \times \text{Out}_x(M_i)$ for each choice M_i in P. The definition takes into account the fact that an input and an output in the same choice cannot interact, by subtracting $\text{Mix}_x(P)$ from the product of the number of inputs and outputs on x.

3   Graphical Representation

This section presents a graphical representation for the stochastic π-calculus, and explains why additional syntax constraints are needed to define a corresponding graphical execution model. The principle of the graphical representation is to display each process P as a *node* in a graph and to draw an *edge* from the node to each nested process in P. This allows the syntax tree of a given process to be represented as a tree of nodes. In addition, each definition in the environment assigns a unique *identifier* to a node. The identifiers are used to define additional edges between nodes, as in standard graph notations.

The graphical representation of the stochastic π-calculus is defined in Fig. 1 and Fig. 2, and is based on an abbreviated syntax for the calculus, presented in Definition 4. The abbreviated syntax is equivalent to the syntax of the stochastic π-calculus presented in Definition 1, but uses a more compact notation for restriction, parallel composition, choice and union. As an example, Figure 3 uses the graphical representation to visualise a stochastic π-calculus model of a gene with inhibitory control, as presented in [2].

The graphical representation described so far is essentially a static way of visualising systems of the stochastic π-calculus. The next stage is to define a dynamic representation, in order to visualise system execution. The principle of the dynamic representation is to add a token to each node in the graph that corresponds to a currently executing process. For example, in Fig. 3 a token is added to the *Gene* node to represent the execution of a single gene, and a new token is added to the *Protein* node each time a new protein is created. Similarly, a token needs to be added to the corresponding node whenever the gene becomes blocked after doing an input on a. However, in order for a token to be added, the node needs to be associated with a suitable identifier. This can be achieved by augmenting the model in Fig. 3 with the definition $Blocked(a, b) = \tau_u.Gene(a, b)$ and by replacing $?a.\tau_u.Gene(a, b)$ with $?a.Blocked(a, b)$. In the general case, each choice needs to be defined separately in the environment, so that a token can be added to the appropriate node during execution. It turns out that this simple constraint is sufficient to derive a graphical execution model for the stochastic π-calculus, as shown in the next section.

$$P ::= \nu z \sum_{i=1}^{N} \pi_i.P_i \quad \text{Choice} \qquad\qquad E ::= X(m) = P \quad \text{Definitiom}$$
$$\mid \quad \nu z \prod_{i=1}^{M} P_i \quad \text{Parallel} \qquad\qquad\quad \mid \bigcup_{i=1}^{N} E_i \quad \text{Union}$$
$$\mid \quad \nu z\, X(n) \qquad \text{Instance}$$

Definition 4. *Abbreviated Syntax of* $S\pi$, *where* $N \geq 0$ *and* $M \geq 2$. A sequence of zero or more restricted names is abbreviated to a tuple z, which may be empty. A choice between zero or more actions $\pi_1.P_1 + \ldots + \pi_N.P_N + \mathbf{0}$ is abbreviated to a sum $\sum_{i=1}^{N} \pi_i.P_i$. The choice can also be written $\pi_1.P_1 + \ldots + \pi_N.P_N$ if $N \geq 1$. A parallel composition of two or more processes $P_1 \mid \ldots \mid P_M$ is abbreviated to a product $\prod_{i=1}^{M} P_i$. Finally, a union of zero or more environments $E_1, \ldots, E_N$ is abbreviated to $\bigcup_{i=1}^{N} E_i$. The abbreviated syntax is used as the basis for the graphical representation.

	Definition	Union
E	$X(m) = P$	$E_1, \ldots, E_N$
E	**P**	**E1** $\cdots$ **EN**

Fig. 1. Graphical representation of environments in $S\pi$. Each process in the environment represents a *node* in a graph, and each definition assigns an *identifier* to a given node. The identifiers are used to define *edges* between nodes, as in standard graph notations. A definition $X(m) = P$ is displayed as the process P, where the name X is used as an identifier for P. By convention, any edges leading to X are connected to the node of P. A union of environments $E_1, \ldots, E_N$ is displayed by drawing the environments $E_1, \ldots, E_N$ next to each other. Edges between nodes in the environments are determined by the node identifiers.

	Choice	Parallel	Instance
P	$\nu z\, (\pi_1.P_1 + \ldots + \pi_N.P_N)$	$\nu z\, (P_1 \mid \ldots \mid P_M)$	$X(m) = P \vdash \nu z\, X(n)$
P	z **X** $\pi 1$ πN **P1** $\cdots$ **PN**	z **P1** $\cdots$ **PM**	z {n/m} **X**

Fig. 2. Graphical representation of processes in $S\pi$. A choice $\pi_1.P_1 + \ldots + \pi_N.P_N$ with restricted names z is displayed as an elliptical node with label z and with edges to processes $P_1, \ldots, P_N$. Each edge to a process P_i is labelled with an action π_i and denotes an alternative execution path in the system. The node can also be annotated with an optional name X. A parallel composition $P_1 \mid \ldots \mid P_M$ with restricted names z is displayed as a rectangular node with label z and with edges to processes $P_1, \ldots, P_M$. Each edge to a process P_i denotes a concurrent execution path in the system. An instance $X(n)$ with restricted names z is displayed as a rectangular node with label z and with an edge to the process identified by X. If $X(m) = P$ and $m \neq n$ then the tip of the edge is labelled with the substitution $\{n/m\}$. This represents the passing of parameters from one process to another. If z is empty then edges from a choice or parallel composition can be connected directly to node X by omitting the rectangle.

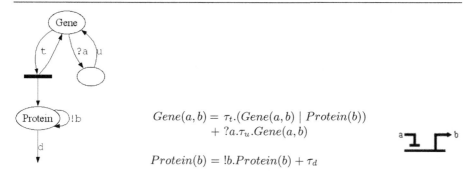

$$Gene(a,b) = \tau_t.(Gene(a,b) \mid Protein(b))$$
$$+ \ ?a.\tau_u.Gene(a,b)$$

$$Protein(b) = !b.Protein(b) + \tau_d$$

Fig. 3. A stochastic π-calculus model of a gene with inhibitory control, as presented in [2]. The gene can transcribe a protein by first doing a stochastic delay at rate t and then executing a new protein in parallel with the gene. Alternatively, it can block by doing an input on its promoter region a and then unblock by doing a stochastic delay at rate u. The transcribed protein can repeatedly do an output on the promoter region b, or it can decay at rate d. The gene is parameterised by its promoter region a, together with the promoter region b that is recognised by its transcribed proteins. The functional behaviour of the gene can be visualised using a corresponding high-level representation (right), which abstracts away from the internal dynamics. According to the reduction rules of the calculus, the output $!b$ of the transcribed protein can interact with the input $?b$ of a corresponding $Gene(b,c)$, which becomes blocked as a result. This simple model of a gene can be used to build arbitrarily complex networks, as described in [2]. An example of one such network is presented in Sec. 4.

4   Graphical Calculus

This section presents the graphical stochastic π-calculus, which formalises the syntax constraints identified in Sec. 3. The graphical calculus is shown to be reduction equivalent to the stochastic π-calculus of Sec. 2, ensuring that the two calculi have the same expressive power. The syntax of the graphical stochastic π-calculus (GSπ) is presented in Definition 5, and a corresponding abbreviated syntax is presented in Definition 6. The graphical calculus GSπ is a subset of the calculus Sπ, with the additional constraint that each choice is defined separately in the environment. Similarly, the graphical representation of GSπ is a subset of the graphical representation of Sπ, as shown in Fig. 4 and Fig. 5.

The graphical calculus can also be used as the basis for a graphical execution model. In this setting, a system $E \vdash P$ is displayed in two parts, a static environment E which remains constant over time, and a dynamic process P which is updated after each execution step. The environment E is displayed using the static representation of environments and processes defined in Fig. 4 and Fig. 5, whereas the process P is displayed using a dynamic representation, defined in Fig. 6. The principle of the dynamic representation is to display each instance $X(n)$ of a definition $X(m) = P$ by attaching a substitution token ${}_{\{n/m\}}$ to the node identified by X. In addition, a dotted edge is drawn from each restricted

$P, Q ::=$	$\nu x\, P$	Restriction	$E ::=$	$X(m) = D$	Definition, $\mathrm{fn}(P) \subseteq m$
	$P \mid Q$	Parallel		E_1, E_2	Union
	$\mathbf{0}$	Null		$\emptyset$	Empty
	$X(n)$	Instance			
			$D ::=$	P	Process
$M ::= \pi.P + M$		Action		M	Choice
	$\mathbf{0}$	Null		$\nu x\, D$	Restriction

Definition 5. *Syntax of* GSπ. This is a subset of the syntax of Sπ, with the additional constraint that processes in GSπ can only contain empty choices, and definitions in GSπ can only contain a choice at the top-level. The constraints ensure that each choice is defined separately in the environment.

$P ::=$	$\nu z\, \mathbf{0}$	Null	$E ::=$	$X(m) = \nu z \sum_{i=1}^{N} \pi_i.P_i$	Choice
	$\nu z \prod_{i=1}^{M} P_i$	Parallel		$X(m) = P$	Process
	$\nu z\, X(n)$	Instance		$\bigcup_{i=1}^{N} E_i$	Union

Definition 6. *Abbreviated syntax of* GSπ, *where* $N \geq 0$ *and* $M \geq 2$. This is a subset of the abbreviated syntax of Sπ, and is used as the basis for the graphical representation.

	Choice	Process	Union
E	$X(m) = \nu z\, (\pi_1.P_1 + \ldots + \pi_N.P_N)$	$X(m) = P$	$E_1 \mid \ldots \mid E_N$
E		P	E1 $\cdots$ EN

Fig. 4. Graphical representation of environments in GSπ, which is a subset of the graphical representation of environments in Sπ. For a definition of a choice, the node can also be annotated with the name X of the definition, or with the name and parameters $X(m)$. Note that all node annotations are optional.

	Null	Parallel	Instance
P	$\nu z\, \mathbf{0}$	$\nu z\, (P_1 \mid \ldots \mid P_M)$	$X(m) = P \vdash \nu z\, X(n)$
P			

Fig. 5. Graphical representation of processes in GSπ, which is a subset of the graphical representation of processes in Sπ

	Null	Parallel	Instance
P	$\nu z\, \mathbf{0}$	$\nu z\,(P_1 \mid \ldots \mid P_M)$	$X(m) = P \vdash \nu z\, X(n)$
P		z $/\ \backslash$ $/\quad\ \backslash$ **P1** $\cdots$ **PM**	$\mathbf{X}_{\{n/m\}} \,\text{-- } z$

Fig. 6. Dynamic graphical representation of processes in GSπ. A null process $\mathbf{0}$ with restricted names z is not displayed. An instance $X(n)$ of a definition $X(m) = P$ is displayed by placing a substitution token $_{\{n/m\}}$ next to the node identified by X. For clarity, the node is highlighted when at least one token is present, and any restricted names z are connected to the token by a dotted edge. A collection of parallel processes $P_1 \mid \ldots \mid P_M$ with restricted names z is displayed by drawing a dotted edge from z to each of the processes $P_1, \ldots, P_M$. This represents the formation of a complex between the processes, where the names z can be used to split the complex. If P_i is an instance $X(n)$ then the dotted edge is connected to the corresponding substitution token.

name to all of the tokens that share this name, in order to represent the formation of complexes. For example, a process $\nu x\,(\,X_1(n_1) \mid X_2(n_2)\,)$ where $X_1(m_1) = P_1$ and $X_2(m_2) = P_2$ is displayed by placing tokens $_{\{n_1/m_1\}}$ and $_{\{n_2/m_2\}}$ next to the nodes identified by X_1 and X_2, respectively. A dotted edge is drawn from the name x to both tokens, in order to represent the formation of a complex between X_1 and X_2. The resulting graph is displayed as: $X_1{}_{\{n_1/m_1\}} \cdots x \cdots_{\{n_2/m_2\}} X_2$.

Additional syntactic sugar can be defined for the dynamic representation, in order to improve the display of processes. For example, if N identical substitution tokens are attached to the same node, they can be replaced by a single token preceded by the number N. Furthermore, if the substitution token is empty it can be omitted, leaving just the number N. Similarly, if there are N copies of a restriction $\nu x\, P$ they can be replaced by a single copy of the restriction, where the name x is preceded by the number N. The scope of a restricted channel can be further clarified by only drawing a dotted edge to a token if it contains a free occurrence of the channel name. For example, a restriction $\nu x_1 \nu x_2\,(P_1 \mid P_2 \mid P_3)$ where $x_1 \notin \mathrm{fn}(P_3)$ and $x_2 \notin \mathrm{fn}(P_1)$ can be displayed as: $P_1 \cdots x_1 \cdots P_2 \cdots x_2 \cdots P_3$. The graphical representation is more informative than the corresponding textual syntax, since it clearly shows that P_1 and P_3 do not share any restricted names. In contrast, to verify this property for the textual syntax one needs to check which names occur inside which processes, and whether any of the names are shared. The extra clarity is not a particular property of the calculus, but simply a consequence of the fact that the graphical representation uses two dimensions, whereas the textual syntax uses just one.

More generally, if multiple substitution tokens of different values are attached to the same node X, a separate copy of the graph connected to X can be spawned

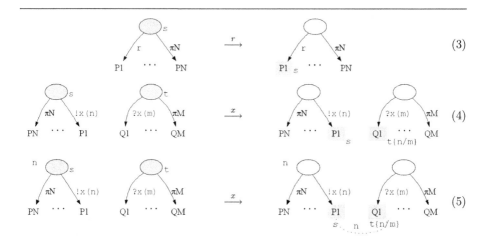

Fig. 7. Example graphical reductions in GSπ, where $P_1, \ldots, P_N$ and $Q_1, \ldots, Q_M$ are assumed to represent choices. A given process is executed graphically by first applying one of the calculus reduction rules and then displaying the resulting process.

for each token of a given value. This can be used to visualise the execution of different types of components in the system, where a token of a given value corresponds to a particular type of component. At the finest level of granularity, a separate graph can be spawned for each individual token, in order to visualise the execution of individual components in the system. In this setting, only a single token is present in the graph at a given instant. This allows successive nodes in the graph to be highlighted after each reduction step, in the style of state machines.

Since the graphical calculus GSπ is a subset of the calculus Sπ, reduction in GSπ can be defined using the rules for Sπ presented in Definition 3. The only required change is to replace P with D in rule (11), since definitions in GSπ are of the form $X(m) = D$. A graphical execution model is obtained by applying these rules to a given process in GSπ, and then displaying the resulting process after each reduction step. Figure 7 illustrates a number of example graphical reductions, based on the reduction rules of Definition 3. Figures 8 and 9 illustrate the execution of a single gene and a network of genes, respectively, based on the model in Fig. 3. During execution, it is also useful to expand instances of definitions that are not choices, so that tokens are only attached to nodes that are waiting to execute. This can be achieved by defining an additional normalisation rule, such that if $X(m) = P$ then the process $X(n)$ is expanded to $P_{\{n/m\}}$, where P does not contain a choice of actions.

So far, the graphical stochastic π-calculus has been used for both the static and dynamic visualisation of calculus processes. The next stage is to prove its equivalence with respect to the stochastic π-calculus, in order to ensure that the

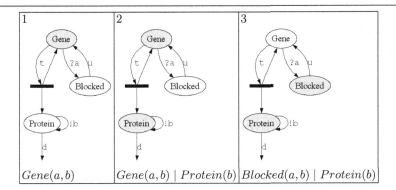

$$Gene(a,b) = \tau_t.(Gene(a,b) \mid Protein(b)) + ?a.Blocked(a,b)$$
$$Blocked(a,b) = \tau_u.Gene(a,b)$$
$$Protein(b) = !b.Protein(b) + \tau_d$$

Fig. 8. Execution trace for a gene with inhibitory control, based on Fig. 3, where each choice is defined separately in the environment. The sequence of transitions is given by $1 \xrightarrow{t} 2 \xrightarrow{?a} 3 \xrightarrow{u} 2$. All substitution tokens in the graphs are empty, since the arguments of each instance are equal to the formal parameters. Parallel execution is represented by highlighting two different nodes on the same graph at the same time.

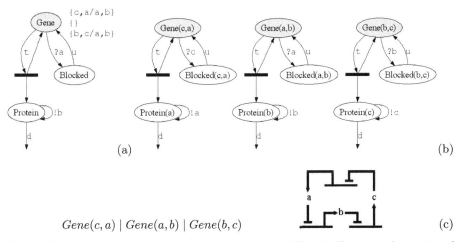

Fig. 9. Constructing a simple network using the gene of Fig. 8. The network consists of three genes that mutually repress each other, and was previously genetically engineered in living bacteria [3]. The network has been dubbed the *repressilator*, since the mutual repression of the three genes gives rise to alternate oscillations in the expression levels of the corresponding proteins. The network is displayed by adding substitution tokens $\{c,a/a,b\}$, $\{a,b/a,b\}$ and $\{b,c/a,b\}$ to the node identified by *Gene*, as shown in (a). By default, the parameters are not shown explicitly on the node label but can be optionally included, as stated in Fig. 4. For clarity, a separate graph can be generated for each token (b), where the names of the parameters are used to distinguish between the different genes. A high-level graphical representation of the network is also given (c).

$$(E \vdash P) \triangleq (E), E' \vdash P' \qquad (13)$$
$$\text{where } E' \vdash P' = (P)$$

$$(\nu z \, \mathbf{0}) \triangleq \emptyset \vdash \nu z \, \mathbf{0} \qquad (14)$$

$$(\nu z \, M) \triangleq (X(n) = \nu z \, M) \vdash X(n) \qquad (15)$$
$$\text{where } X \text{ fresh} \quad M \neq \mathbf{0} \quad n = \mathrm{fn}(\nu z \, M)$$

$$(\nu z \, \textstyle\prod_{i=1}^{M} P_i) \triangleq \bigcup_{i=1}^{M} E_i \vdash \nu z \, \textstyle\prod_{i=1}^{M} P_i' \qquad (16)$$
$$\text{where } E_i \vdash P_i' = (P_i)$$

$$(\nu z \, X(n)) \triangleq \emptyset \vdash \nu z \, X(n) \qquad (17)$$

$$(X(m) = \nu z \, \textstyle\sum_{i=1}^{N} \pi_i.P_i) \triangleq \bigcup_{i=1}^{N} E_i, X(m) = \nu z \, \textstyle\sum_{i=1}^{N} \pi_i.P_i' \qquad (18)$$
$$\text{where } E_i \vdash P_i' = (P_i)$$

$$(X(m) = P) \triangleq E, X(m) = P' \qquad (19)$$
$$\text{where } E \vdash P' = (P) \quad P \neq \nu z \, M$$

$$(\textstyle\bigcup_{i=1}^{N} E_i) \triangleq \bigcup_{i=1}^{N} (E_i) \qquad (20)$$

Definition 7. *Encoding* $S\pi$ *to* $GS\pi$. The function $(E \vdash P)$ encodes a given system $E \vdash P$ in $S\pi$ to a corresponding system in $GS\pi$ (13). The encoding relies on a function (P), which encodes a process P in $S\pi$ to a process and environment in $GS\pi$ as follows. An empty choice $\nu z \, \mathbf{0}$ is unchanged. A fresh definition is created for each non-empty choice $\nu z \, M$, and the choice is replaced by an instance of this definition (15). Each process P_i in a parallel composition $\nu z \, \prod_{i=1}^{M} P_i$ is replaced by its encoding, and any new definitions are added to the environment (16). An instance $\nu z \, X(n)$ is unchanged. The encoding also relies on a function (E), which encodes an environment E in $S\pi$ to an environment in $GS\pi$ as follows. Each process P_i in a choice $\nu z \, \sum_i \pi_i.P_i$ is replaced by its encoding, and any new definitions are added to the environment (18). A process P that is not a choice is replaced by its encoding, and any new definitions are added to the environment. (19). Finally, each environment E_i in a union $\bigcup_{i=1}^{N} E_i$ is replaced by its encoding (20).

$$[E \vdash P] \triangleq E \vdash P \qquad (21)$$

Definition 8. *Decoding* $GS\pi$ *to* $S\pi$. Since the graphical calculus $GS\pi$ is a subset of the calculus $S\pi$, the decoding is simply the identity function.

two calculi can be used interchangeably. This can be achieved by defining an encoding from the calculus $S\pi$ to the graphical calculus $GS\pi$, as presented in Definition 7, where the function $(E \vdash P)$ encodes a given system $E \vdash P$ in $S\pi$ to a corresponding system in $GS\pi$.

Lemma 1 ensures that the encoding is well-defined. The lemma states that if a system $E \vdash P$ is in the calculus $S\pi$ then its encoding $(E \vdash P)$ is in the graphical calculus $GS\pi$.

Lemma 1. $\forall E, P \in S\pi.(E \vdash P) \in GS\pi$

Proof. By straightforward induction on the definition of encoding in $S\pi$.   □

Lemma 2 ensures that the graphical calculus $GS\pi$ is a subset of the calculus $S\pi$. The lemma states that if a system $E \vdash P$ is in the graphical calculus $GS\pi$, then it is also in the calculus $S\pi$. This allows reduction in $GS\pi$ to use the same rules as reduction in $S\pi$.

Lemma 2. $\forall E, P \in GS\pi.E \vdash P \in S\pi$

Proof. By straightforward induction on the syntax of $GS\pi$. By definition, the calculus $GS\pi$ requires each choice to be defined separately in the environment, which is nothing more than a syntactic constraint on the calculus $S\pi$.   □

Theorem 1 ensures that the syntax of the graphical calculus is preserved by reduction. The theorem states that if a system $E \vdash P$ in $GS\pi$ can reduce to $E \vdash P'$ then the resulting system is also in $GS\pi$. This ensures that a given process can be graphically displayed after each reduction step.

Theorem 1. $\forall E, P \in GS\pi.E \vdash P \xrightarrow{\alpha} E \vdash P' \Rightarrow E \vdash P' \in GS\pi$

Proof. By straightforward induction on the definition of reduction in $GS\pi$. It is clear that if each choice is defined separately in the environment then this property will also hold after a reduction, since the reduction rules do not expand definitions of choices. This is the only additional constraint that needs to be preserved with respect to reduction in $S\pi$.   □

Finally, Theorem 2 and Theorem 3 ensure that the graphical calculus $GS\pi$ and the calculus $S\pi$ are reduction equivalent. This ensures that the two calculi have the same expressive power, and can therefore be used interchangeably.

Theorem 2. $\forall E, P \in GS\pi.E \vdash P \xrightarrow{\alpha} E \vdash P' \Rightarrow [\![E \vdash P]\!] \xrightarrow{\alpha} [\![E \vdash P']\!]$

Proof. The proof is immediate, since the graphical calculus $GS\pi$ is a subset of the calculus $S\pi$, where the decoding $[\![E \vdash P]\!]$ is given in Definition 8 as the identity function.   □

Theorem 3. $\forall E, P \in S\pi.E \vdash P \xrightarrow{\alpha} E \vdash P' \Rightarrow (\![E \vdash P]\!) \xrightarrow{\alpha} (\![E \vdash P']\!)$

Proof. The proof is by straightforward induction on the definition of reduction in $S\pi$. The encoding $(\![E \vdash P]\!)$ merely creates a separate definition $X(n) = \nu z\, M$ in the environment E for each choice $\nu z\, M$ in the system. Moreover, rule (11) ensures that if a given process can perform a reduction, then the same reduction can be performed if the process is defined separately in the environment. Therefore, any reductions that are possible in the system $E \vdash P$ will also be possible in the corresponding encoding. Note that the definitions created in the encoding $(\![E \vdash P]\!)$ can have different names to those created in $(\![E \vdash P']\!)$. Furthermore, the encoding $(\![E \vdash P']\!)$ can have less definitions than the encoding $(\![E \vdash P]\!)$, e.g. if some of the choices in $(\![E \vdash P]\!)$ are reduced. Therefore, in order to ensure that $(\![E \vdash P]\!) \xrightarrow{\alpha} (\![E \vdash P']\!)$ the proof assumes that systems $E \vdash P$ of the graphical calculus are equal up to renaming of definitions and up to garbage-collection of unused definitions.   □

5   Biological Examples

This section uses the graphical stochastic π-calculus to model a couple of example biological systems, namely a bistable gene network [4] and a mapk signalling cascade [8]. A visual comparison between the stochastic π-calculus models and their corresponding reaction equations is provided in Appendix B.

5.1   Bistable Gene Network

In [4], a number of gene networks were evolved in silico to perform specific functions. At each stage in the evolution, various criteria were used to select the networks that best matched the desired behaviour. One of the networks was evolved to perform the function of a bistable switch, as summarised in Fig. 10. The evolved network was shown to be considerably more stable than the simpler, more intuitive network in which two genes mutually repress each other.

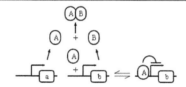

Fig. 10. A bistable gene network obtained by evolution in silico, as presented in [4]. The genes a and b can transcribe proteins A and B respectively, at constitutive transcription rates. Proteins A and B can bind irreversibly to produce the complex AB, which eventually degrades. Protein A can also bind reversibly to gene b, in order to inhibit the transcription of B. Initially, if A binds to b then production of A stabilises at a high level, since B is produced at a much lower rate. Alternatively, if A binds to B then production of B stabilises at a high level, since each subsequent A that is produced immediately binds to B and is degraded.

A graphical stochastic π-calculus model of this system is presented in Fig. 11, and the corresponding code for the model is presented in Fig. 22 of Appendix A. The model is directly executable, in contrast with the informal diagram of Fig. 10. Example execution traces for the model are shown in Fig. 12, which help to clarify the overall system function. Stochastic simulation results for the model are shown in Fig. 13, which match those presented in [4]. The results indicate that the system does indeed behave as a bistable switch.

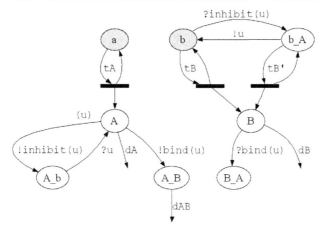

$z = inhibit, bind$
$a(z) = \tau_{tA}.(A(z) \mid a(z))$
$A(z) = \nu u$
$\quad(\tau_{dA}$
$\quad + !bind(u).A\_B(u)$
$\quad + !inhibit(u).A\_b(u, inhibit, bind))$
$A\_b(u, inhibit, bind) = ?u.A(z)$
$A\_B(u) = \tau_{dAB}$

$b(z) = \tau_{tB}.(B(z) \mid b(z))$
$\quad + ?inhibit(u).b\_A(u)$
$b\_A(u) = \tau_{tB'}.(B(z) \mid b\_A(u))$
$\quad + !u.b(z)$
$B(z) = \tau_{dB}$
$\quad + ?bind(u).B\_A(u)$
$B\_A(u) = \mathbf{0}$

$$a(z) \mid b(z)$$

Fig. 11. A graphical stochastic π-calculus model of the bistable gene network presented in [4]. The corresponding textual representation of the network is also given. Each gene a and b is modelled as a separate process with parameters z. Gene a can transcribe a protein A by doing a stochastic delay at rate tA and then executing a new process A in parallel with the gene. Protein A can either degrade by doing a stochastic delay at rate dA, or bind to gene b by doing an output on channel $inhibit$, or bind irreversibly to protein B by doing an output on channel $bind$. When protein A binds to gene b it sends a private channel u and then executes the process A_b, which can unbind from the gene by doing an input on u. When protein A binds irreversibly to protein B it executes the process A_B, which can degrade by doing a stochastic delay at rate dAB. Thus, protein A is *neutralised* by protein B. Conversely, gene b can either transcribe a protein B by doing a stochastic delay at rate tB, or bind to protein A by doing an input on channel $inhibit$. When gene b binds to protein A it receives a private channel u and then executes the process b_A, which can either unbind from the protein by doing an output on u, or transcribe a protein B at a much slower rate tB'. Thus, gene b is *inhibited* by protein A. Protein B can either degrade by doing a stochastic delay at rate dB, or bind irreversibly to protein A by doing an input on channel $bind$.

5.2   Mapk Cascade

In [8], a model of the mitogen-activated protein kinase (mapk) cascade was presented, and the cascade was shown to perform the function of an

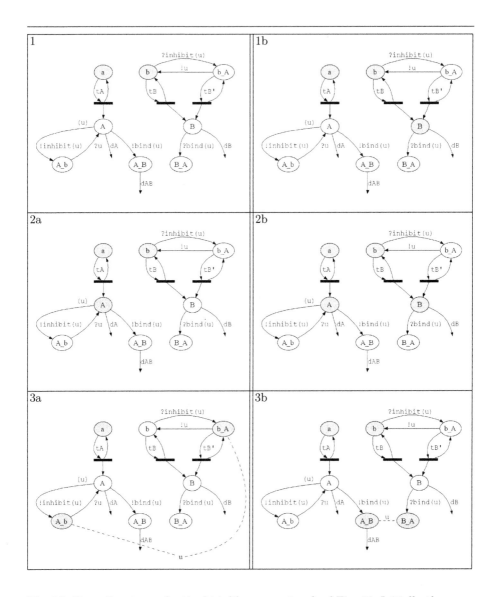

Fig. 12. Execution traces for the bistable gene network of Fig. 11. Initially there are two genes a and b that can transcribe proteins A and B at rates tA and tB, respectively (1). The transcription rate tB is only slightly faster than tA, giving a similar probability for transcribing either protein A or B. If protein A is transcribed first (2a) it can bind to gene b and inhibit the production of protein B (3a). Since protein B is transcribed at a much slower rate tB', a higher proportion of protein A is produced. Alternatively, if protein B is transcribed first (1b), any subsequently transcribed protein A (2b) can bind irreversibly to protein B and be degraded (3b). Since protein B is transcribed faster than protein A, a higher proportion of protein B is produced.

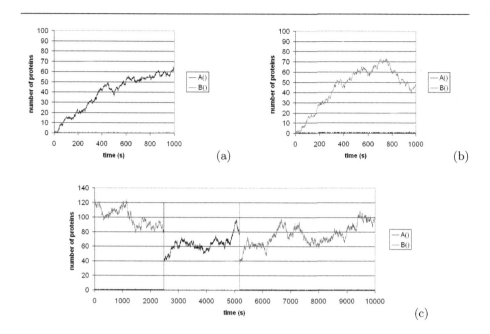

Fig. 13. Simulation results for the bistable gene network of Fig. 11, which show the evolution of the number of proteins over time. The results were obtained by executing the code from Fig. 22 of Appendix A using the SPiM simulator, assuming that the rates are in s^{-1}. Initially, there is a single copy of each gene a and b, with a similar probability of transcribing either protein A or protein B. Depending on the initial transcriptions, the system will either transcribe a high proportion of protein A (a) or a high proportion of protein B (b). When a high proportion of a given protein is transcribed, it suppresses the other protein and the system remains in a stable state. It is possible to toggle between two stable states by injecting a large amount of protein into the system after a given time interval. For example, a system that has a stable production of protein B can be "switched" by artificially injecting a large amount of protein A at time $t \simeq 2500$, and then "switched" again by injecting a large amount of protein B at time $t \simeq 5000$ (c).

ultrasensitive switch. The cascade was studied using a set of reaction equations, which were converted to ordinary differential equations. The equations were solved numerically, and the response curves for the cascade were shown to be steeply sigmoidal. The basic function of the cascade is summarised in Fig. 14.

A graphical stochastic π-calculus model of this system is presented in Fig. 17, and the corresponding code for the model is presented in Fig. 23 of Appendix A. The model represents the reaction between an enzyme E and a substrate K

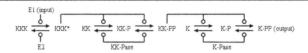

Fig. 14. A model of the mitogen-activated protein kinase (mapk) cascade, as presented in [4]. Initially the cascade contains a large reservoir of substrates KKK, KK and K. When a single enzyme E1 is added, it drives the transformation of KKK to KKK*, which in turn drives the transformation of KK to KK-P to KK-PP, which in turn drives the transformation of K to K-P to K-PP. The effect of these transformations is to produce a rapid increase in the output level of K-PP when an input E1 is added. The transformations can also be driven in the reverse direction by the enzymes E2, KK-Pase and K-Pase, respectively. This allows the output level of K-PP to revert back to zero when the input E1 is removed, so that the cascade can be re-used.

in two stages, as shown in Fig. 15. First, the enzyme binds to the substrate, after which it can either unbind or transform the substrate into a product. An execution trace of a reaction between an enzyme and a substrate is shown in Fig. 16. Stochastic simulation results for the mapk cascade are shown in Fig. 18. The results highlight the increase in signal response as the cascade is traversed from KKK, to KK to K, in accordance with the predictions of [8]. Further simulations across a range of values indicate that the overall function of the system is robust to changes in reactions rates. Even when all of the rates were set to a nominal value of 1.0, the system still behaves as an ultrasensitive switch. Such robustness in system behaviour is perhaps not a coincidence, given that the cascade is used to trigger important processes such as cell division in living organisms.

In previous work, the stochastic π-calculus was used to construct a high-level library of genes, which was used to build networks of varying size and complexity [2]. In principle, a similar approach can also be applied to signalling pathways, such as the mapk cascade in Fig. 17. The cascade is a fairly regular system that consists of proteins with only two types of behaviour, namely enzyme and substrate. The complexity of the system lies in the way multiple combinations of behaviours can be defined for the same protein. The ability to combine behaviours in this way can be modelled more directly by defining a high-level library of enzymes and substrates, as shown in Fig. 19. The library uses simple syntactic sugar, which enables a stochastic π-calculus model for the mapk cascade to be constructed by a combination of calls to the library, as shown in Fig. 20. Taking things a step further, one can also envisage a high-level graphical representation for the library, as illustrated in Fig. 20. In general, one can envision multiple high-level (graphical) libraries for different types of systems, such as gene networks and signalling cascades, all defined in terms of a single underlying (graphical) programming language.

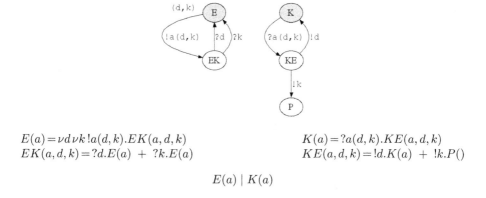

$$E(a) = \nu d \nu k \, !a(d,k).EK(a,d,k) \qquad\qquad K(a) = ?a(d,k).KE(a,d,k)$$
$$EK(a,d,k) = ?d.E(a) \; + \; ?k.E(a) \qquad\qquad KE(a,d,k) = !d.K(a) \; + \; !k.P()$$

$$E(a) \mid K(a)$$

Fig. 15. A stochastic π-calculus model of enzymes and substrates. The reaction between an enzyme E and a substrate K takes place in two stages. First, the enzyme binds to the substrate with a given rate a, after which the enzyme can either unbind with rate d, or transform the substrate to a product P with rate k. This is represented by the reaction equation $E + K_{\,d} \rightleftharpoons^a E : K \rightarrow^k E + P$. A reaction of this form is modelled in the stochastic π-calculus by defining separate processes $E(a)$ and $K(a)$ for the enzyme and substrate, respectively. The enzyme E can bind to the substrate by sending private channels d and k on channel a. The bound enzyme can either unbind by doing an input on d, or react by doing an input on k. Similarly, the substrate K can bind to an enzyme by receiving private channels d and k on channel a. The bound substrate can either unbind by doing an output on d, or react by doing an output on k to produce a product P.

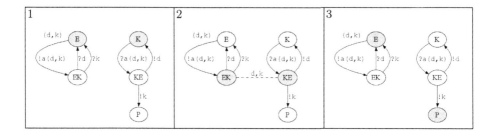

Fig. 16. Execution trace for the enzyme and substrate of Fig. 15. Initially, there is an enzyme E and a substrate K that can interact on channel a (1). The enzyme binds to the substrate by sending private channels d and k on channel a (2). The bound enzyme and substrate can unbind by doing a complementary input and output on channel d, and return to their original state (1). Alternatively, they can react by doing a complementary input and output on channel k. The enzyme returns to its original state, while the substrate is transformed into a product P (3).

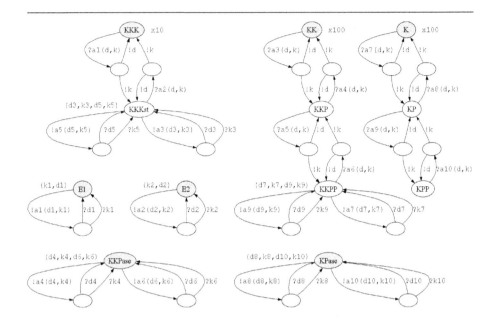

Fig. 17. A graphical stochastic π-calculus model of the mapk cascade presented in [8]. The cascade consists of proteins that can act as enzymes or substrates, as defined in Fig. 15. The process $E1$ can act as an enzyme on a_1, and the process KKK can act as a substrate on a_1 to produce a product $KKKst$. Conversely, the process $KKKst$ can act as a substrate on a_2 to produce a product KKK. It can also act as an enzyme on both a_3 and a_5. The remaining enzymes and substrates are defined in a similar fashion.

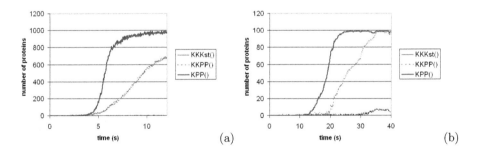

Fig. 18. Simulation results for the mapk cascade of Fig. 17. The results were obtained by executing the code from Fig. 23 of Appendix A, using the SPiM simulator. Simulation (a) was obtained using rates and quantities derived from [8], with $rate(a_i) = 1.0s^{-1}$, $rate(d_i) = rate(k_i) = 150.0s^{-1}$, starting with one of $E1$, $E2$ and $KKPase$, 120 of $KPase$, 3 of KKK and 1200 of KK and K. Simulation (b) was obtained by setting all the rates to a nominal value of 1.0, starting with the quantities in Fig. 17. Both simulations exhibit an increase in signal response as the cascade is traversed from KKK to KK and K. Functionally similar response profiles were observed for the output KPP in both simulations, in spite of the differences in simulation conditions.

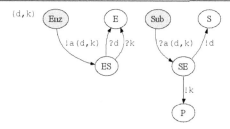

$$Enz(E, a) = \nu d \nu k\, !a(d, k).ES(E, a, d, k) \qquad Sub(S, P, a) = ?a(d, k).SE(S, P, a, d, k)$$
$$ES(E, a, d, k) = ?d.E() \; + \; ?k.E() \qquad\qquad SE(S, P, a, d, k) = !d.S() \; + \; !k.P()$$

Fig. 19. A library of enzymes and substrates, based on the definitions in Fig. 15. The library uses a higher-order variant of the stochastic π-calculus, in which process names can be passed as parameters. The definition of an enzyme Enz is parameterised by the name of the enzyme E, while the definition of a substrate Sub is parameterised by the names of the substrate S and the product P. This allows multiple enzyme and substrate behaviours to be defined for a given protein, by simple combinations of calls to the library. For example, $X() = Sub(X, P, a2) + Enz(X, a3) + Enz(X, a5)$ defines a protein X that can act as a substrate on $a2$ to produce a product P, as an enzyme on $a3$, or as an enzyme on $a5$. The definition relies on additional syntactic sugar for placing an instance inside a choice, where $\nu z'\,(X(n) + N)$ is short for $\nu z z'\,(M + N)$, assuming $X(n) = \nu z\, M$ and $z \cap z' = \emptyset$.

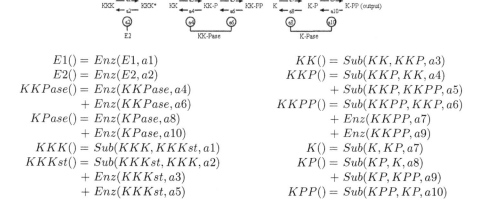

$$E1() = Enz(E1, a1) \qquad\qquad KK() = Sub(KK, KKP, a3)$$
$$E2() = Enz(E2, a2) \qquad\qquad KKP() = Sub(KKP, KK, a4)$$
$$KKPase() = Enz(KKPase, a4) \qquad + \; Sub(KKP, KKPP, a5)$$
$$+ \; Enz(KKPase, a6) \qquad KKPP() = Sub(KKPP, KKP, a6)$$
$$KPase() = Enz(KPase, a8) \qquad\qquad + \; Enz(KKPP, a7)$$
$$+ \; Enz(KPase, a10) \qquad\qquad + \; Enz(KKPP, a9)$$
$$KKK() = Sub(KKK, KKKst, a1) \qquad K() = Sub(K, KP, a7)$$
$$KKKst() = Sub(KKKst, KKK, a2) \qquad KP() = Sub(KP, K, a8)$$
$$+ \; Enz(KKKst, a3) \qquad\qquad + \; Sub(KP, KPP, a9)$$
$$+ \; Enz(KKKst, a5) \qquad KPP() = Sub(KPP, KP, a10)$$

Fig. 20. High-level program code for the mapk cascade of Fig. 17. The code is constructed by calls to the library of enzymes and substrates defined in Fig. 19. The structure of the code gives a clear indication of the function of each protein in the cascade. A corresponding high-level graphical representation for the code is also given. The representation is similar to the biological diagram of Fig. 14, but also contains explicit channel names to denote possible interactions. If the stochastic π-calculus model is *closed* by restricting channels $a_1, \ldots, a_{10}$ then the set of possible interactions is fixed, and we obtain exactly the diagram of Fig. 14.

6   Implementation

The variant of the stochastic π-calculus described in this paper has been used to implement the current version of the SPiM programming language, which is used to simulate models of biological systems [15]. The language extends the syntax of the calculus by allowing mutually recursive processes to be defined at arbitrary levels of nesting. This gives rise to a more scalable syntax, which facilitates programming of large systems. A collection of mutually recursive processes is of the form:

$$\text{let } X_1(m_1) = P_1 \text{ and } \dots \text{ and } X_N(m_N) = P_N \text{ in } Q$$

This is encoded into the calculus by expanding the scope of each definition $X_i(m_i) = P_i$ to the top level, adding parameters to each top-level definition to ensure that $\text{fn}(P_i) \subseteq m_i$, and renaming process definitions where necessary to ensure that all top-level definitions are distinct. The transformations are based on standard encodings presented in [22,11,21]. A core syntax of the SPiM programming language is presented in Appendix A.

The implementation can display a process of the graphical stochastic π-calculus by exporting to an open graph syntax such as DOT [5]. DOT is a textual syntax for representing directed graphs, which can be rendered using the Graphviz DOT layout engine. A symbolic core syntax for DOT graphs is described in Definition 9. An encoding $\{|E \vdash P|\}$ for generating a DOT graph from a system $E \vdash P$ in GSπ is presented in Definition 10. The encoding maps each definition of X to a corresponding node with identifier X. This allows mutually recursive definitions to be encoded compositionally, since the DOT layout engine can link edges to nodes based on their identifiers.

Theorem 4. $\forall E, P \in \text{GS}\pi.\{|E \vdash P|\} \in \text{DOT}$

Proof. By straightforward induction on the definition of encoding in DOT.   □

The way in which nodes, edges and labels are displayed can be customised for a given DOT graph. A node X that corresponds to a choice is displayed as an ellipse with label X, whereas a node that corresponds to a parallel composition is displayed as a solid rectangle. A node X with toplabel z is displayed with label z near the top left of the node. An edge $X \xrightarrow{\pi}_\sigma Y$ from a node X to a node Y is displayed as a directed edge from X to Y, with the label π at the midpoint of the edge and the label σ at the head of the edge. A subgraph $^z\{G\}$ is displayed by creating a new text node with name z and drawing a dotted edge to each of the nodes in G. If the number of nodes in G is sufficiently large then an alternative representation can be used, in which the nodes are enclosed in a dotted rectangle with label z.

The encoding has been used to implement a graph generating tool, which produces a DOT graph from a given source file written in the SPiM language. First, the SPiM program is encoded to a process of the graphical calculus by adding new definitions according to Definition 7. The resulting process is then encoded to a corresponding DOT graph, according to Definition 10. The graphs

$$G ::= X \xrightarrow{\pi}_\sigma Y \quad \text{Edge from node } X \text{ to } Y \text{ with label } \pi \text{ and headlabel } \sigma$$
$$| \ X \longrightarrow_\sigma Y \quad \text{Edge from node } X \text{ to } Y \text{ with headlabel } \sigma$$
$$| \quad {}^z X \qquad \text{Node } X \text{ with toplabel } z$$
$$| \quad X_\sigma \qquad \text{Node } X \text{ with bottomlabel } \sigma$$
$$| \quad {}^z\{G\} \qquad \text{Subgraph } G \text{ with label } z$$
$$| \ \bigcup_{i=1}^{N} G_i \quad \text{Union of graph declarations } G_1; \ldots ; G_N \text{ where } N \geq 0$$

Definition 9. *Symbolic Syntax of* DOT *Graphs.*

$$\{\!| E \vdash P |\!\} \triangleq \{\!| E |\!\}_E ; \{\!| P |\!\}_E \tag{22}$$

$$\{\!| \nu z \prod_{i=1}^{M} P_i |\!\}_E \triangleq {}^z\{\bigcup_{i=1}^{M} \{\!| P_i |\!\}_E\} \tag{23}$$

$$\{\!| \nu z \, \mathbf{0} |\!\}_E \triangleq \emptyset \tag{24}$$

$$\{\!| \nu z \, X(n) |\!\}_E \triangleq {}^z\{X_{\{n/m\}}\} \tag{25}$$
$$\text{where } X(m) = D \in E$$

$$\{\!| \bigcup_{i=1}^{N} E_i |\!\}_E \triangleq \bigcup_{i=1}^{N} \{\!| E_i |\!\}_E \tag{26}$$

$$\{\!| X(m) = \nu z \sum_{i=1}^{N} \pi_i . P_i |\!\}_E \triangleq {}^z X ; \bigcup_{i=1}^{N} X \xrightarrow{\pi_i} \lfloor P_i \rfloor_E \tag{27}$$

$$\{\!| X(m) = \nu z \prod_{i=1}^{M} P_i |\!\}_E \triangleq {}^z X ; \bigcup_{i=1}^{M} X \longrightarrow \lfloor P_i \rfloor_E \tag{28}$$

$$\{\!| X(m) = \nu z \, Y(n) |\!\}_E \triangleq {}^z X ; X \longrightarrow \lfloor Y(n) \rfloor_E \tag{29}$$

$$\lfloor X(n) \rfloor_E \triangleq {}_{\{n/m\}} X \tag{30}$$
$$\text{where } X(m) = D \in E$$

$$\lfloor P \rfloor_E \triangleq Y ; \{\!| Y(m) = P |\!\}_E \tag{31}$$
$$\text{where } P \neq X(n) \quad Y \text{ fresh} \quad m = \text{fn}(P)$$

Definition 10. *Encoding from* GSπ *to* DOT. The function $\{\!| E \vdash P |\!\}$ generates a DOT graph from a given system $E \vdash P$ in GSπ. The encoding relies on a function $\{\!| E' |\!\}_E$ and a function $\{\!| P |\!\}_E$, which generate a DOT graph from an environment E' and a process P, respectively. Both functions take the initial environment E as a parameter, which is needed for looking up definitions. The encoding also relies on a function $\lfloor P \rfloor_E$, which ensures that each process P has a corresponding process identifier when drawing an edge to P. This is because the DOT syntax requires each node in the graph to have a unique identifier. If P is of the form $X(n)$ then the identifier X is used. Otherwise, a fresh definition is generated, and the definition name is used as the identifier for P.

in this paper were generated using this tool, and further examples of generated graphs are available from [15]. In practice, some of the elements in the high-level DOT syntax of Definition 9 need to be fine-tuned to improve layout, but the additional modifications are mostly straightforward.

Finally, an abstract machine has been defined for the variant of the stochastic π-calculus presented in this paper, based on the abstract machine presented in [16]. The abstract machine has been used to implement a simulator for the calculus, based on the current implementation available from [15]. In a future version of the simulator, we plan to adapt the encoding of Definition 10 to generate a DOT graph from a machine term after each execution step, in order to render a graphical debugger for visualising the current state of a simulation.

7   Related Work

Pioneering work on Statecharts [7] highlighted the need for a scalable, self-contained graphical representation of concurrent systems. More recent work proposed a synchronous variant to Statecharts, in which concurrent processes can synchronise on shared labels [1]. Our graphical representation uses a similar principle, in contrast with foundational work on graphical representations for the π-calculus [10], which uses more elaborate rules for graph re-writing. In general, graphical representations for process calculi are still an active area of research. For example, [12] describes an automata-based representation for the π-calculus, in which each state of the system is represented as a node in the graph of an automaton. In this paper we adopt a less ambitious but perhaps more scalable approach, which allows new copies of a graph to be generated on demand. From a biological perspective, each new copy represents a new molecule or component, whose internal behaviour is described by a separate graph. Molecules can interact by synchronising on common channels and can also degrade, after which the corresponding graph is deleted. The use of substitution tokens in the graphical calculus is also reminiscent of Petri Nets [14], where each token represents a separate entity in the system.

Preliminary informal ideas on a graphical representation for the stochastic π-calculus were previously presented in [16]. This paper formalises and extends these ideas to produce a novel representation, in which different node types are used to distinguish between stochastic choice and parallel composition. An extended abstract for this paper is presented in [17].

The reduction semantics of [16] relies on a notion of structural congruence for the re-ordering of processes. Although this gives rise to a simplified definition of reduction, it cannot be used in the context of the graphical calculus, since it does not preserve the syntax of processes. In particular, the following structural congruence rule allows $X(n)$ to be instantiated with D, which may contain a choice:

$$X(n) = D \quad \Rightarrow \quad X(n) \equiv D_{\{n/m\}}$$

This violates the syntax of the graphical calculus, since a choice should only occur inside a definition of the environment. In contrast, the transition system of Definition 3 does not violate the syntax of the graphical calculus, since the corresponding rule (11) allows a reduction to occur without instantiating $X(n)$:

$$X(m) = D \quad D_{\{n/m\}} \xrightarrow{\alpha} P' \quad \Rightarrow \quad X(n) \xrightarrow{\alpha} P'$$

8   Conclusion

This paper presented a graphical representation for the stochastic π-calculus, which was used to model a bistable gene network and a mapk signalling cascade.

One of the benefits of the representation is its ability to highlight the existence of cycles, which are a key feature of biological systems. Another benefit is its ability to animate interactions between system components, in order to visualise system dynamics. Such graphical animations are particularly valuable when debugging complex system models.

There are various areas for future work. One issue is to investigate how high-level libraries for different types of biological systems could be built on top of the stochastic π-calculus, as discussed in Sec. 5. It would be interesting to define high-level graphical representations for these libraries, inspired by diagrams such as [13] that are currently being used by biologists.

Another area for future work is to explore ways of minimising the occurrence of substitution labels in the graphical representation of a given process. Such labels are needed whenever a definition is instantiated with arguments that are different from the formal parameters. Interestingly, for the examples considered in this paper, it was always possible to rename the formal parameters in a collection of mutually recursive definitions so that they were same as the applied arguments. For example, in the gene network of Fig. 8 the arguments for $Gene(a,b)$, $Protein(b)$ and $Blocked(a,b)$ were such that the substitution labels in the corresponding graphical representation were all empty. It would be interesting to define algorithms for parameter renaming in the general case, in order to minimise the occurrence of substitution labels.

A somewhat unexpected property of the graphical calculus is that it can potentially be used as the basis for an efficient execution algorithm for the stochastic π-calculus. In particular, the requirement to define each choice separately in the environment is a way of partially mapping out the state space of the system. Thus, instead of generating a new copy of a given process, one can simply keep track of the number of identical copies being executed. In this setting, two processes are considered identical if they instantiate the same process definition with the same parameters. This optimisation would be particularly useful when executing large numbers of identical processes, and could be formally described in terms of the graphical calculus presented in this paper.

In the short term, we plan to use our graph generation tool to implement a graphical debugger for the SPiM simulator. In the longer term, it would be interesting to develop a tool for drawing graphical models, which could automatically generate the corresponding π-calculus code. One can also envisage an interactive visualisation environment, in which disjoint graphs can be displayed separately or collapsed to a single node by clicking on the graph. Such features are crucial for the scalability of a graphical representation, since they allow a user to visualise parts of the system in a modular fashion, rather than trying to visualise the entire system at once. This ongoing research on graphical interfaces can be used to complement the existing textual interface to the simulator, to help make modelling and simulation of biological systems more accessible to non computer scientists.

References

1. Ch. Andre. Synccharts: A visual representation of reactive behaviors. research report tr95-52, University of Nice, Sophia Antipolis, 1995.

2. Ralf Blossey, Luca Cardelli, and Andrew Phillips. A compositional approach to the stochastic dynamics of gene networks. *Transactions in Computationial Systems Biology*, 3939:99–122, January 2006.

3. Michael B. Elowitz and Stanislas Leibler. A synthetic oscillatory network of transcriptional regulators. *Nature*, 403(6767):335–338, January 2000.

4. Paul Francois and Vincent Hakim. Design of genetic networks with specified functions by evolution in silico. *PNAS*, 101:580–585, 2004.

5. Emden R. Gansner and Stephen C. North. An open graph visualization system and its applications to software engineering. *Software-Practice and Experience*, 1-5, 1999.

6. Daniel T. Gillespie. Exact stochastic simulation of coupled chemical reactions. *J. Phys. Chem.*, 81(25):2340–2361, 1977.

7. David Harel. Statecharts : A Visual Formalism for Complex Systems. *Sci. Comput. Prog.*, 8:231–274, 1987.

8. Chi-Ying F. Huang and James E. Ferrel Jr. Ultrasensitivity of the mitogen-activated protein kinase cascade. *PNAS*, 93:10078–10083, 1996.

9. Paola Lecca and Corrado Priami. Cell cycle control in eukaryotes: a biospi model. In *BioConcur'03*. ENTCS, 2003.

10. Robin Milner. Pi-nets: A graphical form of π-calculus. In *ESOP'94*, pages 26–42, 1994.

11. Robin Milner. *Communicating and Mobile Systems: the π-Calculus*. Cambridge University Press, May 1999.

12. Ugo Montanari and Marco Pistore. History-dependent automata: An introduction. *Lecture Notes in Computer Science*, 3465:1–28, 2005.

13. Kanae Oda, Yukiko Matsuoka, Akira Funahashi1, and Hiroaki Kitano. A comprehensive pathway map of epidermal growth factor receptor signaling. *Molecular Systems Biology*, 1:E1–E17, May 2005.

14. Carl Adam Petri. *Kommunikation mit Automaten*. PhD thesis, Bonn: Institut für Instrumentelle Mathematik, Schriften des IIM Nr. 2, 1962. Second Edition:, New York: Griffiss Air Force Base, Technical Report RADC-TR-65–377, Vol.1, 1966, Pages: Suppl. 1, English translation.

15. Andrew Phillips. *The Stochastic Pi-Machine*. Available from http://www.doc.ic.ac.uk/~anp/spim/.

16. Andrew Phillips and Luca Cardelli. A correct abstract machine for the stochastic pi-calculus. In *Bioconcur'04*. ENTCS, August 2004.

17. Andrew Phillips and Luca Cardelli. A graphical representation for the stochastic pi-calculus. In *Bioconcur'05*, August 2005.

18. C. Priami, A. Regev, E. Shapiro, and W. Silverman. Application of a stochastic name-passing calculus to representation and simulation of molecular processes. *Information Processing Letters*, 80:25–31, 2001.

19. Corrado Priami. Stochastic π-calculus. *The Computer Journal*, 38(6):578–589, 1995. Proceedings of PAPM'95.

20. A. Regev, W. Silverman, and E. Shapiro. Representation and simulation of biochemical processes using the pi- calculus process algebra. In R. B. Altman, A. K. Dunker, L. Hunter, and T. E. Klein, editors, *Pacific Symposium on Biocomputing*, volume 6, pages 459–470, Singapore, 2001. World Scientific Press.

21. Davide Sangiorgi and David Walker. *The π-calculus: a Theory of Mobile Processes*. Cambridge University Press, 2001.

22. David N. Turner. *The Polymorphic Pi-Calculus: Theory and Implementation*. PhD thesis, LFCS, June 1996. CST-126-96 (also published as ECS-LFCS-96-345).

A   Program Code

$$Dec ::= \textbf{new } x\{@r\} : t$$ Channel Declaration
$$| \textbf{ type } n = t$$ Type Declaration
$$| \textbf{ val } m = v$$ Value Declaration
$$| \textbf{ run } P$$ Process Declaration
$$| \textbf{ let } D_1 \textbf{ and } \dots \textbf{ and } D_N$$ Definitions, $N \geq 1$

$$D \quad ::= X(m_1, \dots, m_N) = P$$ Definition, $N \geq 0$

$$P \quad ::= ()$$ Null Process
$$| (P_1 | \dots | P_M)$$ Parallel, $M \geq 2$
$$| X(v_1, \dots, v_N)$$ Instantiation, $N \geq 0$
$$| \pi\{; P\}$$ Action
$$| \textbf{ do } \pi_1\{; P_1\} \textbf{ or } \dots \textbf{ or } \pi_M\{; P_M\}$$ Choice, $M \geq 2$
$$| (Dec_1 \dots Dec_N P)$$ Declarations, $N \geq 0$

$$\pi \quad ::= !x \{(v_1, \dots, v_N)\}$$ Output, $N \geq 0$
$$| ?x \{(m_1, \dots, m_N)\}$$ Input, $N \geq 0$
$$| \texttt{delay@}r$$ Delay

Fig. 21. The core SPiM language, where optional elements are enclosed in braces {}

```
val tA = 0.20 val dA = 0.002
val tB = 0.37 val dB = 0.002
val tB' = 0.027 val dAB = 0.53
new bind@0.72:chan new inhibit@0.19:chan(chan)
let a() = delay@tA; ( A() | a() )
and A() = (
  new u@0.42:chan
  do delay@dA
  or !bind; A_B()
  or !inhibit(u); A_b(u)
)
and A_b(u:chan) = ?u; A()
and A_B() = delay@dAB
let b() =
  do delay@tB; ( B() | b() )
  or ?inhibit(u); b_A(u)
and b_A(u:chan) =
  do !u; b()
  or delay@tB'; B(); b_A(u)
and B() = do delay@dB  or ?bind
run (a() | b())
```

Fig. 22. Program code for the bistable gene network of Fig. 11

```
let E1() = (
  new k1@rk1:chan new d1@rd1:chan
  !a1(d1,k1); do ?d1; E1() or ?k1; E1()
)
let E2() = (
  new k2@rk2:chan new d2@rd2:chan
  !a2(d2,k2); do ?d2; E2() or ?k2; E2()
)
let KKK() = ?a1(d,k); (do !d; KKK() or !k; KKKst())
and KKKst() = (
  new d3@rd3:chan new k3@rk3:chan
  new d5@rd5:chan new k5@rk5:chan
  do ?a2(d,k); (do !d; KKKst() or !k; KKK())
  or !a3(d3,k3); (do ?d3; KKKst() or ?k3; KKKst())
  or !a5(d5,k5); (do ?d5; KKKst() or ?k5; KKKst())
)
let KK() = ?a3(d,k); (do !d; KK() or !k; KKP())
and KKP() =
  do ?a4(d,k); (do !d; KKP() or !k; KK())
  or ?a5(d,k); (do !d; KKP() or !k; KKPP())
and KKPP() = (
  new d7@rd7:chan new k7@rk7:chan
  new d9@rd9:chan new k9@rk9:chan
  do ?a6(d,k); (do !d; KKPP() or !k; KKP())
  or !a7(d7,k7); (do ?d7; KKPP() or ?k7; KKPP())
  or !a9(d9,k9); (do ?d9; KKPP() or ?k9; KKPP())
)
let K() = ?a7(d,k); (do !d; K() or !k; KP())
and KP() =
  do ?a8(d,k); (do !d; KP() or !k; K())
  or ?a9(d,k); (do !d; KP() or !k; KPP())
and KPP() = ?a10(d,k); (do !d; KPP() or !k; KP())
let KKPase() = (
  new d4@rd4:chan new k4@rk4:chan
  new d6@rd6:chan new k6@rk6:chan
  do !a4(d4,k4); (do ?d4; KKPase() or ?k4; KKPase())
  or !a6(d6,k6); (do ?d6; KKPase() or ?k6; KKPase())
)
let KPase() = (
  new d8@rd8:chan new k8@rk8:chan
  new d10@rd10:chan new k10@rk10:chan
  do !a8(d8,k8); (do ?d8; KPase() or ?k8; KPase())
  or !a10(d10,k10); (do ?d10; KPase() or ?k10; KPase())
)
run (10 of KKK() | 100 of KK() | 100 of K())
run ( 1 of E2() | 1 of KKPase() | 1 of KPase() | E1())
```

Fig. 23. Program code for the mapk cascade of Fig. 17

B   The Stochastic π-Calculus vs. Reaction Equations

This appendix gives a visual comparison between the stochastic π-calculus and reaction equations, using the example biological systems described in the main text. The stochastic π-calculus allows the description of a biological system to be decomposed into distinct components, where each component is described by a separate connected graph. Each node in the graph represents a state of the component, and each labelled edge represents a potential interaction with another component. The interactions between components are determined by the complementarity of actions on the edges, and do not need to be given explicitly. This allows new components to be added directly, without modifying the existing system. As a result, large and complex systems can be defined incrementally, by direct composition of simpler components. In contrast, reaction equations require the interactions between components to be defined explicitly, resulting in a highly connected graph. If a new component is added to the system, each interaction with an existing component needs to be defined by an additional edge to the component. If each new component can interact with multiple existing components, this leads to a combinatorial explosion in the number of edges.

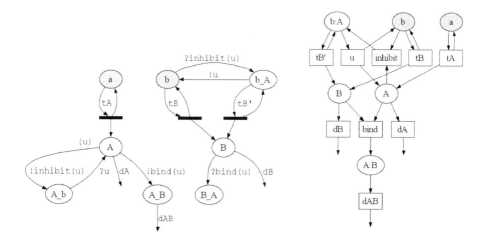

Fig. 24. Visual comparison between stochastic π-calculus processes (left) and reaction equations (right) for the bistable gene network of Fig. 11

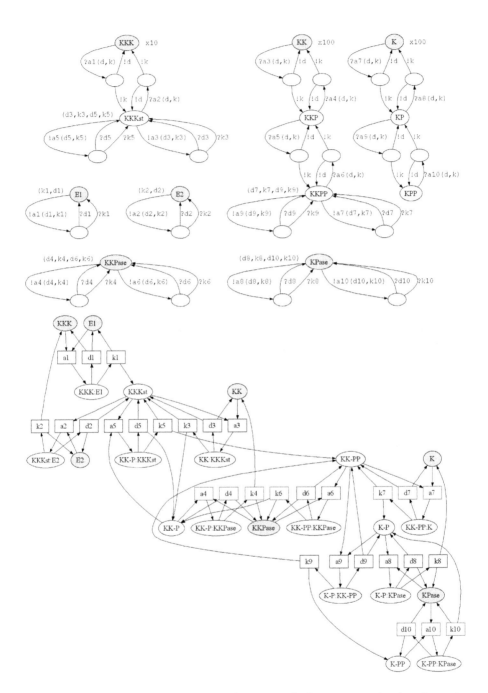

Fig. 25. Visual comparison between stochastic π-calculus processes (top) and reaction equations (bottom) for the mapk cascade of Fig. 17

On Differentiation and Homeostatic Behaviours of Boolean Dynamical Systems

Élisabeth Remy and Paul Ruet

CNRS - Institut de Mathématiques de Luminy,
163 avenue de Luminy, Case 907, 13288 Marseille Cedex 9 (France)
{remy, ruet}@iml.univ-mrs.fr

Abstract. We study rules proposed by the biologist R. Thomas relating the structure of a concurrent system of interacting genes (represented by a signed directed graph called a regulatory graph) with its dynamical properties. We prove that the results in [10] are stable under projection, and this enables us to relax the assumptions under which they are valid. More precisely, we relate here the presence of a positive (resp. negative) circuit in a regulatory graph to a more general form of biological differentiation (resp. of homeostasis).

1 Introduction

The activity of a biological cell is to a large extent controlled by genetic regulation, which is an interacting process involving proteins and DNA (genes). We are interested here in genetic regulatory networks which abstract from the detailed genome-protein interaction by focussing on the genome and by considering interactions between genes. Such a simplification is somehow justified by the importance of DNA as a program which is present in all the cells of an organism (whereas the concentrations in proteins and in RNA transcribed from DNA vary according to the cell and the time). Genetic regulatory networks have the structure of a signed directed graph, where vertices represent genes and directed edges come equipped with a sign ($+1$ or -1) and represent activatory or inhibitory effect.

This paper deals with properties relating the structure of such a concurrent system of interacting genes with its dynamics. We shall consider here discretised Boolean dynamics,[1] where the activity of a gene in a specific cell is measured by the concentration of the RNA transcribed from DNA, a quantity called the expression level of the gene and assumed to be either 1 (gene expressed) or 0 (gene not expressed). Hence the state of a system of n genes is modelled by an n-tuple $x \in \{0, 1\}^n$. The concurrent nature of these biological objects is clearly

---

[1] Discrete approaches are increasingly used in biology because of the qualitative nature of most experimental data, together with a wide occurrence of non-linear regulatory relationships (e.g., combinatorial arrangements of molecular bindings, existence of cooperative or antagonist regulatory effects).

C. Priami et al. (Eds.): Trans. on Comput. Syst. Biol. VII, LNBI 4230, pp. 153–162, 2006.
© Springer-Verlag Berlin Heidelberg 2006

demonstrated for instance by a mapping to standard Petri nets [2,9], of which genetic regulatory graphs can be considered as a subsystem.

The starting point of this work consists in two simple rules stated by the biologist R. Thomas and relating the structure of regulatory graphs to their asymptotic dynamical properties [17]:

1. a necessary condition for multistability (i.e., the existence of several stable fixed points in the dynamics) is the existence of a positive circuit in the regulatory graph (the sign of a circuit being the product of the signs of its edges): this corresponds to cell differentiation processes;
2. a necessary condition for the existence of an attractive cycle in the dynamics is the existence of a negative circuit: this corresponds to homeostasis (sustained oscillatory behaviours, e.g., cell cycle or circadian rhythms).

These rules have given rise to mathematical statements and proofs mostly in a differential dynamical formalism [8,14,4,15], and more recently in the discrete Boolean formalism [1,10]. By proving in this paper that these properties are stable under projection (in a sense that we make precise in Lemma 1), we generalise the results in [10] by showing that the existence of positive and negative circuits actually follows from weaker assumptions (Theorems 3 and 4). In the case of positive circuits for instance, the condition corresponds to a more general form of differentiation than in [10].

We do not make explicit in this introduction how regulatory graphs and dynamics are defined in terms of each other. This is done in Section 2. Let us simply observe here that instead of starting from processes which are graphs and studying their dynamics (which is typically graph rewriting, see [3] in the case of protein-protein interaction), we start here with a given dynamics and derive a regulatory graph at each point of the phase space (via a discrete form of Jacobian matrix). In particular, our approach can be used to infer circuits in regulatory networks. It is also possible to consider a fixed global "topology" of interacting genes, e.g., by taking the union of the graphs over points in the phase space, and to view our local graphs as annotations of the global one (where an interaction is "active" in a certain region of the phase space). Observe however that these more global graphs need not immediately correspond to the usual interaction graphs considered by biologists: for instance, as noticed in [16], the positive circuits occurring in [5,7] are not regulatory feedback circuits, and the regulatory graphs defined in [6] are the same as ours only up to self-regulations.

We believe that the kind of properties at hand in this paper should serve as a basis to study more refined models, which could in particular take into account stochastic phenomena and metabolic pathways.

2   Thomas' Rules and Stability Under Projection

2.1   Preliminaries

We start by recalling here the definitions which enable to associate regulatory graphs to a dynamics. The paper is self-contained, though more details can be found in [10].

Let n be a positive integer. The integers $1, \ldots, n$ denote genes. A *state* of the system is an $x = (x_1, \ldots, x_n) \in \{0, 1\}^n$, where x_i is the (discretised) expression level of gene i: $x_i = 1$ when gene i is expressed, 0 otherwise. For $\beta \in \{0, 1\}$, we define $\bar{\beta}$ by $\bar{0} = 1$ and $\bar{1} = 0$. For $x \in \{0, 1\}^n$ and $I \subseteq \{1, \ldots, n\}$, $\bar{x}^I \in \{0, 1\}^n$ is defined by $(\bar{x}^I)_i = x_i$ for $i \notin I$ and $(\bar{x}^I)_i = \overline{x_i}$ for $i \in I$. When $I = \{i\}$ is a singleton, $\bar{x}^{\{i\}}$ is denoted by $\bar{x}^i$.

Dynamics. We are interested in the dynamics of the system consisting in the n interacting genes. Consider a map $f : \{0, 1\}^n \to \{0, 1\}^n$, $f(x) = (f_1(x), \ldots, f_n(x))$. For each $x \in \{0, 1\}^n$ and $i = 1, \ldots, n$, $f_i(x)$ denotes the value to which x_i, the expression level of gene i, tends when the system is in state x. We assume that the system evolves according to the (non-deterministic) *asynchronous dynamics* $\{(x, \bar{x}^i)$ s.t. $x \in \{0, 1\}^n, x_i \neq f_i(x)\}$, i.e., the expression level of only one gene is updated at each step. Other dynamics can be considered, like the (deterministic) synchronous dynamics $\{(x, f(x))$ s.t. $x \in \{0, 1\}^n\}$ where all the expression levels x_i are simultaneously updated to $f_i(x)$ in one step. But as argued in [10], the asynchronous one is more realistic, and Theorem 2 for instance does not hold for the synchronous one. Observe that kinetic parameters are not taken into account in the discrete approach considered in this paper; however the model could be enriched by temporal delays: this would enable to recover kinetic informations.

A *cycle (for f)* is a sequence of states $(x^1, \ldots, x^r)$ such that for each $i = 1, \ldots, r$, the pair (x^i, x^{i+1}) belongs to the (asynchronous) dynamics. Indices are taken here modulo r, i.e., $r + 1 = 1$. A cycle $(x^1, \ldots, x^r)$ is completely described by one of its points, say x^1, and its *strategy*, which is the map $\varphi : \{1, \ldots, r\} \to \{1, \ldots, n\}$ such that

$$x^{i+1} = \overline{x^i}^{\varphi(i)}.$$

A cycle $(x^1, \ldots, x^r)$ with strategy φ is said to be a *trap cycle* when, once in the cycle, one cannot escape any more, i.e., for all $i = 1, \ldots, r$:

$$f(x^i) = \overline{x^i}^{\varphi(i)}.$$

Regulatory Graphs. A *regulatory graph* is a signed directed graph with vertex set $\{1, \ldots, n\}$, i.e., a directed graph with a sign, $+1$ or -1, attached to each edge. To $f : \{0, 1\}^n \to \{0, 1\}^n$ and $x \in \{0, 1\}^n$, we associate a regulatory graph $G(f)(x)$ with an edge from j to i when

$$f_i(\bar{x}^j) \neq f_i(x),$$

with positive sign when

$$x_j = f_i(x),$$

and negative sign otherwise. The intuition for the first condition is straightforward, and actually the graph underlying $G(f)(x)$ (obtained by forgetting the signs) has adjacency matrix the *discrete Jacobian matrix* of f at x defined in [11,12] and recently used in [13] for proving a discrete version of Jacobian conjecture. The intuition for the second condition is that the edge is positive when the values x_j and $f_i(x)$ either both increase or both decrease.

If $I \subseteq \{1, \dots, n\}$, an I-*circuit* is a circuit $(n_1, \dots, n_k)$ such that $n_1, \dots, n_k \in I$. If $J \subseteq I$, a J-circuit is clearly an I-circuit. The *sign of a circuit* is the product of the signs of its edges.

If G is a regulatory graph and $I \subseteq \{1, \dots, n\}$, the *restriction of G to I* is the regulatory graph obtained from G by removing any vertex not in I and any edge whose source or target is not in I.

Thomas' Rules. The following results have been proved in [10].

Theorem 1. *Let $f : \{0,1\}^n \to \{0,1\}^n$. If f has at least two fixed points, then there is an $x \in \{0,1\}^n$ such that $G(f)(x)$ has a positive circuit. More precisely, if f has two fixed points a and b, and if I is such that $b = \overline{a}^I$, then there is an $x \in \{0,1\}^n$ such that $G(f)(x)$ has a positive I-circuit.*

Theorem 2. *If $f : \{0,1\}^n \to \{0,1\}^n$ has a trap cycle $(x^1, \dots, x^r)$ with strategy φ, then $G(f)(x^1) \cup \cdots \cup G(f)(x^r)$ has a negative I-circuit with $I = \{\varphi(1), \dots, \varphi(r)\}$.*

Examples of biological situations illustrating these two kinds of dynamical properties have been studied for instance in [2]: drosophila cell cycle for an example of homeostasis and negative circuit, flowering of arabidopsis for an example of differentiation and positive circuit.

2.2 Stability Under Projection

We show that the regulatory graphs defined in Section 2.1 are stable under projection in the following sense.

Given $I \subseteq \{1, \dots, n\}$, let m be the cardinality of I, $m \leqslant n$, and let $\pi_I : \{0,1\}^n \to \{0,1\}^m$ be the projection on $\{0,1\}^m$. If $f : \{0,1\}^n \to \{0,1\}^n$ and $s : \{0,1\}^m \to \{0,1\}^n$ is a *section* of π_I (i.e., $\pi_I \circ s$ is the identity), let

$$f_{I,s} = \pi_I \circ f \circ s : \{0,1\}^m \to \{0,1\}^m.$$

Let us say that I is *compatible with f* when for all $x, y \in \{0,1\}^n$, $\pi_I(x) = \pi_I(y)$ implies $\pi_I(f(x)) = \pi_I(f(y))$. In that case, all the maps $f_{I,s}$, for s a section of π_I, are equal, and we may let $f_I : \{0,1\}^m \to \{0,1\}^m$ be their common value: f_I is then also given by

$$f_I(z) = \pi_I(f(x))$$

for $x \in \{0,1\}^n$ any point *over* z, i.e., such that $\pi_I(x) = z$.

Lemma 1. *Let $f : \{0,1\}^n \to \{0,1\}^n$, $I \subseteq \{1, \dots, n\}$ and $z \in \{0,1\}^m$. If s is a section of π_I, then $G(f_{I,s})(z)$ coincides with the restriction of $G(f)(s(z))$ to I. In particular, when I is compatible with f, $G(f_I)(z)$ is the restriction of $G(f)(x)$ to I for $x \in \{0,1\}^n$ any point over z.*

Proof — Let $i, j \in I$. The regulatory graph $G(f_{I,s})(z)$ contains an edge from j to i if, and only if,

$$(f_{I,s})_i(\overline{z}^j) \neq (f_{I,s})_i(z).$$

But $(f_{I,s})_i(z) = f_i(s(z))$ because

$$\pi_i \circ \pi_I = \pi_i$$

for $i \in I$, and $(f_{I,s})_i(\overline{z}^j) = f_i\left(\overline{s(z)}^j\right)$ because

$$s(\overline{z}^j) = \overline{s(z)}^j$$

for $j \in I$. Hence $G(f_{I,s})(z)$ has an edge from j to i if, and only if, $G(f)(s(z))$ has. The edge in $G(f_{I,s})(z)$ is positive if, and only if,

$$z_j = (f_{I,s})_i(z),$$

and the edge in $G(f)(s(z))$ is positive if, and only if,

$$s(z)_j = f_i(s(z)).$$

These conditions are equivalent for $i, j \in I$.   □

This Lemma asserts a sort of commutation property: the regulatory graph associated to the projected dynamics is the restriction of the initial regulatory graph. Observe however that the projection does not commute with the dynamics. Indeed, let us define the asynchronous dynamics of $f_{s,I}$: a pair $(z, z') \in \{0,1\}^m \times \{0,1\}^m$ with $z \neq z'$ is in the dynamics when there exists $x' \in \{0,1\}^n$ such that $z' = \pi_I(x')$ and $(s(z), x')$ belongs to the asynchronous dynamics of f. The point is that a pair (x, x') in the dynamics of f may satisfy $\pi_I(x) = \pi_I(x')$ (when $x' = \overline{x}^i$ with $i \notin I$) and hence not be mapped to a pair in the dynamics of $f_{s,I}$.

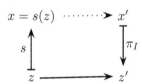

Remark that when I is compatible with f, the equivalence relation $\sim$ induced by the projection π_I between states ($x \sim y$ if, and only if, $\pi_I(x) = \pi_I(y)$) is a bisimulation for the asynchronous dynamics: indeed, it can be checked that if $x \sim y$ and (x, x') is in the dynamics of f, then there exists y' such that $x' \sim y'$ and (y, y') is in the dynamics of f.

Lemma 1 enables us to relax the conditions of validity of Theorems 1 and 2, as we shall see in the following sections.

3   Disjoint Stable Subspaces and Positive Circuits

The process of biological differentiation does not necessarily correspond to multi-stationarity. Consider for instance the process which controls the lysis-lysogeny decision in the bacteriophage lambda. The dynamics has a single fixed point (lysogeny) and a trap cycle (lysis): these two stable subspaces can be viewed as a differentiation phenomenon, and we would like this to imply the existence of a positive circuit (which exists indeed in the regulatory graph associated to our example, between genes C1 and Cro). In this Section we show that holds in general for Boolean dynamics.

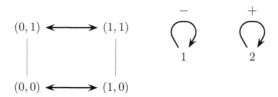

Fig. 1. On the left, a dynamics for $n = 2$ with no fixed point is pictured on a framed square, and a bold arrow from state x to state $\bar{x}^i$ means that $x_i \neq f_i(x)$. The x-axis carries the expression level of gene 1 and the y-axis the expression level of gene 2. On the right, a positive loop on gene 2 in the (constant) regulatory graph, in accordance with Theorem 3.

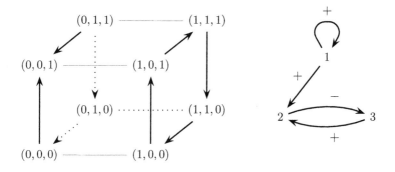

Fig. 2. On the left, a dynamics with a single fixed point $(0, 0, 1)$; dotted lines are only supposed to ease visualising the 3-cube. On the right, the regulatory graph associated to the state $(1, 1, 1)$ has a positive loop on 1, in accordance with Theorem 3.

Theorem 3. *Let $f : \{0, 1\}^n \to \{0, 1\}^n$, $I \subseteq \{1, \dots, n\}$ and s a section of π_I. If $f_{I,s}$ has at least two fixed points, then there is an $x \in \{0, 1\}^n$ such that $G(f)(x)$ has a positive circuit. More precisely, if $f_{I,s}$ has two fixed points a and b, and if $J \subseteq I$ is such that $b = \bar{a}^J$, then there is an $x \in \{0, 1\}^n$ such that $G(f)(x)$ has a positive J-circuit.*

Proof — By Theorem 1, there is a $z \in \{0, 1\}^m$ such that $G(f_{I,s})(z)$ has a positive J-circuit, and Lemma 1 suffices to conclude.   □

The following obvious Lemma states that multistationarity of f_I corresponds to the existence of disjoint subspaces which are stable under f, clearly a more general form of biological differentiation than multistationarity.

Lemma 2. *Let $f : \{0,1\}^n \to \{0,1\}^n$, $I \subseteq \{1, \ldots, n\}$ and $z \in \{0,1\}^m$. When I is compatible with f, z is a fixed point for f_I if, and only if, the subspace $\pi_I^{-1}(z)$ is stable under f.*

For instance, the dynamics given in Figures 1 and 2 do not have multistability, but projecting the dynamics on the y-coordinate ($I = \{2\} \subseteq \{1,2\}$) in the first case and on the x-coordinate ($I = \{1\} \subseteq \{1,2,3\}$) in the second case, gives rise to multistability and this explains in both cases the existence of a positive circuit in the regulatory graph associated to some state.

A possible generalisation of Theorem 3 would be that positive circuits are necessary for the genuine coexistence of disjoint attractors (in our framework: disjoint sets of states which are stable under the dynamics), a conjecture which still remains to be demonstrated.

It is worth observing that this stability under projection is independent from the framework. For instance, it may be applied to the differential framework in [15]. Indeed, let $\Omega \subseteq \mathbb{R}^n$ be a product of open intervals in $\mathbb{R}$ and $f : \Omega \to \mathbb{R}^n$. The projection $p_I : \mathbb{R}^n \to \mathbb{R}^m$, where m is the cardinality of I, is given by

$$(p_I(x))_i = \begin{cases} x_i & \text{if } i \in I, \\ 0 & \text{otherwise,} \end{cases}$$

and compatibility of $I \subseteq \{1, \ldots, n\}$ with f is defined in the same way as in the Boolean case: for all $x, y \in \Omega$, $p_I(x) = p_I(y)$ implies $p_I(f(x)) = p_I(f(y))$. In that case, we may let $f_I : \mathbb{R}^m \to \mathbb{R}^m$ be defined by $f_I(z) = p_I(f(x))$ for $x \in \Omega$ any point over z. When f is continuously differentiable, C. Soulé associates to any $x \in \Omega$ a regulatory graph $G(f)(x)$ as follows: there is a positive (resp. negative) edge from j to i when the (i,j) entry $J(f)(x)_{i,j}$ of the Jacobian matrix is positive (resp. negative).

Now, when I is compatible with f, we have $(\partial(f_I)_i/\partial x_j)(z) = (\partial f_i/\partial x_j)(x)$ for x any point over z, hence the Jacobian matrix $J(f_I)(z)$ is a submatrix of $J(f)(x)$ and we get the following analogous of Lemma 1: if $x \in \Omega$ is any point over z, then $G(f_I)(z)$ is the restriction of $G(f)(x)$ to I. This implies the following slight generalisation of Theorem 1 in [15]: if $I \subseteq \{1, \ldots, n\}$ is compatible with f and f_I has at least two nondegenerate zeros (points a such that $f_I(a) = 0$ and $\det J(f_I)(a) \neq 0$), then there exists $x \in \Omega$ such that $G(f)(x)$ has a positive circuit.

4   Dynamic Cycles and Negative Circuits

Theorem 4. *Let $f : \{0,1\}^n \to \{0,1\}^n$, $I \subseteq \{1, \ldots, n\}$ and s a section of π_I. If $f_{I,s}$ has a trap cycle $(z^1, \ldots, z^r)$ with strategy φ, then*

$$G(f)(s(z^1)) \cup \cdots \cup G(f)(s(z^r))$$

has a negative J-circuit with $J = \{\varphi(1), \ldots, \varphi(r)\}$.

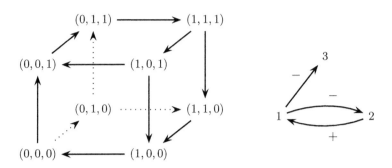

Fig. 3. On the left, a dynamics with no trap cycle. On the right, the regulatory graph associated to state $(0,0,0)$ has a negative circuit, in accordance with Theorem 4.

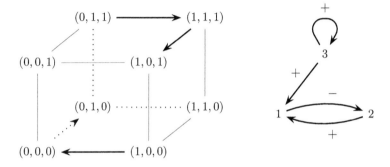

Fig. 4. On the left, a dynamics with no cycle at all. On the right, the regulatory graph associated to state $(1,0,0)$ has a negative circuit, in accordance with Theorem 4.

Proof — By Theorem 2, $G(f_{I,s})(z^1) \cup \cdots \cup G(f_{I,s})(z^r)$ has a negative circuit with vertices $\varphi(1), \ldots, \varphi(r)$. Since $\varphi(1), \ldots, \varphi(r) \in I$, by Lemma 1, this negative circuit is also in $G(f)(s(z^1)) \cup \cdots \cup G(f)(s(z^r))$. □

Figure 3 gives an example of dynamics with many dynamical cycles, none of which is a trap, hence Theorem 2 cannot be applied to infer some negative circuit. We observe that $I = \{1, 2\} \subseteq \{1, 2, 3\}$ is compatible with f: the two horizontal cycles are in parallel planes. Then by projecting on I, we get a trap cycle, and this explains the negative circuit involving genes 1 and 2. In the present case, the negative circuit occurs in the regulatory graph $G(0, 0, 0)$ associated to a single state.

Figure 4 gives the more radical example of a dynamics with no cycle. Take $I = \{1, 2\} \subseteq \{1, 2, 3\}$ (which is not compatible with f in this case) and let s be defined by:

$$s(1, 0) = (1, 0, 0)$$
$$s(0, 0) = (0, 0, 0)$$
$$s(0, 1) = (0, 1, 1)$$
$$s(1, 1) = (1, 1, 1).$$

Then $f_{I,s}$ has a trap cycle, which is obtained by gathering the dynamics on the two horizontal planes. We get a negative circuit, which occurs actually in the regulatory graph $G(1,0,0)$ associated to a single state.

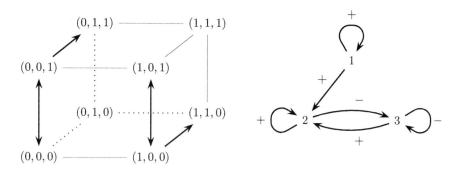

Fig. 5. On the left, a dynamics with both differentiation and homeostasis in different projections. On the right, the regulatory graph associated to state $(0,0,0)$.

A non trivial example of a dynamics with differentiation (multistationarity when projected on $\{1\}$, whence a positive self-loop on $\{1\}$) and homeostasis (trap cycle when projected on $\{3\}$, whence a negative self-loop on $\{3\}$) is given in Figure 5.

Acknowledgements. We thank Christophe Soulé and Denis Thieffry for helpful discussions.

References

1. J. Aracena. *Modèles mathématiques discrets associés à des systèmes biologiques. Application aux réseaux de régulation génétiques.* Thèse de doctorat, Université Joseph Fourier, Grenoble, 2001.
2. C. Chaouiya, É. Remy, P. Ruet, and D. Thieffry. Qualitative modelling of genetic networks: from logical regulatory graphs to standard Petri nets. In *Application and Theory of Petri Nets*, volume 3099 of *Lecture Notes in Computer Science*, pages 137–156. Springer, 2004.
3. V. Danos and C. Laneve. Graphs for core molecular biology. In *Computational Methods in Systems Biology*, volume 2602 of *Lecture Notes in Computer Science*, pages 34–46. Springer, 2003.
4. J.-L. Gouzé. Positive and negative circuits in dynamical systems. *Journal of Biological Systems*, 6:11–15, 1998.
5. R. Karmakar and I. Bose. Graded and binary responses in stochastic gene expression. Technical report, arXiv:q-bio. OT/0411012, 2004.
6. F. Li, T. Long, Y. Lu, Q. Ouyang, and C. Tang. The yeast cell-cycle network is robustly designed. *Proceedings of the National Academy of Sciences of the United States of America*, 2004.

7. N. I. Markevich, J. B. Hoek, and B. N. Kholodenko. Signaling switches and bistability arising from multisite phosphorylation in protein kinase cascades. *Journal of Cell Biology*, 2004.

8. E. Plahte, T. Mestl, and S. W. Omholt. Feedback loops, stability and multistationarity in dynamical systems. *Journal Biological Systems*, 3:409–413, 1995.

9. É. Remy, P. Ruet, L. Mendoza, D. Thieffry, and C. Chaouiya. From logical regulatory graphs to standard Petri nets: dynamical roles and functionality of feedback circuits. In *Transactions on Computational Systems Biology*, Lecture Notes in Computer Science. Springer, 2005. To appear.

10. É. Remy, P. Ruet, and D. Thieffry. Graphic requirements for multistability and attractive cycles in a Boolean dynamical framework. *Under review*, 2005. Prépublication Institut de Mathématiques de Luminy 2005-08. Available at http://iml.univ-mrs.fr/~ruet/papiers.html.

11. F. Robert. *Discrete iterations: a metric study*, volume 6 of *Series in Computational Mathematics*. Springer, 1986.

12. F. Robert. *Les systèmes dynamiques discrets*, volume 19 of *Mathématiques et Applications*. Springer, 1995.

13. M.-H. Shih and J.-L. Dong. A combinatorial analogue of the Jacobian problem in automata networks. *Advances in Applied Mathematics*, 34(1):30–46, 2005.

14. E. H. Snoussi. Necessary conditions for multistationarity and stable periodicity. *Journal of Biological Systems*, 6:3–9, 1998.

15. C. Soulé. Graphic requirements for multistationarity. *ComPlexUs*, 1:123–133, 2003.

16. C. Soulé. Mathematical approaches to gene regulation and differentiation. *Manuscript*, 2005.

17. R. Thomas. On the relation between the logical structure of systems and their ability to generate multiple steady states and sustained oscillations. In *Series in Synergetics*, volume 9, pages 180–193. Springer, 1981.

A Specification Language and a Framework for the Execution of Composite Models in Systems Biology

Ofer Margoninski, Peter Saffrey, James Hetherington,
Anthony Finkelstein, and Anne Warner*

Centre for Mathematics and Physics in the Life Sciences and Experimental Biology
(CoMPLEX), University College London, Gower Street, London, WC1E 6BT
`omargoni@cs.ucl.ac.uk`

Abstract. When modelling complex biological systems it is often desirable to combine a number of distinct sub-models to form a larger composite model. We describe an XML based language that can be used to specify composite models and a lightweight computational framework that executes these models. The language supports specification of structure and implementation details for composite models, along with the interfaces provided by each sub-model. The framework executes each sub-model in its native environment, allowing extensive reuse of existing models. It uses mathematical and computational connectors and translators to unify the models computationally. Unlike other suggested approaches for model integration, our approach does not impose one modeling scheme, composition algorithm or underlying middleware framework. We demonstrate our approach by constructing a composite model describing part of the glucose homeostasis system.

1 Introduction

Recent years have seen the proliferation of mathematical models used to describe biological phenomena. Among others, models have been proposed for describing metabolic processes, signalling pathways, transport processes and various electro-physiological systems. While many detailed models describing various biological aspects have been suggested, very few models describe a complete physiological system, organism or organ, across scales. Such large scale models can, theoretically, be created by integrating together existing detailed models describing sub-aspects of the desired system[12], but the lack of suitable tools for model integration in Systems Biology has made this task, so far, nearly impossible. This paper describes such a tool. In presenting this tool, we use the structured view of models and modelling activity of the *meta-model* suggested by Finkelstein et. al. in [1].

Models exist in a great variety of schemes and formats including differential equations, stochastic and process algebra models, each of which have their attendant facilities and tool support. However, it is possible to view each model

---

* We thank the DTI for supporting this research through the UCL Beacon Project.

C. Priami et al. (Eds.): Trans. on Comput. Syst. Biol. VII, LNBI 4230, pp. 163–184, 2006.
© Springer-Verlag Berlin Heidelberg 2006

as a specification for possible computations. Each model can be executed by a software tool, or an *engine*. Using the model and a set of inputs, or *context* the engine provides a set of outputs, or an *interpretation*. By mapping the outputs of one model into the inputs of another, we can construct a *composite model*. Repeatedly composing such models together can produce *composite models* that are arbitrarily large and complex. The basic building blocks of such models, which can not be further decomposed are known as *elementary models*. Elementary models are constructed in a modelling environment such as Mathematica or XPPAUT.

1.1 The Composite Model Description Language

We have developed an XML based language, the Composite Model Description Language (CMDL), that allows the description of composite and elementary models, so that they can be used within our framework. CMDL also enables the specification of composite models themselves.

For all models, A CMDL file can be used to describe the functionality and the interfaces provided by the model. CMDL allows each sub-model to have multiple interfaces to capture models that have more than one functionality, for example: an ODE model can be solved to plot its dynamical variables versus time, or analyzed to find its bifurcation points. CMDL also can be used to provide attribution annotation and to link the behaviour of a model to the biological phenomena, or *aspects* it represents, to allow for more convenient collation and reuse. Thus, CMDL is MIRIAM[25] compliant. As suggested in the MIRIAM proposal, we use existing ontologies to minimise ambiguity.

For composite models, A CMDL description also specifies the model architecture and implementation details: What sub-models are used, how they are connected together, and in what order they should be executed.

CMDL has been designed to provide biological, mathematical and computational information about a model and to make that information easily accessible to all parties.

1.2 The Computational Framework

We have also developed a lightweight computational framework that enables the execution of composite models specified in CMDL. Individual models are executed on their native tools and are integrated by the framework. Usually they need not be modified in order to be used by the framework. The framework utalizes *translators* to take account of inevitable differences in input and output formats, including differences in timescale. It uses *smart connectors* to resolve any feedback present in the composite model structure. Each part of the framework is generic and based on well defined interfaces, so it can easily be replaced by user-defined algorithms and translations. Our framework utilizes existing middleware infrastructure, such as dynamic link libraries or Web Services[37] for communicating between the different components. We do not presume the existence of any specific infrastructure, and the framework can potentially run on many different middleware infrastructures. At the moment we support only the integration of ODE models, but the framework can be easily extended to support the integration of models developed in other schemes by the development of appropriate connectors.

This paper proceeds as follows. Firstly, we review the current state of the art in model integration in Systems Biology. We then describe the Composite Model Description Language and the model integration framework in more detail. We conclude by describing a composite model of glucose homeostasis that we have specified and executed using the framework.

2   Related Work

2.1   Approaches Originating in Systems Biology

At the moment, there exists no component middleware specifically designed for the integration of models in Systems Biology. While our proposal shares some concepts with Cell-ML[9],[23], SBML[28],[29] and the Systems Biology Workbench (SBW)[31], it also differs from them in several crucial aspects.

CellML[9],[23] was designed with the view of enabling modellers in Systems Biology to specify composite models composed of a number of sub-models. CellML requires the definition of input and output variables for each model; model composition is achieved by connecting inputs and outputs from separate models. CellML, however, does not allow specification of how the composed model should be executed, detailed descriptions of the model interfaces, or the integration of models which are not ODE models, or which are specified in a format other then CellML. Thus, while CellML may be quite adequate for the conceptual representation of a composite model, composed of several ODE based sub-models, it does not, currently, fulfil our need for a composite model description language, which is more generic, on the one hand, and implementation oriented, on the other hand.

The other currently prominent modelling language for Systems Biology is SBML - The Systems Biology Markup Language[28],[29]. It attempts to standardize the expression of ODE based models of cellular systems, concentrating on chemical reactions. SBML is a rich language in this environment and has good take up within the community. However SBML currently does not allow for modularization, has no support for interface specification, and does not support linkage with models created in other tools and languages. Thus, SBML can not be used to integrate existing, heterogeneous models. We view our proposal as complementary to SBML. We use the SBML annotation scheme, and existing SBML models can be easily wrapped with a CMDL description in order to facilitate their integration with other models.

SBW[31] is a generic middleware for the integration of software tools, used in Systems Biology. It was not designed specifically to facilitate the integration of models, and is actually a quite generic middleware architecture, similar to CORBA[10].

Several tools exist to support model construction and simulation specifically in Systems Biology. E-Cell[17],[34],[33] is a whole-cell and multi-cell simulation tool based on an object oriented approach . While it enables the creation of models using a few different schemes, such as reaction-diffusion, S-System and flux distribution analysis schemes, it does not support the integration of models created in other tools. Also, currently only one connecting algorithm, which is embedded in the software itself, is supported.

The XS-system[2] enables the construction of models of cellular networks from a set of building blocks representing syntheses, degradations, reversible reactions and enzymatic reactions. The resulting model is represented as a set of ODEs, specifying the rate equations for the various substances involved. Representation using SDEs (stochastic Differential Equations), timed automata or hybrid automata is also supported, but in a rather limited manner. The XS-system is designed to support the construction of models from a pre-existing set of existing, elementary, building blocks rather than allowing the user to integrate models created in different tools.

BioSpice[5], [6] is a collaborative project of American universities and research centres. It aims to build a comprehensive software environment that integrates a suite of analytical, simulation and visualisation tools related to cellular systems biology. At the moment, the tool suite focuses on individual model construction and analysis and does not address model integration.

2.2   Approaches Originating in Software Engineering

There are a number of frameworks aimed at integrating heterogeneous components for simulation. The High Level Architecture (HLA) [21] is a general purpose architecture for simulation reuse and interoperability, developed for the Defense Modeling and Simulation Office (DMSO). HLA uses a central service to coordinate a number of models via a standard time-step interface. However, there is no explicit language to describe model connections and only the time-step interface is supported.

Generic component frameworks, such as CORBA[10], COM[11], Java Beans[18], and more recently, Web Services[37] include an Interface Definition Language (IDL), such as IDL for CORBA and COM, and WSDL[38] for Web Services, used to specify the functional interfaces exposed by the components. Process execution languages, such as BPEL-WS[4] , enable a multiple component execution to be specified. These frameworks do not, however, allow detailed annotation of the nature of each component necessary both for heterogeneous model integration and understanding of biological models. They also have poor support for specifying the architecture of the overall model.

The concept of interconnecting components exist in many Architectural Description Languages (ADLs), for example Darwin[13], [14], [15] and Wright[39], including the possibility of a rich set of component connectors. However, these languages can not be used for specifying the biological aspects the models represent, or how the models should be executed.

The Unified Modelling Language [35],[36] is a very comprehensive model description language, designed mainly for modelling software systems. The main focus is on modelling in detail the code itself and not the aspects, or phenomenon, that the code relates to. It is also difficult, in UML, to present an overall view of the different functionalities a certain model has, as opposed to a detailed representation of its interfaces. UML is also not well suited for representing the overall component architecture of a system — ADLs are better suited for this purpose.

We focus on the integration of currently existing approaches and techniques in Systems Biology, such as ontologies and model description languages, with Software Engineering tools and techniques such as ADLs, IDLs, process execution languages and component frameworks. Through this integration we build a framework for the representation and execution of composite models in Systems Biology.

2.3   Approaches Originating in Other Scientific Fields

The General Coupling Framework, GCF[19] enables the creation of composite models out of individual model components, developed in a variety of programming languages. Like CMDL, GCF supports the description of the interfaces of the individual components, as well as the architecture of the overall model. Unlike CMDL, GCF focuses on the integration of software modules written in programming languages such as C, Fortran or Java, and requires 'put' and 'get' calls to be placed into the individual modules source code before they can be used within the framework. Currently GCF uses a time-stepping algorithm, embedded within the architecture, in order to perform the simulation.

The Cape-Open standard[8] is a specification for a collection of middleware interfaces, aimed at enabling the integration of models and modelling tools in the chemical industry. The interfaces enable the integration of different Unit Operations Modules, modelling the activity of a unit operation within a chemical plant, and numerical solvers, within the same simulation environment, called the Simulator Executive. There is no proposed standard for the specification of composite models, and it is assumed each Simulator Executive would use its own proprietary methods for that.

3   The Composite Model Description Language

The Composite Model Description Language (CMDL) is an XML schema for *model description files*. For all models, the CMDL file contains a section describing the biological phenomenon described by the model, a section describing the functionalities and interfaces provided by the model, and a section describing some relevant meta-data. For composite models, the model description file also includes a specification of how the model should be implemented: What submodels are included, how they should be connected together, what connectors should be used, and in what order should they be executed.

3.1   The Model Interface Description

The top level element in any CMDL file is the model element, which has an id attribute. A model contains meta-data, phenomenon and functionality elements as it's immediate sub-nodes. A composite model would also contain sub-models elements, which are used to specify the submodels used in the model.

Meta-Data. The Meta-Data section contains the attribution annotation, as required by the MIRIAM[25] standard proposal. It includes a citation of the reference description or scientific paper with which the model is associated, details of the model creators, date and time of creation and a statement about the terms of distribution. These details are specified using RDF, in the same manner as in SBML[9],[23] models.

Phenomenon. The phenomena element links the model with the biology it represents. It is used to precisely specify what biological phenomena are described by the model, in accordance with the MIRIAM[25] proposal. It is composed of a list of phenomenon elements describing the biological processes depicted by the model. Each phenomenon element contains a textual description, and possibly one or more references to terms from the same or different ontologies, which together serve to define the phenomenon. We use the SBML annotation element[30] to refer to these terms. For example, a model describing Insulin stimulus of hepatocytes and the resulting signalling cascade will include the phenomena "Detection of hormone stimulus" (GO term 9720), and "Insulin receptor signalling pathway" (GO term 8286).

A phenomenon element also contains compartment and aspect elements. They are used to specify where within the organism the mentioned phenomenon, or process, occurs and the concrete *measurables* that the model describes. These measurables are the main modelling results, to be compared to the results obtained in experiments or by executing other models for validation purposes. They usually correspond to the main variables imported and exported by the model. Aspects specified by the sub-models, which may be of less interest for the overall model, need not be listed.

While our concept of compartments is similar to that of SBML, and the SBML species element can be viewed as a subtype of our aspect element, we use compartment and aspect elements only for annotation and not for the actual specification of the model itself. Compartments and aspects may again be specified by making references to terms in various relevant ontologies. For example, the cytoplasm of a hepatocyte can be specified by the combination of terms hepatocyte(CELL:OBO term 182), and cytoplasm (GO term 5737) .

Functionalities. The functionalities section serves to describe the interfaces provided by the model. It describes, given what inputs, what outputs are provided by the model. The same model may be interpreted in many different ways, using the same or different sets of inputs and engines, to give different predictions or results. For example, an ODE model can be run in a simulation, when provided with all the required parameter values, or analyzed for its null clines and bifurcation points. Thus, a model may provide several different *functionalities*. These functionalities may be specified at different levels of detail: At the highest level, the *broad functionality* level specifies what predictions a model can make (output aspects) based on what data (input aspects). This level of specification provides a basic summary of model behaviour that may be useful to biologists in particular.

The next level is the *mathematical functionality* level, which is used mainly to specify the mathematical format of the model's inputs and outputs. This is done by assigning at least one *variable* to each aspect. A variable in CMDL is used to provide, usually quantitative, information regarding an aspect. For example, a variable may serve to describe the concentration of Calcium over time or the frequency of Calcium oscillations. A variable can be of many different types - It can be, for example, a scalar, a vector, tensor, a matrix, a probability distribution or a time track - describing how the value of a dynamical variable is changing with time. By assigning a variable of a certain type to an aspect, we specify exactly how this aspect is described, mathematically, by the model. MathML may be used to describe the precise format of a variable. For example, We can use MathML to specify that $Ca = F(t)$, where $t0 < t < t1$. A variable should have units, unless the dimension it describes is 'dimensionless' such as, 'the number of particles' .

The mathematical functionality also includes a list of required parameters. The difference between parameters and variables is that usually the value of parameters remains fixed during the course of an interpretation of a model, while the values of variables may change. Currently we use the SBML syntax for specifying parameters. However, the parameter value may be specified in a separate, auxiliary, parameter values file. The enables the framework to run multiple instances, or copies, of the same model with different parameters.

A mathematical functionality may also specify the mathematical scheme in which the model is implemented: For example, chemical reactions can be mathematically described either deterministically as a set of ODE's or stochastically using Gillepsi's algorithm.

The mathematical functionality description level is useful both to biologists and mathematicians using the model.

The most detailed level is the *computational interface* description. The computational interface specifies the type of interface supported - for example Web Services, DLL libraries or a simple output file, the name of the interface supported, and a reference to a file containing the actual interface specification. This would be a WSDL file for Web Services, or a C/C++ header file in the case of a DLL library. These files specify the precise data structures of the variables involved. In the case of Web Services, the WSDL file also specifies the location of the sub models to be used by using the WSDL 'binding' element.

The interface referenced should be one which is currently supported by the orchestrator and at least some existing connectors, in order for the model to be used within our framework. Information at this level is for use by the computer scientists responsible for implementing a composite model using this model as one of its components.

A broad functionality may contain several different mathematical functionalities and each mathematical functionality may in turn contain several different computational interfaces. Thus, the different functionalities for each model form a tree hierarchy.

3.2   Specifying Composite Models

In order to execute a composite model we need to specify what model instances, translators and connectors should be used. We then need to map out the connections between these elements, specifying how the inputs required by each model instance are satisfied. Finally, we need to specify in what order the model instances and the connections should be invoked, and which specific computational interfaces should be called. Thus, in a manner similar to BPEL[4] we provide a process description notation with many features reminiscent of an executable language. Like an executable programming language a CMDL model is unambiguous, provided that all of the internal models it is composed of are unambiguous. In other words, a CMDL model will always yield the same results for a specific set of inputs, provided that the elementary models it is composed of behave in this manner. The key difference between languages such as CMDL or BPEL and programming languages used to describe executable internal processes is that a CMDL or BPEL file also calls for the execution of internal processes, or in our case elementary models, without specifying how these internal processes or elementary models actually handle the data - this is assumed to be specified by the modelling language in which the elementary model is specified.

   While the CMDL specification is detailed enough to support execution of the composite model by our framework, it is also designed to enable mathematicians and biologists to gain a broad understanding of how the model is put together.

Specifying the Model Architecture. The first thing to be specified is the model components to be used. A model component is an *instance* of a submodel executing on an engine, similar to the instance of an object in object oriented programming. Many instances can be created from the same submodel, perhaps using different parameters for each, each forming its own component. For example, in order to model a liver cell plate, comprised of many hepatocyte cells, one model component can be used to model each cell. All of these model components can be created from the same hepatocyte cell model, using the same or different sets of parameters. Different parameters may be used, for example, to reflect biological differences between periportal and periveneous cells.

   Connections specify the topology of the network of models. *Horizontal connections* specify the connections between the sub-models - which output variables of which models are used as inputs for other models. *Vertical connections* map the variables of the overall model into the variables of the different components it is composed of. For each variable mapping, we may specify a *translation*. This can be a simple scaling of the variable, or a more complex transformation. For horizontal connections which form a feedback loop, we also specify which smart connector should be used to resolve the feedback.

3.3   Specifying the Algorithm Used to Solve the Model

The algorithm for executing a composite model is specified using a 'sequence' construct, similar to that found in BPELWS[4]. The sequence element contains a list of invocation elements. Each invocation element specifies either the invocation of a specific mathematical functionality on one of the pre-declared model components, or the invocation of a smart connector, used to solve several model components which are interdependent on one another. Currently, the only flow of control supported is a simple linear one. In the future we plan to support additional flow control elements already supported by BPELWS, such as those used to implement loops and branches.

4   Example of a Model Specification File

The appendix contains an example composite model specification file. The model described is of the generation of calcium oscillations in liver hepatocytes as a result of hormonal stimulation. The model depicted forms part of a more comprehensive model of this process, which will be described later.

The model file first defines the phenomena depicted by the model - the glucagon stimulated signalling cascade. The phenomena is defined both through a textual definition and through references to terms in the relevant ontologies. We also specify the compartments in which the phenomena of interest occurs - the hepatocyte membrane and cytoplasm. The last part of the phenomena element lists the actual aspects, or measurables, depicted by the model. In this case these are the activation level of G-Protein and the concentration of intracellular calcium.

The model is a composite model composed of two sub-models, listed within the 'submodels' tag. The first model describes the hormone binding to the G-Protein receptor, resulting in the release of PhosphoLipase into the cell, and the second model describes how PhosphoLipase causes Calcium oscillations.

The model has one functionality, predicting G-Protein activation levels and cytoplasmic concentration of Calcium, as a function of the concentration of Glucagon in the blood, over time. This functionality is specified in precise mathematical terms in the 'mathematical functionality' section: It provides timetracks of Calcium concentration and G-Protein activation level, and requires a timetrack of Glucagon levels. The units of the variables involved are also specified.

As we can see in the 'implementation' section, to implement this functionality, we create one instance of each sub-model, and then link together the two instances, feeding the PhosphoLipase concentration from the G-protein receptor model into the Calcium model, and feeding back the Calcium concentrations from the Calcium model into the G-protein model. The model instances are linked together using a waveform relaxation connector. The sequence of execution steps for this functionality contains only one step - the execution of the connector.

5   The Model Integration Framework

Models specified in the CMDL language are executed by the orchestrator. The orchestrator serves mainly as a workflow co-ordination service. It executes the composite model by launching and executing the elementary sub-models on their respective engines, such as Xppaut and Mathematica, and passing data between them as required. The orchestrator communicates with the various engines through *engine wrappers* - pieces of software that expose the functionality of the different engines in a standard manner. The orchestrator uses *connectors* to solve together models which are interdependent on one another, and *translators* to carry out necessary data transformations between the models. The orchestrator is used in conjunction with a set of supporting information services, used to store data required for model runs, such as parameter values, as well as results obtained from model execution and, in the future, the CMDL files themselves. A separate paper about these information services is in preparation.

5.1   The Core Computational Elements

The Engine Wrappers. Individual instances of elementary models are executed by the software tools, or *engines*, in which they were originally developed. Accommodation of specific modelling tools within our framework is done through wrappers. Wrappers expose the functionality of the modelling tool in a standard way to the rest of the framework. Wrappers expose interfaces used to launch new model components and enable access to and the execution of computational interfaces of components already launched. Internally, the wrappers use the proprietary command set of the modelling tool in question to provide these operations. We currently have available wrappers for Mathematica[24], Xppaut [40], and for a C++ library used to numerically integrate differential equations using the numerical recipes[27] library.

The Orchestrator. At the core of the framework is an *orchestrator*, which is used for executing composite models. The orchestrator serves mainly as a coordinator or process execution service. It reads the details of the composite model from the composite model specification file and then launches the sub-models and executes them according to the instructions provided in the file. The orchestrator maintains the global (composite) model variables, and passes them as inputs to the sub-models as required.

The composite model file may also specify the use of connectors and translators. These are called by the orchestrator in order to link together models, where the outputs of one model can not be linked to the inputs of the other model in a straightforward manner.

Connectors. A connector serves to numerically integrate two models where such an integration is not trivial. For example, integrating two or more ODE models which are interdependent and which were implemented on different tools, as in our case studies. Several different connectors can be used to achieve the same task. For example, for integrating ODE models, one can use either a connector implementing a wave form relaxation algorithm[22] or a step wise integrator as described by [34].

The wave form relaxation algorithm uses a 'seed' function to guess the solution to one model and then iterates between solving each model, refining the overall solution to convergence. A step wise integrator runs all the models at once, performing the numerical integration using a method such as Euler's method or RangKutta. Each of these algorithms requires a different mathematical interface (see section 3.1).

The different connectors are best suited for use in different scenarios: A waveform connector typically executes at most a few dozen calls on each model, but each call is computationally intensive, as a complete simulation is performed, and requires the transfer of substantial amounts of data. A stepwise integration algorithm may make millions of calls on each model, but each call is computationally quick and requires the transfer of only a few values. Given these characteristics, a waveform connector may be more suitable for connecting together models residing on different, remote machines, while a stepwise integrator may prove to be more efficient when all models reside on the same machine.

Connectors may also be used in order to integrate together models developed in different schemes. For example, a connector can be built in order to connect together a Discrete Event (DEVS) model with an ODE model. Such a connector may generate events for the DEVS model when certain variables in the ODE model cross certain thresholds. It may also modify the values of certain parameters in the ODE equations when certain events occur. Such a connector may be used to link a DEVS model of an intracellular signalling system with an ODE model depicting gap-junctions and the flow of different chemical species through it. Similarly, connectors can be devised for stochastic models, based on suitable mathematical algorithms.

In addition to connectors, *translators* are used to take account of inevitable differences in input and output formats, such as differences in the units used by different models for the same variable, differences in timescale, or differences in the data structures used by the different model implementations.

The aim of this free-form approach is to allow each model component to be based on the most natural and appropriate scheme, rather than forcing each model into a unified system such as ODEs or discrete events.

To conclude, our framework is modular not only in the deconstruction of models, but in the components of the framework itself. Users of the framework are free to select from an existing range of connectors and translators or build their own, in order to achieve greater efficiency or the ability to integrate new types of models.

Underlying Infrastructure. Our computational framework does not presume any specific underlying middleware infrastructure. Currently, the engine wrappers we have built expose their interfaces either through dll library calls, or through web services[37]. Thus an orchestrator, or a connector, can both communicate efficiently with modelling tools residing on the local machine, and with modelling tools residing on other machines, perhaps in remote locations. Future engine wrappers may expose their functionality through other component middleware infrastructures, such as COM, CORBA[10] or SBW[31] .

5.2 Supporting Services

The computational framework is supported by a number of *information services* that provide information about each model used during the integration and then collect the results during a model run. Parameters required for the interpretation of a model are obtained from the context service, which serves as a central repository for parameter values to be used in biological modeling. The results, or *interpretations*, of the models are stored by the interpretation service. We envision a central model repository, such as 'BioModels.net'[7] being used to store existing models. One should be able to systematically search the repository in order to find desired sub-models required for the creation of a new composite model. We have implemented prototype versions of the context and interpretation services. Their functionality is exposed both via web services, to support communication with the rest of the framework, and through a web based user interface, which enables users to manually query the services for parameter values, or the results of previous model runs. The context and interpretation services will be described in greater detail in a future publication.

5.3 Example

Figure 1 shows a view of our *model integration framework*, which is used to execute *composite models*, specified in CMDL. In the figure we can see the two sub-models of the model depicted in section 4, executing on their respective tools, Xppaut and Mathemtatica. Since the two models are interdependent, they are integrated by

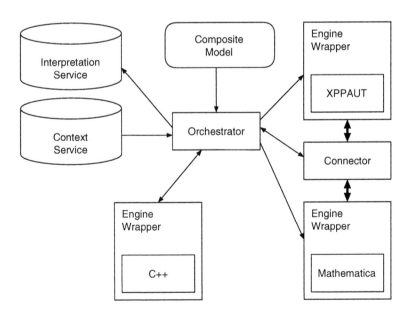

Fig. 1. Model Integration Framework

means of a connector. The orchestrator is responsible for launching the models and the connector, for passing to them the necessary input values and model parameters, and for collecting the results and storing them on the interpretation service.

6   Using CMDL to Model Glucose Homeostasis

We are part of a research project at University College London whose aim is to produce a physiological model of the liver which is integrated across scales[41]. As part of the project, we have recently used CMDL, along with our model execution framework, in order to specify and execute a composite model describing glucose homeostasis[42]. Glucose is the readily available fuel, or source of energy, which is being supplied by the blood to all cells in the body. Glucose is stored in the liver, in the form of glycogen. Glycogen buildup and release in the liver is controlled by two hormones, Insulin and Glucagon, secreted by the Pancreas.

Our model is able to predict glucose levels in the blood, as a function of the dietary regime, and various other parameters, such as the affinity of liver cells receptors to Insulin. We have used new and existing models to create our composite model of glucose homeostasis. Currently our model includes basic models of hormone secretion by the Pancreas and glucose transport in the blood stream, along with a quite detailed model of glucose release or intake by the liver, as a function of current glucose and hormone levels in the blood. This detailed model is in turn composed of 5 sub-models, describing the membrane receptors, the second messengers responses within the cell, and the actual build-up and breakdown of glycogen. The model and the sub-models it is composed of will be described in detail in a subsequent publication.

As these models are interdependent on each other and form a feedback loop, we have used a waveform relaxation connector in order to solve them together. The models also use different units and different time scales. We have thus used two simple scaling translators when connecting the models. One is used for adjusting the time scales between the different models, and the other is used to scale the other, time dependent variables.

By replacing some of the model components with simpler or more elaborate models, we try to determine how sensitive is glucose homeostasis to details in the description of the different sub-systems involved, specifically the receptor mechanisms and second messenger cascades in liver hepatocytes. We are trying to ascertain whether a good approximation of glucose homeostasis can be achieved by using relatively simple models of those sub-systems, or whether a detailed, mechanistic model of them is required. By removing or changing some of the model components, we try to ascertain what is the role of the different control mechanisms, such as hormonal control and direct glucose control, in maintaining glucose homeostasis.

7   Conclusions

We have presented CMDL, an XML Composite Model Description Language. CMDL integrates elements from ontologies, mathematical description languages such as MathML, interface description languages such as WSDL[38], Architecture Description languages and process execution languages, in order to provide a full description and specification of composite models in Systems Biology, moving from a broad description of the phenomenon depicted by the model and the functionalities provided by it, through an architectural description of the implementation, down to the precise details required for model execution. While we have borrowed heavily from well known techniques used to describe these different levels, we are currently unaware of any other attempt to integrate them together in a similar manner.

We have also presented a lightweight computational framework that is able to execute composite models specified in CMDL. It enables the integration of models, executing on a variety of different tools, and potentially executing on different machines in different locations. Unlike some other currently existing frameworks, our framework does not assume a specific model integration algorithm. Different connectors and translators can be used to connect the models together, and model composers can select the connector or translator which is most suitable to the task at hand and to the available facilities and model executing tools. The same overall composite model architecture can be implemented in radically different ways - the sub-models can be integrated using a C++ framework, with all models running on the same machine, or be integrated using Web Services, with different models running on distributed machines.

We have used our framework to implement a composite model of glucose homeostasis, composed of several existing models. These models run on a variety of different time scales, use different units for the variables involved, and are interdependent on one another. To tackle those issues, we have used a variety of connectors and translators. This model is now being actively used for scientific exploration.

One of our principal aims was to build a model integration framework which is easy to use. Unlike other suggested frameworks, such as SBW[31] or GCF[19], our framework does not require the writing of any program code on behalf of the modellers. We are currently building graphical user interface tools that can be used to specify and display the composite model specification files. Even without these tools, only about two days of work were required to write the CMDL files for the composite glucose homeostasis model, and launch the integrated model, by a person who was not familiar before-hand with XML or CMDL.

While up until now we have used our framework mainly to integrate ODE models, with the provision of suitable connectors and translators, our framework can be used to integrate discrete event, and perhaps process algebra models, as well.

References

1. A. Finkelstein, J. Hetherington, L. Li, O. Margoninski, P. Saffrey, R. Seymour, and A. Warner "Computational Challenges of Systems Biology", in *IEEE Computer* 2004, vol. 37(5), pp. 26-33
2. M. Antoniotti, F. Park, A. Policriti "Model building and model checking for biochemical processes", in *Cell Biochemistry and Biophysics* 38, 2003 pp 271-186

3. E. Bugianesi et. al. "Quantification of Gluconeogenesis in Cirrhosis: Response to Glucagon" GASTROENTEROLOGY 1998; Vol. 115 pp. 1530-1540
4. Specification: Business PRocess Execution Lanugage for Web Services Version 1.1 Available at: `http://www-106.ibm.com/developerworks/library/ws-bpel/`
5. BioSpice, at `https://community.biospice.org/`
6. B. Mishra et. al. "A Sense of Life: Computational and Experimental Investigations with Models of BioChemical and Evolutionary processes" in *OMICS* Vol. 7(3) 2003
7. The BioModels database at `http://www.ebi.ac.uk/biomodels/`
8. The CAPE-OPEN Laboratories Network, at `http://www.colan.org/`
9. CellML at `http://www.cellml.org`
10. The OMG Corba's web site - `http://www.corba.org`
11. The Distributed Component Object Model, by Microsoft, at `http://www.microsoft.com/com/tech/DCOM.asp`
12. P. V. Coveney and P. W. Fowler "Modelling biological complexity: a physical scientist's perspective" in *Interface* 2005, vol. 2, pp 267-280
13. J. Magee, N. Dulay and J. Kramer "Structuring Parallel and Distributed Programs", in *IEE Software Engineering Journal* Vol 8, No. 2 March 1993 pp 73-82
14. J. Magee, N. Dulay, S. Eisenbachand J. Kramer "Specifying Distribute Software Architectures" in *Proceedings of the Fifth European Software Engineering Conference, ESEC 95* 1995, pp 137-153
15. J. Kramer and J. Magee "Exposing the Skeleton in the Coordination Closet", in *Proceedings of the Second International Conference on Coordination Languages and Models* 1997 LNCS vol. 1282 pp 18-31
16. Dublin Core Metadata Initiative, at `http://dublincore.org/`
17. `http://www.e-cell.org`
18. Enterprise Javabeans Technology `http://java.sun.com/products/ejb/`
19. R.W. Ford et. al. "GCF: A General Coupling Framework" in Concurrency and Computation: Practice and Experience, 2006 vol. 18 pp. 163-181
20. Gene Ontology Consortium "An Introduction to Gene Ontology" at `http://www.geneontology.org/GO.doc.html`
21. The High Level Architecture `https://www.dmso.mil/public/transition/hla/`
22. Linzhong Li and Steve Baigent, "Integrating biosystems using waveform relaxation", submitted to bioinformatics
23. Catherine M. Lloyd, Matt D. B. Halstead and Poul F. Nielsen, CellML: its future, present and past, Progress in Biophysics and Molecular Biology, Volume 85, Issues 2-3, June-July 2004, Pages 433-450. (http://www.sciencedirect.com/science/article/B6TBN-4BT1658-2/2/109054184e74743e7ad3371bae71dd56)
24. Mathematica, Wolfram Research, described at `http://www.wolfram.com/products/mathematica/index.html`
25. N. L. Novere, A. Finney et. al. "Minimum information requested in the annotation of biochemical models (MIRIAM)", 2005, Nature Biotechnology, vol 23, pp. 1509 - 1515.
26. O. L. Munk et. al. "Liver Kinetics of Glucose Analogs Measured in Pigs by PET: Importance of Dual-Input Blood Sampling", Journal of Nuclear Medicine, 2001, vol 42 pp. 795-801
27. W. H. Press et. al. "Numerical Recipes in C: The Art of Scientific Computing", Cambridge University Press, 1992
28. SBML: Systems Biology Markup Language, 2003; at `http://www.sbml.org`
29. M. Hucka et. al. "The systems biology markup language (SBML): a medium for representation and exchange of biochemical network models" Bioinformatics Vol. 19 no. 4 2003 PP 524-531

30. N. L. Novere, A. Finney "A simple scheme for annotating SBML with references to controlled vocabularies and database entries", 2005, available at `www.ebi.ac.uk/compneur-srv/sbml/proposals/AnnotationURI.pdf`

31. SBW: The Systems Biology Workbench Project, at `http://www.sbw-sbml.org/the_project.html`

32. S. Schuster, M. Marhl, T. Hofer "Modelling of simple and complex calcium oscillations" em European Journal of Biochemistry 2002, vol 269(5) page 1333

33. K. Takahashi et. al. "Computational Challenges in Cell Simulation: A Software Engineering Approach", in *IEEE Intelligent Systems*, pp 64 - 71, SepetemberOctober 2002

34. "A multi-algorithm, multi-timescale method for cell simulation", K. Takahashi, K. Kaizu, B. Hu, M. Tomita, *Bioinformatics*, 20(4), 538-546, (2004).

35. G. Booch, J. Rumbaugh, I. Jacobson, "The Unified Modeling Language User Guide", Addison-Wesley, 1999

36. The Unified Modeling Language, a specification of the Object Management Group `http://www.uml.org`

37. "New to Web Services", by IBM, at `http://www-106.ibm.com/developerworks/webservices/newto/websvc.html` The W3C Web Services Activity at `http://www.w3.org/2002/ws/`

38. Web Services Description Language at `http://www.w3.org/TR/wsdl`

39. R. Allen, D. Garlan "A Formal Basis for Architectural Connection" in *ACM Transactions on Software Engineering and Methodology* July 1997

40. Bard Ermentrout, "Simulating, Analyzing, and Animating Dynamical Systems: A Guide to Xppaut for Researchers and Students", SIAM, 2002

41. The UCL Beacon Project, 2003; http://grid.ucl.ac.uk/biobeacon/php/index.php

42. Peter J. Klover and Robert A. Mooney, "Hepatocytes: critical for glucose homeostasis", *The International Journal of Biochemistry and Cell Biology*, Volume 36, Issue 5, May 2004, Pages 753-758.

Appendix - The Hepatocyte Glucagon G-Protein Calcium Model Encoded in CMDL

```xml
<?xml version="1.0" encoding="UTF-8"?>

<model id="Glucagon_GProtein_Calcium"
    xmlns="http://www.cs.ucl.ac.uk/biobeacon/CMSL1.0#">

    <rdf:RDF xmlns:bqs="http://www.cellml.org/bqs/1.0#"
        xmlns:dc="http://purl.org/dc/elements/1.1/"
        xmlns:dcterms="http://purl.org/dc/terms/"
        xmlns:rdf="http://www.w3.org/1999/02/22-rdf-syntax-ns#"
        xmlns:vCard="http://www.w3.org/2001/vcard-rdf/3.0#">
        <!-- Meta Data goes here - Format is the same as in SBML/BIOMODELS models -->
        <!-- ... -->
    </rdf:RDF>
    <phenomenon xmlns:sbml="http://www.sbml.org/sbml/level2">

        <phenomena id="Glucagon_Stimulated_Sig_Cascade" metaid="ph1">
            <!-- The main phenomena describe by the model -->
            <description>
                GLucagon hormonal stimulation of hepatocytes, and the
                resulting internal signaling cascade
            </description>
            <annotation>
```

```
<!-- Link the phenomena to detection of Hormone Stimulus as listed in the Gene
    Ontology -->
<rdf:RDF xmlns:dc="http://purl.org/dc/elements/1.1/"
    xmlns:dcterms="http://purl.org/dc/terms/"
    xmlns:rdf="http://www.w3.org/1999/02/22-rdf-syntax-ns#">
    <rdf:Description rdf:about="#ph1">
        <dc:isVersionOf>
            <rdf:Bag>
                <!-- Detection of Hormone Stimulus -->
                <rdf:li
                    rdf:resource="http://www.geneontology.org/#GO009720" />
            </rdf:Bag>
        </dc:isVersionOf>
    </rdf:Description>
</rdf:RDF>
</annotation>
<!-- Now list the compartments in which the above mentioned phenomena, described
    by the model, occurs-->
    <!-- First the Hepatocyte membrane, which we link to the Open Biomedical Ontologies term
        hepatocyte and to the Gene Ontology term membrane -->
<sbml:compartment id="Hepatocyte_Membrane"
    metaid="Hepatocyte_Membrane">
    <annotation>
        <rdf:RDF xmlns:dc="http://purl.org/dc/elements/1.1/"
            xmlns:dcterms="http://purl.org/dc/terms/"
            xmlns:rdf="http://www.w3.org/1999/02/22-rdf-syntax-ns#">
            <rdf:Description
                rdf:about="#Hepatocyte_Membrane">
                <dc:isPartOf>
                    <rdf:Bag>
                        <!-- hepatocyte -->
                        <rdf:li
                            rdf:resource="http://obo.sourceforge.net/#OBO:0000182" />
                    </rdf:Bag>
                </dc:isPartOf>
                <dc:isVersionOf>
                    <rdf:Bag>
                        <!-- membrane -->
                        <rdf:li
                            rdf:resource="http://www.geneontology.org/#GO:0005886" />
                    </rdf:Bag>
                </dc:isVersionOf>
            </rdf:Description>
        </rdf:RDF>
    </annotation>
</sbml:compartment>
<!-- Next the hepatocyte cytoplasm, linked to the Open Biomedical Ontolgies term hepatocyte and
to the Gene Ontology cytoplasm -->
<sbml:compartment id="Hepatocyte_Cytoplasm"
    metaid="Hepatocyte_Cytoplasm">
    <annotation>
        <rdf:RDF xmlns:dc="http://purl.org/dc/elements/1.1/"
            xmlns:dcterms="http://purl.org/dc/terms/"
            xmlns:rdf="http://www.w3.org/1999/02/22-rdf-syntax-ns#">
            <rdf:Description
                rdf:about="#Hepatocyte_Cytoplasm">
                <dc:isPartOf>
                    <rdf:Bag>
                        <!-- hepatocyte -->
                        <rdf:li
                            rdf:resource="http://obo.sourceforge.net/#OBO:0000182" />
                    </rdf:Bag>
                </dc:isPartOf>
                <dc:isVersionOf>
                    <rdf:Bag>
                        <!-- cytoplasm -->
                        <rdf:li
                            rdf:resource="http://www.geneontology.org/#GO:0005737" />
```

```
                </rdf:Bag>
              </dc:isVersionOf>
          </rdf:Description>
       </rdf:RDF>
    </annotation>
</sbml:compartment>
<!-- Now we list the aspects, the concrete measurables depicted by the model and which are
part of the depicted phenomena -->
<!-- First is G-Protein activation level, again linked to the corresponding term in the
Gene Ontology -->
<aspect id="G_Protein_Activation_Level"
    metaid="G_Protein_Activation_Level">
    <aspect_id>9234675</aspect_id>
    <annotation>
       <rdf:RDF xmlns:dc="http://purl.org/dc/elements/1.1/"
           xmlns:dcterms="http://purl.org/dc/terms/"
           xmlns:rdf="http://www.w3.org/1999/02/22-rdf-syntax-ns#">
           <rdf:Description
              rdf:about="#G_Protein_Activation_Level">
              <dc:isVersionOf>
                 <rdf:Bag>
                    <!-- G-Protein Activation -->
                    <rdf:li
                        rdf:resource="http://www.geneontology.org/#GO:0004930" />
                 </rdf:Bag>
              </dc:isVersionOf>
              <dc:isVersionOf>
                 <rdf:Bag>
                    <!-- Activation level -->
                    <rdf:li
                        rdf:resource="http://www.measurableproperties.org/#Activation_Level" />
                 </rdf:Bag>
              </dc:isVersionOf>
           </rdf:Description>
       </rdf:RDF>
    </annotation>
    <text_definition>
       Activation level of hepatocyte G Protein
    </text_definition>
    <description>
       The activation level of a G Protein activated by external hormone stimuli.
    </description>
</aspect>
<!-- Another aspect described by the model is the concentration of
    intracellular calcium. This time we define the term through a
    reference to the term 'Calcium' in the CHEBI ontology.  -->
<sbml:specie id="Intracellular_Calcium"
    name="Intracellular Calcium Concentration"
    metaid="Instracellular_Calcium"
    compartment="Hepatocyte_Cytoplasm">
    <aspect_id>9234675</aspect_id>
    <annotation>
       <rdf:RDF xmlns:dc="http://purl.org/dc/elements/1.1/"
           xmlns:dcterms="http://purl.org/dc/terms/"
           xmlns:rdf="http://www.w3.org/1999/02/22-rdf-syntax-ns#">
           <rdf:Description
              rdf:about="#Instracellular_Calcium">
              <dc:isVersionOf>
                 <rdf:Bag>
                    <!-- Calcium -->
                    <rdf:li
                        rdf:resource="http://www.ebi.ac.uk/#CHEBI:22984" />
                 </rdf:Bag>
              </dc:isVersionOf>
              <dc:relation>
                 <rdf:Bag>
                    <!-- Concentration -->
                    <rdf:li
```

```
                                rdf:resource="http://www.measurableproperties.org/#Concentration" />
                        </rdf:Bag>
                    </dc:relation>
                </rdf:Description>
            </rdf:RDF>
        </annotation>
        <text_definition>
            The concentration of intracellular Calcium in Hepatocytes
        </text_definition>
        <description>
            Calcium acts as an important second messenger.
            Changes in concentration and specifically
            oscillations occur as a result of hormonal stimulus, and
            in turn affect enzymatic activity within the cell
        </description>
    </sbml:specie>
  </phenomena>
</phenomenon>

<!-- The list of submodels of which this model is composed -->
<submodels>
    <submodel description_file="./G_Protein.xml"
        name="GProtein_activation" />
    <submodel description_file="./Calcium_cAMP.xml"
        name="PieceWise_Linear_Model_of_Calcium_Oscillations" />
</submodels>

<!-- This model has only one functionality, or possible usage. It can be used to
predict G-Protein activation levels and intracellular Calcium concentrations as a
function of blood Glucagon levels -->
<functionality
    name="G_Protein activation and Calcium levels as a function of hormone stimulus">
    <UsingAspects>
        <!-- One may refer here to aspects already defined in the phenomenon section, and
    also define additional aspects. Aspects can be defined simply by referring to the
        aspect id in the parameter and aspect repository. -->
        <aspect id="Blood_Glucagon_Levels">
            <aspect_id>875446</aspect_id>
        </aspect>
    </UsingAspects>
    <ProvidingAspects>
        <aspect_ref id="Intracellular_Calcium_Level" />
        <aspect_ref id="G_Protein" />
    </ProvidingAspects>

    <!-- Here we list the functionalities of the submodels this model uses in order to implement
        its own functionality -->
    <using>
        <functionality
            functionality="G_Protein  activation level as a function of Hormone Stimuli and Calcium"
            model="G_Protein" />
        <functionality
            functionality="Calcium  concentration as a function of G_Protein activation level"
            model="PieceWise_Linear_Model_of_Calcium_Oscillations" />
    </using>

<!-- The mathematical functionality term defines the functionality in precise mathematical terms.
    We specify that the output of the model contains timetrack (Function depicting how a
    variable changes through time) of G-Protein activation levels and of Calcium concentrations.
    The input is a timetrack of blood hormone levels -->
    <mathematical_functionality
        name="G_Protein activation level and  Calcium level vs. time as a function of
        hormone stimulation">

        <!-- We may specify the scheme that the model is implemented in - in this case,
            Ordinary Differential Equations -->
        <scheme composite="yes" type="differential_equations" />
```

```
<!-- Here we define units that will be used later on. The specification
    is similar to that of CellML -->
<units name="milli_mole_per_liter">
    <unit prefix="milli" units="mole" />
    <unit exponent="-1" units="litre" />
</units>

<!-- The variable type that appears here applies to all variables within
this mathematical functionality, unless a variable
    is explicitly declared to be of another type. Thus
    we specify here that all the variables are of type
    timetrack -->
<variable>
    <type name="timetrack" />
</variable>

<!-- List of output and input variables. Note that each variable
is linked to the aspect it describes. -->
<outputVars>
    <variable initial_value="0.0" id="G_Protein_Level"
        units="pure_number">
        <aspect_ref id="G_Protein" />
    </variable>
    <variable initial_value="0.0" id="Calcium_Level"
        units="milli_mole_per_liter">
        <aspect_ref id="Intracellular_Calcium_Level" />
    </variable>
</outputVars>
<inputVars>
    <variable initial_value="0.0" id="Hormone_Level"
        units="milli_mole_per_liter" />


</inputVars>

<!-- Parameters are similar to input variables, the main difference being
that their value remains fixed through out the course of the simulation -->
<parameters>
    <parameter units="milli_mole_per_liter" id="IP3_ER"
        name="IP3 concentration threshhold in Endoplasmic Reticulum">
        <aspect_id>9865543</aspect_id>
        <type name="scalar" />
    </parameter>
    <parameter units="milli_mole_per_liter"
        id="Resting_GProtein"
        name="Resting concentration of inactive G-protein">
        <aspect_id>8754433</aspect_id>
        <type name="range" />
    </parameter>
</parameters>

<!-- Here the description of the interface provided by the
mathematical functionality ends, and we proceed to
describe how this functionality is actually implemented.
The orchestrator reads the 'implementation' section
and executes it in order to execute the model -->
<implementation>

    <!-- The model instances/components participating in the computation -->
    <!-- In this simple example we have one component per model,
    but one may specify mulitple components launched for the same model.
    For example, one may specify a composite multi-cellular model using
    multiple instances of the same cellular model -->
    <component model="GProtein_activation"
        id="G_Protein_Component" />
    <component
        model="PieceWise_Linear_Model_of_Calcium_Oscillations"
        id="Calcium_Component" />
```

```
<!-- Next we map out the connections between the models. We first specify
which components are connected to each other, and which functionalities
and interfaces of each component are being used. Then
we actually map output variables into input variables -->
<!-- This connection is a 'horizontal' connection, it links
sub-models on the same level -->
<CMSL_connection id="GProtein_Calcium_Coupling"
    type="horizontal">
    <map_components>
        <mapped_component
            functionality="G_Protein and PLC activation level as a function of Calcium"
            mathematical_functionality="G_Protein and PLC activation levels vs. time
            as a function of Calcium"
            component="G_Protein_Component" id="G_Protein" />
        <mapped_component
            functionality="Calcium levels as a function of PLC activity levels"
            mathematical_functionality="Calcium levels as a function of PLC activity levels vs. time"
            component="Calcium_Component" id="Calcium" />
        <map_variable>
            <source mapped_component="G_Protein"
                variable="PhosphoLipase" />
            <dest mapped_component="Calcium"
                variable="PhosphoLipase" />
        </map_variable>
        <map_variable>
            <source mapped_component="Calcium"
                variable="Calcium_Concentration" />
            <dest mapped_component="G_Protein"
                variable="Calcium_Level" />
            <translator>
                <scaling default_value="100.0"
                    name="Glucose_scaling" />
            </translator>
        </map_variable>
    </map_components>
</CMSL_connection>
<!-- This is a 'vertical' connections, wiring of the submodels variables to
the 'global' model variables -->
<CMSL_connection type="vertical">
    <map_components>
        <mapped_component
            functionality="G_Protein  activation level as a function of Calcium"
            component="G_Protein_Component" id="G_Protein" />
        <mapped_component id="Self" />
        <map_variable>
            <source mapped_component="G_Protein"
                variable="G_Protein" />
            <dest mapped_component="Self"
                variable="G_Protein" />
        </map_variable>
    </map_components>
</CMSL_connection>
<CMSL_connection type="vertical">
    <map_components>
        <mapped_component
            functionality="Calcium_Level as a  function of GProtein activation"
            id="Calcium" component="Calcium_Component" />
        <mapped_component id="Self" />
        <map_variable>
            <source mapped_component="Calcium"
                variable="Calcium_Concentration" />
            <dest mapped_component="Self"
                variable="Calcium_Level" />
        </map_variable>
    </map_components>
</CMSL_connection>
```

```
<!-- Now we specify what connector we use to actually implement the connection
    between the two models. In this case we use a waveform relaxation connector -->
<CMSL_connector id="GProtein_Calcium_Coupling">
    <integration_method name="Waveform_relaxation" />
    <implement_connection
        connection="GProtein_Calcium_Coupling" />
</CMSL_connector>

<!-- This is the specification of the algorithm the orchestrator has to follow in order
    to execute this functionality. -->
<sequence>
    <invoke name="step1">
        <CMSL_connector
            connector="GProtein_Calcium_Coupling" />
    </invoke>
</sequence>
</implementation>

<!-- The last section in the mathematical functionality definition is the computational interface
section. It describes the precise data format of the model's inputs and outputs -->
<computational_interfaces>
    <implementation id="imp1">
        <engine name="C++_Orchestrator" version="0.1" />
        <!-- Here we specify additional data that the orchestrator may require in order
            to execute the invocations, such as the computational interfaces to be used by the
            connector -->
        <engine name="C++_Orchestrator" version="0.1" />
        <invoke step="step1">
            <CMSL_connector
                name="GProtein_Calcium_Coupling">
                <use_interface mapped_component="G_Protein"
                    id="G_Protein_Interface" />
                <use_interface mapped_component="Calcium"
                    id="Calcium_cAMP_Interface" />
            </CMSL_connector>
        </invoke>

    </implementation>

    <!-- Here we define the computational interface for the (top level) model. In this case it is
        simply an output file -->
    <computational_interface id="G_Protein_Calcium_LZ"
        type="output_file">
        <subtype id="TimeTrack_Interface" implemention="imp1"/>
    </computational_interface>

    </computational_interfaces>
    </mathematical_functionality>
    </functionality>
</model>
```

Author Index

Lecture Notes in Bioinformatics